CREATIVITY & COMPASSION

CREATIVITY & COMPASSION

How They Come Together

Edited by John Briggs

Associate Editor Paul Hackett

KARUNA PUBLICATIONS

Published in 2012 by Karuna Publications
An Imprint of Diamond Cutter Press, LLC
55 Powderhorn Drive
Wayne, NJ 07470

Printed in the United States of America

Book design by Clare Cerullo

Library of Congress Cataloging-in-Publication Data is available upon request.

ISBN 978-1-937114-05-3

www.karunapublications.org

Contents

CONTENTS

CONTENTS

To those who have the nature of
compassion
I offer palaces resounding with
melodious hymns,
Exquisitely illuminated by hanging
pearls and gems
That adorn the infinities of space.

—Śāntideva,
Guide to the Bodhisattva's Way of Life 10:18

Preface
Bringing Together Art, Creativity, and the Wisdom of Selflessness

Professor Robert Thurman generously agreed to provide a preface to *Creativity and Compassion* in the form of his answers to a series of questions on the themes of this book. Thurman is a preeminent Buddhist scholar who holds the first endowed chair in Buddhist Studies in the West, the Jey Tsong Khapa Chair in Indo-Tibetan Buddhist Studies at Columbia University. He has been a personal student of the Dalai Lama for over 30 years, has served as his translator, and has written many scholarly and popular books on Indo-Tibetan philosophical and psychological traditions.

The Dalai Lama and other Buddhist thinkers seem to be able to step outside of Buddhism's particular rituals, beliefs, and eschatology and address the human condition in a nonpartisan way that appeals to people of many different religions. What is it about Tibetan Buddhism in particular that makes that possible?

The curriculum of a Tibetan Buddhist monk like His Holiness the Dalai Lama is the curriculum of the ancient Indian Buddhist university of Nālandā, where logic, epistemology, psychology, and in particular extreme philosophical refinement based on the most thorough and profound system of critical evaluation of one's worldview, ideology, or outlook on the world and the self, were developed to a degree greater than any other world civilization. Mastering this curriculum, as His Holiness most wonderfully has, enables a person to always see things from many perspectives, to hold to reason in all things, to respect and seek to understand the views of others, and to always be open to new learning, new insight, new capabilities. This surprises us because we think of Buddhism as a "religion"—that is, a system of belief—and we associate devout people of religions to be absolutist, inflexible if not fundamentalist, those who strongly cling to and advocate a specific view that is most often chosen out of obedience to authority rather than developed through reasoning and experience. In fact, as the marvelous example of His Holiness demonstrates, Buddhism is a civilization, based on mind sciences and ethical disciplines, that leads its best adherents to intellectual openness and emotional dedication to friendliness and compassion for others.

What role does compassion play in the Buddhist worldview? What role does what we call "creativity" play in the Buddhist worldview?

Compassion is central in the Buddhist worldview. Buddhist physics has long maintained the Buddha's central discovery of absolute relativity, the famous "emptiness" being the very opposite of nothingness—a negation of any relative absolute, any sort of state or existence outside of the web of interconnected being and things. This compels persons to shift their absolute concern from some sort of hypothesized escape from the difficulties of relationship into a state of absolute freedom in "God" or "*Nirvāṇa*"—a state beyond the world—to the improvement of the quality of beings in the world. If you are one with beings in the sense that all of you are forever interconnected in an ever-changing infinite life realm, it becomes your absolute concern that others never suffer, because their suffering becomes as intolerable to you as your own. And that is the definition of universal compassion.

Creativity then becomes the result of that compassion, as you have potential infinite energy to do whatever it takes to relieve others (and yourself as interconnected with them) from suffering. In Buddhism, the sixth transcendent virtue is *prajñā*, the superknowing or wisdom of selflessness or emptiness, which is the experiential understanding of the relativity of all things due to every single one of them lacking any intrinsic separate reality. The seventh is *upāya*, which is often mistranslated as "skill-in-means," or dully translated as "method," but which really means "art," creativity in the broadest sense, employing all artful ways of creating whatever is needed, doing whatever it takes, to help others free themselves from suffering. This could be creativity in the arts of healing, building, making things of beauty, performing exalting plays or music, inventing things to benefit others, and even living as a benefit to others, etc. It is "transcendent" as it is driven by transcendent wisdom and so becomes absolute in its determination to transform the relative; it is inexhaustible in its endurance against any odds, inconceivable in its resourcefulness, blissful in its confidence even when confronting the seemingly most intractable disasters, and so on.

Do you think this discussion of the relationship between the concepts of compassion and creativity is an important one? If so, why?

It is important, because otherwise people think Buddhism encourages passivity and inaction in the face of suffering, which is a mistake. By realizing that "art" and "creativity" are key virtues that arise naturally from the attainment of the wisdom of selflessness, science and ethics are brought together. Without people having to become Buddhists, they can look more carefully at their own traditions, even that of secular humanism, and begin to discern perspectives where compassion, altruism, and universal responsibility are not merely unattainable ideals, but realistic and necessary, even essential. This Buddhism embodied as a civilization can contribute by example and through dialogue to the evolving world culture and world ethic. A world ethic that mandates the decrease of consumerism and militarism, the social results of greed and hatred, is essential at this time for human survival on the polluted and overheated planet.

How does compassion relate to other key ideas in Buddhism such as dependent origination or other essential concepts?

Emptiness as the transcendent, non-foundational foundation of physical and mental reality imperatively mandates the infinite and eternal changeable and illusory dependent origination, or relativity, of all migrant beings and inanimate things. A fact—first discovered in our era by Shakyamuni Buddha—unveiled how compassion arises. It arises when the energy that seeks to know reality fully—an energy in quest of security and happiness—discovers its freedom from a trajectory toward the infinite eternal absolute. At that moment the energy seeking reality grasps that the absolute is the transparent fabric of the infinite web of relational being and things. From that realization, compassion bursts forth spontaneously as a universal love willing all beings happiness and universal compassion, willing them to join itself in the bliss of freedom from all suffering.

Do you think it's possible that increasing awareness of compassion and applying that awareness to our creative pursuits in science, technology, the arts, and human systems can make a realistic positive impact on the conflictual world that human thought has created?

You said it all in the way you phrased this question! Yes, a million times yes!

Do you see a creative "art" to the way His Holiness communicates his message of compassion and happiness?

His Holiness's art is based on his refined perception of people arising from his nondual, cognitive-dissonance-reconciling awareness that remains clear about everyone's natural freedom as indivisible from beginningless bliss of Nirvāṇa, while that awareness is simultaneously fully sensitive to each person's specific way of not experiencing themselves as free and satisfied. His Holiness is thus like the best doctor, who can see the incipient health and well-being of the patient, while fully attending to the obstructions in their lifestyle and bodily systems that prevent them from enjoying that health. Such a doctor thus knows simultaneously what should be changed therapeutically, while seeing clearly the target state as already imminent in the life-force of the patient. His Holiness reaches people like that. They can feel a subliminal release that comes from being accepted and blessed when seen for once by someone who sees them as already all right, as one might say, and yet they feel also a more conscious pleasure in having that same someone respect, even share, their problems, and thus be able to give them useful advice, practical instructions as to what they might do effectively about their situation.

Any further thoughts about His Holiness's work and impact?

Thank you for honoring me with the opportunity to reflect in some depth about the amazing person that is His Holiness. I have come to think of him over the years in this way: If Shakyamuni Buddha were to come to a seemingly normal human life in our era, he would be no one more or less than the good friend to all, His Holiness the Dalai Lama, whose great message to us all is constantly given as, in the words he used in his Templeton Prize acceptance speech recently, "I am thankful for your kindness and appreciation of my efforts, but it is very wrong for you all to depend on some other person, no matter how much you may admire him or her. You yourselves can do the very needful actions of altruism, courage, intelligence, and honesty and can overcome all difficulties, no matter how hopeless they may seem. Indeed, you have to take up the universal responsibility for all life and its environment!" And so on. Hopefully we will be remembering that sentiment when we never give up, when we speak truth to power, when we practice what we preach, when we give as much as we can.

Introduction
The Origins of
Our Inquiry

John Briggs

This collection of essays is the fruit of a conversation begun in 2010, when members of the Western Connecticut State University faculty began meeting with members of the Do Ngak Kunphen Ling Tibetan Buddhist Center for Universal Peace (DNKL) in nearby Redding, Connecticut, to discuss inviting His Holiness the Dalai Lama to the WCSU campus.

During those early talks, we shared our conviction that across cultures and time, the great creative arts have both helped us experience our common humanity and inspired us to an awe about the cosmos. This purpose of art is evident in the earliest cave paintings, in the plays of Shakespeare, the symphonies of Beethoven, and the canvasses of Picasso. Even in modern art—which frequently depicts humans alone and out of sync with the universe—our existential solidarity peeks through beneath the alienated surface. Consider the inner psychology expressed by the twisted faces of a Picasso—and the recognition and compassion that those faces evoke.

As artists and scholars, we also shared our deep response to the Dalai Lama's call to recognize the vital importance of compassion, a concept not very well understood in the West. In those early days of our conversation, we felt sure that these two important concepts—creativity and compassion—must be intimately related, though we were not clear how. As we talked, many issues arose that were blocking our understanding. For example, in Western cultures, compassion has been confounded with pity. In Tibetan Buddhist culture—as reflected in the Tibetan language itself—there is no single word to describe what we in our secular culture mean by the words "creative" or "creativity." Even in the Buddhist-rich culture of Bali, there is no such word, though Bali is generally thought of as having a highly artistic culture. Importantly, the Western idea of creativity is strongly associated with the individual ego, whereas Buddhist compassion focuses on a process that leaves the ego behind.

Within months, our conversation expanded to include other university faculty, staff, and students as well as Tibetan Buddhist monks and Geshes (an academic degree from a Tibetan monastic university that is the equivalent of a Doctorate of Religious Philosophy) from our local community.

As our inquiry evolved, we began to grapple with the dark side of the creativity. We had originally thought in terms of creativity as an important spiritual expression unfolding down through the ages. But of course creativity has brought humanity many dreadful things, too. Along with the uses of fire and the insights of religion have come innovative means of torture and destruction; violently escapist entertainment; and the unintended consequences of technology, where an ostensibly advantageous invention can quickly transform into a demonic influence.

On April 20th and 21st, 2012, we shaped our inquiry—our conversation—into a small conference about creativity and compassion, held on the WCSU campus. We asked others to join us. During the two days, students, Buddhists, and academics from various fields in the arts, philosophy, education, law, and psychology gathered into panels to discuss the topics reflected in the five sections of this book—all subtopics under a general heading of how creativity and compassion may fit together to form a synergistic positive force. We asked those attending the conference to come without the notes or prepared papers typically expected at an academic conference. We wanted a conference structure that would encourage us to dialogue freely and forge meaning together from the subtle substances of our individual perspectives. And dialogue freely our conferees did. Afterwards, we asked them to return to the solitude of their own thoughts and organize their insights into the essays for this book. The book also includes essays by several individuals who, though not able to attend the conference, had become part of our conversation.

So, what did we learn? One thing that I believe we all took away from the inquiry is the conviction that without some dynamic conjunction between compassion and creativity, we humans may not be able to solve the lethal problems that face us in the 21st century—climate change, global conflict, the need for prosperity and security, a spiraling descent into materialism and anomie, to name a few—problems that our very inventiveness and creativity have created. Compassion for all sentient beings, as the Buddhists put it, may provide the only sensible framework and enabling force that will allow our overflowing creativity to function sanely.

In her opening remarks to the conference, WCSU Provost Jane McBride Gates pointed out that The Millennium Project, initiated by the Smithsonian Institution and two other organizations, identified 15 challenges for the 21st century, among them: sustainable development and climate change, clean water, democratization, the rich-poor gap, the status of women, energy, and global ethics. She noted that "the challenges are interdependent: an improvement in one makes it easier to address others; deterioration in one makes it harder to address others. Arguing whether one is more important than another is like arguing that the human nervous system is more important than the respiratory system. These challenges are transnational in nature and trans-institutional in solution."

In other words, it will take *both* our creativity and our compassion—working together in feedback and exponentially amplifying each other—to solve them.

Both human creativity and human compassion exist at the nexus of what psychologist John Amoroso and I like to call "the primal paradox." The Dalai Lama speaks frequently to this paradox, though of course he doesn't use the words "primal" or "paradox." For example, one of his more well-known sayings is, "If you want *others* to be happy, practice compassion. If *you* want to be happy, practice compassion." A similar resonance can be found in his book *In My Own Words*, where he writes, "Adopting an attitude of universal responsibility is essentially a personal matter."

We might imagine the primal paradox as like the long single hinge of a door that swings open in two apparently opposite directions. In one direction, the door swings inward to reveal each of us as a separate individual, a solitary ego, struggling to survive and be happy in a world of multifarious, contending egos. In the opposite direction, the door swings outward to reveal our inseparability from others and from the earth. In each direction, our desire and need for love has a different meaning. In fact, we each exist at the hinge itself, both as a separate individual and as inseparably indivisible from everything else.

Variations of this paradox—strongly in evidence in these essays—occur everywhere in religious thought and in human thinking in general. It appears in the Golden Rule in the admonition that you should treat others as you would treat yourself. It occurs as Kant's idea of the "categorical imperative," where the philosopher urged us to act in the world as if our action might suddenly become translated into a "universal law." If I intentionally cut someone off on the highway, imagine that my decision suddenly became a universal law requiring everyone to cut off everyone else on the highway. Kant's imperative was only one of many varied and fascinating formulations of the primal paradox. The Hindu doctrine that the *ātman*, or individual soul, is ultimately the *Brahman*, or universal soul, is another version. A similar paradox even occurs in quantum mechanics, wherein it is impossible to definitively isolate a single subatomic particle from all other particles due to its ultimate indeterminacy and potentially non-local attributes. The paradox occurs in chaos theory, which realizes that in large complex systems in nature "everything causes everything else." Chaos theory, a good description of nature's creativity, should be no surprise to a Buddhist. Compassion is understood as an inevitable force in Buddhism because the Buddha realized that very same chaos theory idea from a different angle: In his doctrine of "dependent origination and emptiness," he observed that no one exists separately; since every phenomenon is the result of a combination of conditions, the individual has no inherent autonomous existence. Achieving this understanding leads naturally to an attitude of tolerance and service to others. In the Buddhist view, compassion is our destiny. Meanwhile, in the Western view, creativity is our inheritance.

In the following pages, the reader will find the results of a kind of "collective creativity" we experienced taking place among us as we inquired into the question of where these two important concepts meet.

We would like now to invite the reader to join us in our inquiry as it continues.

CREATIVITY & COMPASSION

In simple terms, compassion and love can be defined as positive thoughts and feelings that give rise to such essential things in life as hope, courage, determination, and inner strength. In the Buddhist tradition, compassion and love are seen as two aspects of the same thing: Compassion is the wish for another being to be free from suffering; love is wanting them to have happiness.

—His Holiness the Dalai Lama, from *The Compassionate Life*

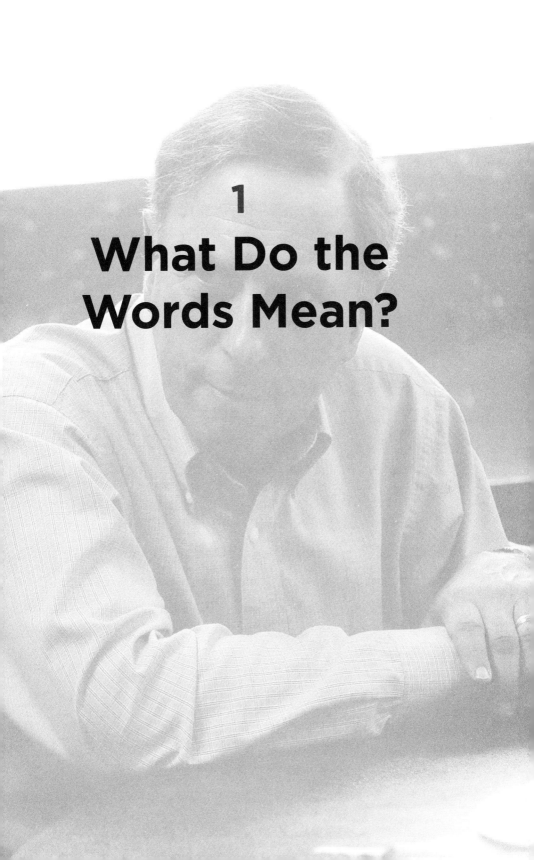

1
What Do the
Words Mean?

རྣམ་དཔྱོད་ཀྱི་ཆལ་དང་སྐྱིད་སྡེ།

ཞ་སྐྱིད།

༈ །དེ་རིང་འདིར་དྲུ་བ་ནི་རྣམ་དཔྱོད་ཀྱི་ཆལ་ཞེར་ན་གང་འདུ་ཞིག་དང་། སྐྱིད་རྗེ་ཟེར་ན་ག་འདུ་ཞིག་ལ་ཚོས་འཛིར་དགོས་མིན། དེ་གཉིས་ཟུང་འབྲེལ་དགོས་པ་གལ་ཆེན་པོ་རེད་དམ་མ་རེད་ཅེས་དྲུ་བ་གསུམ་པོ་འདི་རེར་འདུག་འཛིག་ཏེན་འདིར་ཞི་བདེ་དགོས་ན་དེ་གཉིས་ཟེས་པར་ཟུང་འབྲེལ་དགོས་ཞེས་ལན་འདེབས་རྒྱུ་ཡིན།

སྟོན་ལ་ཚོགས་པ་འདིའི་དམིགས་ཡུལ་དང་འབྲེལ་ནས་ལན་ཚོ་ཚ་ཞེས་ན། སྐྱིད་བདང་འཛིམ་སྐྱིང་འདིར་མི་འཁོར་ཆ་ནས་ཞི་བདེར་མོས་མཐུན་ཡོད་ག་ཨན་ཏུ་ཅང་ཚོང་མཐོ་པོ་རེད་དེ། ཕེན་ཀྱང་འདིར་མིའི་གྲས་འཁོར་དང་བསྟུར་ན་དོན་དག་ལག་ལེན་ཕོག་ཞི་བདེ་སྐྱན་ཐབས་གནང་མཁན་དང་། དེའི་ཐབས་ཞེས་མཁན་ཅུང་བ་ཡོད། དེ་འདུ་ཅུང་ཤས་ཞིག་གིས་འཛིམ་སྐྱིང་འདིར་ཞི་བདེ་སྐྱན་པར་དུས་ཡུན་ཏུ་ཅང་རིང་པོ་འགོར་སྐྱིང་ལ། གཅིག་བྱས་ན་ཅུང་དགས་པའི་རྒྱེན་ཀྱིས་ཁོང་རྣམ་པའི་དམིགས་ཡུལ་དགའ་རྗི་ལམ་ཚམ་ཏུ་འགྱུར་མི་སྐྱིང་པའང་མིན། དེ་འདུ་ཡིན་དུས་ང་ཚོ་བསམ་ཞིག་བྱས་མཐར་འཛིམ་སྐྱིང་ཞི་བདེ་ཡོང་བར་རྒྱུ་རྐྱེན་མང་པོ་ཞིག་ལ་རག་ལས་པ་མ་ཟད་ཕྱོགས་མང་པོ་ཞིག་ལ་མཐུན་རྐྱ་བྱས་ནས་ལས་འགུལ་སྐྱེལ་དགོས་པ་དེ་མེད་དུ་མི་རུང་བའི་ཆ་རྐྱེན་ཞིག་ཏུ་མཐོང་། དེ་ཡང་གཅམ་བཀག་གནང་གཁན་དང་ཕྱག་དེའི་ཚོམ་པ་པོ་ཚོ་གཅིག་པོ་མ་ཡིན་པར།

Combining Creativity and Compassion
An Introduction

Geshe Lobsang Dhargye
Buddhist Monk

T hree questions have been raised by our inquiry: (1) "What is creativity?"; (2) "How do we define what we refer to as 'compassion'?"; and (3) "What is the importance of combining these two qualities?" And the response that has been given is, "If we want to enhance peace and well-being in the world, these two qualities—creativity and compassion—must be practiced in combination."

First, I would like to make a few observations about the main goal of this book. In general, the number of people who share the wish for world peace is certainly very large. However, by comparison, the number of people who are actually trying to implement a method of bringing about this peace and well-being, or who have some knowledge of a method for doing so, is quite small. It is likely, then, that even if the efforts of this smaller group of individuals were to ultimately succeed in bringing about world peace, it will take an extremely long period of time to do so. Or perhaps, due to the limited size of this group, it may be a goal that is nothing more than an impossible dream.

In light of this situation, our investigations have concluded that not only does the possibility of achieving world peace depend upon a great many factors, but we have also recognized that the one indispensable condition is the need for people from many fields of endeavor to work together to promote this effort.

གང་ལྟར་སྐྱེ་ཚོགས་ནང་རྒྱུན་ལྡན་ནས་འབྱག་སྟེན་འདིའི་དགོས་མཁོ་སྣན་ཐབས་ལ་བསམ་
ཞིབ་གནང་མཁན། དཔེར་ན། ཚོན་རིག་པ། བཟོ་ལས་པ། རྒྱུ་རྩལ་པ། རི་མོ་བ། གནས་པ་
དང་གནས་མ། ཨེམ་ཆི། ཚེམ་པ་པོ། ཚོང་ལས་པ། སློབ་གྲྭ་ཁག་ཚོས་ལུགས་མི་སྐྲ་ སྲིད་
དོན་པ། ཞལ་ལག་བཟོ་མཁན་སོགས་ཀྱི་ནང་འབྱན་བླ་བྲལ་བའི་རྣམ་དཔྱོད་ཀྱི་ཤེས་རབ་
དང་། ཡིད་དབང་འཕྲོག་པའི་གསར་བཏོད་པའི་རིགས་ཡོད་སྲིད་ལ། ཡོད་དགོས་པའང་
ཡིན། དེ་ལྟ་བུའི་རྣམ་དཔྱོད་ལྡན་པའི་མི་རྣམས་ཀྱིས་འཛམ་སྐྱིན་འདེ་ལ་ཞེ་བདེས་ཞབས་
འདེགས་བསྐྲུབ་ཐུབ་པ་ཡིན་ན། ཐབ་རྣབས་ཡང་དུ་ཅང་ཆེན་པོ་ཡོང་བར་མཐོང་གི་འདུག་
ཨོན་ཀྱང་དེ་ལ་གལ་ཆེ་བའི་ཆ་རྒྱེན་ཞིག་དགོས་པ་ནི་སྙིང་རྗེའི་ཀུན་སློང་དང། ཡང་ན་
སྙིང་སེམས་ཆུན་དུ་གཏོང་རྒྱུ་ནི་དེས་པར་ཏུ་དགོས་པ་ཞིག་རེད། རྒྱུ་ཚན་ཡོངས་སློང་དང་
གཏུམ་སྐྲན་ལུགས་གྲགས་ཡོན་ཐབས་ཚམ་གྱི་བསམ་བློ་དེ་འདི་ནི་ད་བར་ཐལ་ཆེར་ལ་ཡོང་བསྟང་
པ་ཞིག་རེད། ད་བར་ཐལ་ཆེར་གྱི་རྣམ་དཔྱོད་བཟང་པོ་དེ་འདོད་ཞེན་དང་། ཡང་ཁོང་
ཁྲོ། ཡང་ན་འཕེན་འཛིན། ཐུག་དོག་སོགས་ཀྱི་གནས་དབང་ཨོག་བཀོལ་སྤྱོད་བྱས་དང་བྱེད་
བཞིན་ཡོང་ལ། དེ་འདིའི་གནས་དབང་དུ་སོང་བའི་རྣམ་དཔྱོད་ཀྱི་ནུས་སྟོབས་ལས་འབྱུང་
བའི་གསར་གཏོད་རིགས་གང་འདུ་བྱུང་ནའང་ཕྱོགས་ཡོངས་ནས་ཕུན་སུམ་ཚོགས་པ་ཞིག་
དང་། ཐག་གཅིག་ཏུ་དགའ་ཞེན་བྱེད་འོས་པ། མིའི་བདེ་སྐྱིད་ཡར་རྒྱས་ནས་གོན་འཕེལ་འགྲོ་
ཐུབ་པ་དེ་བས་ཁག་པོ་རེད། དེ་ལས་སྙིང་རྗེའི་ཀུན་སློང་དེ་ཡོད་ན་རང་གནས་གཞིས་ཕན་
དང་། གཏུམ་སྐྲན་ལུགས་སོགས་རང་ལུགས་ཀྱིས་ཡོང་གི་ཡོད་དུས་སྙན་གཅིག་གིས་ནང་
མང་པོ་དག་བསྐྲེད་ཡོང་ཐུབ་པ་ལྟར་རེད།

དཔེར་ན་རི་མོ་མཁན་མཁས་པ་ཞིག་ལ་ཆ་མཚོན་ན། དུས་རྣམ་ཡང་རི་མོ་མི་འགྲོ་
གཏུམ་ཆན་མིག་གཉིས་སྤང་མིག་གིས་བགྲད་པ་དང་། ལག་ན་མདའ་མདུང་གྲི་སོགས་
འཕྱར་བ་ཞིག་འགྲོ་བཞིན་པའི་མི་དེ་ལ་རྣམ་ཞིག་སྐྱིད་རྗེའི་བསམ་པ་ཞིག་སྐྱེས་ན། ཁོ་ཞིང་
གཏུམ་དྲག་ཆན་གྱི་སྲང་མིག་གིས་ལྟ་བའི་མི་སྣག་པའི་བྱུད་བཞིན་ཁྲོ་གཉེར་ཆན་དེ་ཅོ་ཆེ་
འཛིན་ཞིག་ཞིག་གི་ཞལ་རས་ཞིག་ཏུ་འགྱུར་བ་དང་། མདའ་མདུང་དེ་ཚོ་མི་ཏོག་སོགས་
སུ་བྱུར་ནས་འཛིན་སྟེན་འདི་ན་དགའ་འཁྲུག་གི་རྣམ་ཏོག་གང་པོ་ཞིག་ལ་སྤྱོད་འགོག་བྱེད་

6

Moreover, this is not something just for commentators and writers to pursue; it is an effort that can and must also be pursued by those individuals in society who possess unrivalled intelligence and creativity and who are always thinking about ways to produce things that are needed in the world. This group would include scientists, engineers, actors, artists, musicians, singers, doctors, writers, businessmen, educators, religious leaders, politicians, and those who work in the culinary arts. If the brightest people from these fields were able to work together in support of world peace, I do believe a great deal of progress would be made, yet I also think that one essential condition is for all of us as a society to be motivated by compassion, or at least that we should try to reduce our selfish aims as much as possible.

In the past, most people had the attitude of seeking such things as wealth and fame. Those individuals who possess superior intelligence have also previously been driven by, and continue to be influenced by, such feelings as greed, hatred, resentment, and envy. But the things that are produced by the power of an intelligence that is under the control of such attitudes are not likely to be perfect in every respect, nor deserving of complete admiration, nor capable of bringing about the increase and development of genuine human well-being. However, if these efforts were motivated by compassion, I believe they would benefit both those who made them as well as all others beings, and they would naturally bring about such results as fame. This would be like having a single medicine that is able to cure many illnesses.

For example, consider a skilled artist who always paints figures of angry persons who have eyes that bulge with anger, and who are brandishing in their hands weapons such as arrows, spears, or swords. If this artist were to develop a compassionate mind, his or her compulsion to create unattractive drawings of wrathful, furious persons with wrinkled brows and glaring eyes might change into a disposition favoring illustrations of persons with bright, smiling faces, with the arrows and swords that they previously held being replaced by flowers and the like.

Those of us from Western Connecticut State University and Do Ngak Kunphen Ling Tibetan Buddhist Center for Universal Peace, who have formed the Committee for Compassion and Creativity in the 21st Century, view with great importance the goal of finding ways to promote world peace. Not only is

7

ཐུབ་རེས་རེད། གནས་ཚུལ་ཞིག་མོ་ལེག་ནས་ཏྲི་རྒྱ་ཡིན། དེ་འདྲ་སོང་ཚང་ང་ཚོ་(WCSU
& DNKL) རོ་ནས་(Creativity Compassion) ཚོགས་པ་འདི་འཛུགས་སྐྲུན་ཞི་
བདེར་སྐྱེན་པའི་ཐབས་ལམ་གལ་ཆེན་པོར་རྩེ་བཞིན་ཡོད། གང་ལྟར་དམིགས་ཡུལ་ཆེ་ཆུང་
ཅི་འདུ་ཞིག་བསྐྱབ་དགོས་ནའང་ཐབས་ཤེས་བྱུང་འབྲེལ་གནང་དགོས་པ་འདི་འི་སྐྱོབ་
སྟོང་བྱེད་པའི་བཅུད་རིག་ནང་ཤུགས་ཆེན་པོ་གསུང་གི་འདུག་པར་མ་ཟད། ང་རང་ཡང་
འདིར་དུ་ཆང་མོས་མཐུན་ཡོད་གཞན་ཞིག་ཡིན།

བོད་སྐད་ནང་(Creativity)ཟེར་བའི་དོན་གང་།

དབྱིན་སྐད་ནང་ཡོད་པའི་(Creativity)ཟེར་བའི་ཚིག་འདི་བོད་སྐད་ནང་རྣམ་དཔྱོད་
ཀྱི་རྒྱལ་ལམ། ཨང་ན་དུ་རུ་རྒྱུ་སྐྱེད་པོའི་ཐབས་འཕུལ་ལྟ་བུ་ཞིག་ལ་གོ་དགོས་པར་གསུང་
མཁན་ཡོད་པ་དང་། མང་ཆེ་བས་གསར་བཏོད་ཀྱི་རིག་པ་ཞིག་ལ་འགྲོལ་བཞིན་འདུག
གུས་ནས་རྣམ་དཔྱོད་ཀྱི་རྒྱལ་ཞེས་པ་དེ་འདོད་རྒྱུ་ཡིན། རྣམ་དཔྱོད་དང་རྒྱལ་ཞེས་ཚིག
སྐུབ་གཞིས་ཡོད། རྣམ་དཔྱོད་ཟེར་ན་དོན་དང་དོན་མ་ཡིན་པ་རྣམ་པར་འབྱེད་པའི་རིག
པའམ། ཡུལ་གྱི་དོ་བོ་དང་ཁྱད་པར་ལ་དཔྱོད་པའི་རིག་པ། བཅས་ལ་གོ་བ་དང་། རྒྱལ་ཟེར
ན་སྟོབས་ཤུགས་དང་སྟུ་ཚོགས་པའི་ནུས་མཐུ་ལ་གོ་བ་ཡིན། མདོར་ན་ཡུལ་གྱི་དོ་བོ་དང་
ཁྱད་པར་ལ་ཏྲིག་ཞིག་བྱེད་པའི་ཤེས་རབ་ཀྱི་ནུས་མཐུ་ལ་ཟེར།

གང་ལྟར་ཡང་རྣམ་དཔྱོད་ཀྱི་རྒྱལ་ལས་གང་ཞིག་མེད་པ་ནས་ཡོད་པ་བཟོ་བའམ།
ཨང་ན། ཡོད་པ་གང་ཞིག་གཏོར་བཤིག་གཏོང་བ། དེ་བཞིན་དཀའ་བའི་རིགས་སྟ་རུ་གཏོང་
བ། ཆ་མ་ཚོ་བའི་རིགས་ཆ་ཚང་བར་བཟོས་པ་སོགས་ནི་གཙོ་བོ་མིའི་རྣམ་དཔྱོད་ལས་
ཡོང་བ་ཡིན་དུས། དེ་འདུའི་རྣམ་དཔྱོད་ཀྱི་རྒྱལ་དེ་ལ་དབྱིན་སྐད་ནང་(Creativity)ཟེར
བའི་ཚིག་འདི་ལབ་པ་མིན་འགྲོ། འདི་ནི་འགྲོ་བ་མི་སོ་སོའི་རང་བཞིན་སྐྱེ་སྐྲིས་ལ་ཡོད
པའི་ཤེས་རབ་དང་། ཚེ་འདིའི་སྒྱངས་སྟོབས་ལས་བྱུང་བའི་ཤེས་རབ་གཉིས་དང་འབྲེལ་བ
གཏིང་ཟབ་ཡོད།

མ་ཟད་ཤེས་རབ་ལའང་། ཤེས་རབ་ཆེ་བ། ཤེས་རབ་ཟབ་པ། ཤེས་རབ་གྱུར་བ། ཤེས
རབ་གསལ་བ་བཅས་ཡོད་པ་བཞིན། སོ་སོ་ནས་བྱུང་བའི་རྣམ་དཔྱོད་རྒྱལ་ལའང་མི་འདུ

it stated with great emphasis in my own field of study that, no matter how great or small the goal that one is trying to achieve, it is necessary to apply the two qualities of wisdom and skillful means in combination, but I am also someone who comes here with a desire to offer my very strong support for this topic.

How to render the term "creativity" in Tibetan

Some persons have rendered the English word "creativity" into Tibetan as the expression *nam chö-kyi tsel* [T: *rnam dpyod kyi rtsal*], which literally means "the dynamic energy of intelligence." This word has also been interpreted in Tibetan by a phrase that means "a prolific ability to engender innovative thoughts" [T: *dran rgyu rgod po'i thabs 'phrul*], although most people describe creativity as a kind of awareness that is characterized by inventiveness [T: *gsar gtod kyi rig pa*]. My own belief is that the first expression is the most accurate. This Tibetan term is formed by combining two elements: *nam chö* and *tsel*. *Nam chö* refers to a type of mind that can distinguish between what is true and false, as well as one that has the ability to examine the essential nature and attributes of a particular object. It can also be understood to mean a type of mind that effectively perceives what is good or bad about something. The term *tsel* means a type of power or multifaceted ability. In short, the expression *nam chö-kyi tsel* describes a kind of intellectual power that examines the essential nature and attributes of an object.

In any case, the Tibetan expression *nam chö-kyi tsel*, which literally means "the dynamic energy of intelligence," mainly refers to a kind of human intelligence that is variously used to produce things that did not previously exist, destroy things that do exist, find easier ways of doing things that are difficult, complete things that previously were incomplete, and so forth. Consequently, it is my understanding that the quality described by this Tibetan expression is precisely what is meant by the English word "creativity." This quality also has a strong connection with two kinds of human intelligence: one form of intelligence that occurs innately, and a second that can be developed in this life through learning.

Intelligence also has different aspects, such as those that are described as "great intelligence," "profound intelligence," "quick intelligence," "bright intelligence," and the like.[1] I think these attributes also contribute to different kinds

བ་ཡོང་སྲིད་པ་རེད། དཔེར་ན། པར་གཞི་བྱུས་བཀོད་པ་དེ་ཚོ་གཙོ་བོ་ཤེས་རབ་གསལ་བ་
ལས་བྱུང་བ་དང་། གནས་མ་བྱུ་དང་མཚོ་བྱུ་དེ་དག་ཤེས་རབ་ཟབ་པ་ལས་བྱུང་བ་ལྟ་བུ་རེད།
མི་གཅིག་ལ་ཤེས་རབ་དེ་ཆང་མ་ཆང་ཡོད་པའང་སྲིད་ལ། ཤེས་རབ་སྟ་རེ་མ་གཏོགས་མེད་
པའང་སྲིད།

གང་ཞིག་ལ་སྙིང་རྗེ་ཟེར།

འདིར་སྙིང་རྗེ་ཟེར་ན། ཆད་ཡོད་པའི་སྙིང་རྗེ་ནས་ཆད་མེད་པའི་སྙིང་རྗེ་བར་ཆང་མར་
ཚོས་འཛིན་ཞུ་རྒྱུ་ཡིན། ཆད་ཡོད་པའི་སྙིང་རྗེ་ཟེར་ན། རང་ཉིད་དག" རང་ལ་དགའ་བོ་ཡོད་
པའི་མི་འམ་དུང་འགྲོ་དེ་ལ་དགའ་འལ་འཕྱུད་སྐྱབས་དགའ་འལ་དེ་ལས་སྐྱོབ་ཐབས་དང་
། དེ་ལས་ཐར་འཛིན་ཡོད་པའི་བསམ་པ་དེ་ལ་ཟེར་བས། དེ་ནི་ཏ་ཅང་རྒྱ་ཆུང་ཆུང་གི་སྙིང་
རྗེ་ཞིག་རེད།

བསམ་བློ་དེ་གོང་འཕེལ་བཏང་ནས་རང་གི་གཉེན་ཆན་དང་། དེ་ནས་རང་གི་མཁའ་སྟེ་
གཅིག་པ་ཚོ། དེ་ནས་རང་གི་རྒྱལ་ཁབ་གཅིག་པ་ཚོ། དེ་འདྲ་དེ་འདྲ་བྱུས་ནས་འཛིག་ཧྟེན་
འདིའི་འགྲོ་བ་སེམས་ཅན་ཡོད་ཆད་སྡུག་བསྔལ་ལས་སྐྱོབས་ཐབས་དང་སྡུག་བསྔལ་ལས་
འབྲལ་འདོད་ཡོད་པའི་བསམ་པ། རང་གི་ཁེ་ཕན་དང་མ་འབྲེལ་བའི་བློ་ཞིག་ཏུ་འགྱུར་
སྲིད་པ་རེད། འདི་ནི་བསམ་བློ་གང་འཚམ་རྒྱ་ཆེན་པོ་ཡོད་པའི་སྙིང་རྗེ་ཞིག་རེད། ད་དུང་
དེ་མཐའ་མེད་དུ་འཕེལ་རྒྱ་ཡོད་པ་ཞིག་ལ་ད་གབོང་ཆང་མེད་པའི་སྙིང་རྗེ་ཟེར། མདོར་
བསྡུས་ན་སྙིང་རྗེ་ནི་གཞན་ལ་ཕན་པའི་སེམས་ཡིན། སྙིང་རྗེ་ནི་རང་གཞན་ཐམས་ཅད་སྐྱག་
བསྡལ་དང་བྲལ་འདོད་དང་དེ་ལས་སྐྱོབས་རྒྱའི་འགན་འཁུར་བའི་སེམས་ཤིག་ཡིན། སྙིང་
རྗེ་ནི་རང་གི་ཁེ་ཕན་བློས་གཏོང་བའི་སེམས་ཤིག་ཡིན། སྙིང་རྗེ་ཞེས་པ་འདི་ལ་རང་རང་གི་
འདོད་ཚུལ་དང་མཐུན་པའི་འགྲེལ་བཤད་མི་འདུ་བ་རེ་རྒྱག་བཞིན་ཡོད་ནའང་། གཙོ་བོ་
རང་བཞིན་ལྷུན་སྐྱེས་ལ་སེམས་ཚོར་ཅི་འདུ་ཞིག་ཡོད་པ་དེ་དང་མཐུན་ན་སྙིང་རྗེ་དང། དེ་
དང་མི་མཐུན་ན་སོ་སོས་དགོས་མཁོ་དང་བསྟུན་ནས་བཟོ་བའི་སྙིང་རྗེ་རེད། རང་བཞིན་
ལྷུན་སྐྱེས་དང་མཐུན་ཞེས་པ། དཔེར་ན་ཕ་མས་བུ་གུ་ལ་བརྩེ་བ་སྐྱོད་དུས་རང་གི་ཁེ་ཕན

10

of creativity. For example, the skill of a graphic designer derives mainly from bright intelligence, while the ability to design an airplane, ship, or computer derives from profound intelligence. It is possible for someone to exhibit all of these types of intelligence; sometimes a person may have only one of them.

What is compassion?

In the present context, I would describe compassion as a quality that ranges from a type that is limited in nature to one that is unlimited, while recognizing that that the entire spectrum can be referred to as forms of compassion. "Limited compassion" means an attitude in which a person desires to save or free himself or herself, or someone that he or she likes, or an animal, from circumstances or from some form of difficulty that any of these may be experiencing. But this is a very narrow kind of compassion. It is possible to expand this attitude gradually from a feeling that is held not only toward one's friends and relatives, but also toward all human beings who live in the same geographical area, and then extend it further toward all those who live in the same country, until finally it becomes a feeling that desires to find a way of saving every living being everywhere in the world from every form of suffering and freeing them from their suffering. This attitude can also be one that is entirely free of any desire for personal gain or benefit. Such an attitude would represent a form of compassion that is quite far-reaching. If this attitude can be developed even further than this to a point where it is completely unrestricted, then it becomes what we can call "unlimited compassion."

In its essence, compassion is a type of mind that wants to benefit others, and one that desires to free oneself and others from suffering, and that ultimately takes on the responsibility of saving oneself and others from that suffering. Compassion is also a mind that gives up concern for one's own personal gain or benefit.

Although people may define compassion differently based upon their own individual belief system, the main point to bear in mind as we try to establish a common definition of compassion is whether the description accords with qualities of our mind that are part of our innate nature. Any description that does not accord with this standard can be judged to be one that has been artificially devised to fit the needs of a particular theory. When I say qualities that

དོར་ནས་དུས་རྣམ་ཡང་ཕྱུ་གུའི་བདེ་སྡུག་རྒྱུད་བསྐུལ་པ་འདི་རང་བཞིན་ལྷུན་སྐྱེས་རེད། དུང་འགྲོ་ཚོགས་རང་གི་ཕྱུ་གུར་བརྩེ་བ་སྟོད་སྡངས་འདི་ཡང་ལྷུན་སྐྱེས་རེད། འགྲོ་བ་སེམས་ཅན་ལ་བརྩེ་ཟེར་བ་དེ་ཁ་མས་ཕྱུ་གུ་ལ་བརྩེ་བ་སྟོད་སྡངས་དང་མཚུངས་པ་ཞིག་དགོས་པ་རེད།

རྣམ་དཔྱོད་ཆལ་དང་སྙིང་རྗེ་བྱུང་འབྱེལ་དགོས་པའི་རྒྱུ་མཚན།

འཇིག་རྟེན་འདི་ཡར་རྒྱས་ཡེས་པར་དུ་དགོས་ལ། ཡར་རྒྱས་གཏོང་ཁ་མཁན་གྱི་རྣམ་དཔྱོད་ཅན་ཡང་ཡེས་པར་དགོས། དེ་དང་མཉམ་འགྲོ་བའི་བདེ་སྙིང་ལའང་ཡར་རྒྱས་ཡེས་པར་དགོས། རྒྱུ་མཚན་དེར་རྟེན་རྣམ་དཔྱོད་པ་དང་སྙིང་རྗེ་བྱུང་འབྱེལ་ཡེས་པར་དགོས་ཀྱི་འདུག་ལུ་ཡིན།

དའི་དོ་ཤེས་ཡེས་ཆེ་སེམས་པ་བཟང་པོ་ཞིག་ཡོད། ཁོང་གིས "དུས་རྣམ་ཡང་སྙིང་རྗེ་དང་ཤེས་རབ་བྱུང་འབྱེལ་དགོས། ཤེས་རབ་ཡག་པོ་ཡོད་ལ་སྙིང་རྗེ་མེད་ན་དེ་ཏི་ཡར་རང་བཞིན་ཆགས་རྒྱུ་དང་། སྙིང་རྗེ་ཡོད་ཅིང་ཤེས་རབ་མེད་ན་ཁྲི་ནང་བཞིན་རེད་" ཅེས་གོ་རྒྱུ་ཡོད་པའི་བགའ་མོལ་ཞིག་གསུངས་སྐྱོང་། ཡང་ནང་པའི་གཞུང་ལ་འགའ། མིའི་ནུ་ཚོགས་ཕྱུགས་ཀྱི་འདུ་ཤེས་ཅན[2] ཞེས་རང་གི་མི་ཚེའི་ཀུན་སྙོད་ནང་དག་འདུལ་གཞེན་སྐྱོང་དང་། ཉིན་རེའི་འཚོ་བ་འཕྲོངས་ཐབས། རང་གི་སྲོག་སྲུང་ཐབས་ཁོ་ན་མ་གཏོགས་བསམ་བློ་གཞན་མེད་ན། དེ་འདི་ཞིག་ནི་དུང་འགྲོ་ཚོ་ལའང་གཅིག་མཚུངས་སུ་ཡོད་པས། མིའི་ལུས་ཡིན་གོ་མ་ཆེན་པ་ཞིག་དང་རང་གི་རྣམ་དཔྱོད་བེད་སྤྱོད་གཏོང་མ་ཐུབ་པས་དང་འགྲོའི་བསམ་བློ་དང་གཅིག་པ་རེད་གསུང་གི་ཡོད། ཡང་མིའི་རྣམ་དཔྱོད་ཆ་ཚང་བ་བེད་སྤྱོད་གཏོང་ཐུབ་མཁན་ཡོད་དུང་སྐྱེར་སེམས་ཆེན་པོ་ཡོད་ན་རང་ལ་མ་གཏོགས་འཇིག་རྟེན་སྤྱི་ལ་ཕན་ཐོགས་ཡོང་མི་སྲིད། བྱ་སྤྱོད་དང་པ་རྣམས་སྐྱེར་སེམས་ལ་བརྟེན་ནས་ཡོང་བ་རེད། བྱས་ཙང་ང་ཚོ་སུ་ཡིན་ནའང་འཇིག་རྟེན་འདིའི་འགྲོ་བའི་བདེ་སྙིང་ཡོང་ཐབས་ལ་ཡེས་པར་དུ་བསམ་ཤེས་གནང་དགོས་འདུག དེ་ལ་སྙིང་རྗེའི་བསམ་པ་ལ་དགོས་པར་མཐོང་།

"accord with our innate nature," I mean, for example, that when parents show affection toward their own children, they ignore anything that might bring gain or benefit to themselves and consider only what affects the welfare of their children. This is a mental quality that is part of their innate nature. Animals also have a way of showing affection toward their offspring that is innate. So when we refer to the affection that individuals show toward other sentient beings, it must include a way of showing affection that is like that which parents show toward their children.

Why creativity and compassion should be combined

The world we live in must be improved. We also need intelligent persons who are capable of bringing about this improvement. Moreover, we must also improve the well-being of sentient beings. This is why creativity must be combined with compassion.

I know a certain doctor who has a very insightful mind. I had a conversation with him in which he said something quite meaningful. He told me, "Wisdom and compassion must always go together. An intelligent person who lacks compassion can become like Adolf Hitler. And if we are compassionate but lack intelligence, then we might become like a dog." Wise Buddhist teachers often quote the line, "a person with a human form whose ideas are like those of a beast."[2] This means that if a person's behavior consists only of trying to defeat his or her enemies and support his or her allies, and if he or she doesn't think about anything except how to obtain his or her daily subsistence and how to protect his or her own life, then that person is just like an animal. This person is one who has not taken advantage of his or her human existence and has not used human intelligence to its fullest capacity. Therefore, the thoughts of such a person are said to be the same as those of an animal. Even if a person is able to use all of his or her intelligence, if he or she is very selfish, then that ability will be used only to benefit himself or herself; it will not be possible for him or her to benefit the world in general. Those who engage in evil behavior also do so because of their selfishness. Therefore, it is absolutely necessary for all of us, no matter who we are, to know how to think about the welfare of all sentient beings in the world. This is why we must have a compassionate attitude.

དཔེར་ན། སྐྱེ་སྲུང་ཅན་གྱི་སྲུང་འགྲོ་མཁན་ཞིག་ལ་མཚོན་ན། རང་ལ་རྐུ་མ་རྟོག་གི་
འཁར་སྲུང་ཕོག་དགའ་ལ་དང་སྔག་བསྒྱལ་རིགས་རྒྱུད་རྒྱུང་ལ་བསམ་ཞིག་གཏོང་དགོས་
དུས། རང་ཉིད་ཀྱི་སྐྱེ་དགས་ནས་སྲུག་བསྒྱལ་ནད་སྲུང་བ་དང་སྲུབས་ཉེས་ན་རང་སྲོག་
གཅོད་པའི་ཡོང་སྲིད་པ་རེད། སྐྱེ་སྲུང་མ་ཕར་གོན་ནས་སྙིང་རྗེའི་བསམ་པ་ཞིག་བསྐྱེབས་
ཕུབ་ན་རང་སྲོག་སྐྱོབ་ཕུབ་པ་མ་ཟན་སྲུང་དེག་དེ་འང་ཕུན་སུམ་ཚོགས་པོའི་རང་འབྱུབ་
ཕུག། གང་ཡིན་ཟེར་ན་སེམས་སྐྱོ་བཞིན་པ་ནས་གོན་པ་གཉིས་པ་སྟོ་ས་ཡོད་པ་ཞིག་དུ་གོ་
བ་དང་སེམས་ཕུགས་འཕར་མ་བསྐྱེབས་པའི་རྒྱེན་གྱིས་རེད། གང་ཡིན་ཟེར་ན་སེམས་ཅན་
ལ་བརྩེ་བ་ཕུགས་ཅེན་པོ་ཡོད་ན་སོ་སོ་རང་ཉིད་ཀྱི་ཕུང་པོ་དང་ཁ་བྲལ་ཕུབ་ནའང་སེམས་
ཅན་དེ་དག་བློས་གཏོང་ཕུབ་ཀྱི་མེད། འདི་ནི་སྐྱོ་སེམས་དང་ཕན་སེམས་བྱུང་འབྲེལ་བྱེད་
པའི་འབྲས་བུ་ཡིན།

ང་ཚོ་གོན་པའི་ནང་ནའང་སྲུག་བསྒྱལ་དང་སུན་སྲུང་གི་སྐོར་བྲིས་པའི་དེག་མང་པོ་
ཡོད་ལ་སྒོག་མཁན་ཡང་ཉུང་ཉུང་མ་རེད། དེག་དེ་དག་སྒོག་པའི་མཐར་མི་དེ་འཇིག་རྟེན་
འདིའི་ཕུན་ཚོགས་གང་འདུ་ཞིག་ཡོད་ནའང་དེ་ལ་ཆགས་ཞེན་མེད་པར་སུན་སྲུང་ཕུགས་
ཅེན་པོ་བསྐྱེབས་ནས་རང་ཉིད་གཅིག་པོ་སློག་སྐྱབ་བྱེད་རྒྱུའི་ལས་འཚོལ་བ་ལས་རང་
སློག་ཏོར་བ་མེད། དེ་ནི་བསྐྱབ་བྱའི་ནང་སྐྱེ་སྲུང་བསྐྱེབས་པའི་རྗེས་སུ་གོམ་པ་དང་པོ་དང་
། གཉིས་པ་སོགས་འགྲོ་སའི་ལམ་སྟོན་ཡོད་པའི་རྒྱུ་མཚན་གྱིས་རེད། དེ་ཡང་ཆོམ་པ་པོས་
ཉམས་མྱོང་ཕོག་ནས་བྲིས་པ་རེད། དེ་མཐའ་མ་དུག་དགའ་སློ་ཆད་མེད་ཕོག་གནས་ཡོད་
པ་དང་། དེ་ཡང་སྐྱིང་རྗེའི་བསམ་པ་ཡོད་པའི་རྒྱེན་གྱིས་རེད། དེ་ལྷ་བུའི་བསམ་པ་ཡོད་ན
རང་གཞན་གཉིས་ཀར་ཕན་ཕོགས་པ་གོང་དུ་ཞུས་པ་བཞིན་རེད། དེ་དཔེ་མཚོན་གཅིག་
རེད།

དེ་མཚུངས་ནས་གོང་དུ་ཞུས་པའི་འཇིག་རྟེན་འདིའི་འགྲོ་བ་ལ་དགོས་མཁོ་སྐྱན་
མཁན་ཚོར་ཚང་མེད་པའི་སྙིང་རྗེ་ཞིག་ཡོད་ན་རབ་དང་། དེ་མ་བྱུང་ཡང་རྒྱ་ཆེན་པོའི་སྙིང་
རྗེའི་བསམ་པ་དེ་སྐྱེ་ཕུབ་ན་ང་ཚོའི་དགོས་མཁོ་རྣམས་ལས་སྣ་པོས་སྐྱབ་ཕུབ་ཀྱིས་རེད།
འགྲོ་བ་མི་ཡིན་ན་དེ་འདུའི་བསམ་པ་སྐྱེས་སྲིད་པ་མ་ཟད་འབྱུང་སྐྱིང་བཞང་རེད། འོན

For example, consider a person who habitually writes sad stories. If the author must always think about circumstances that only involve misfortune and suffering, then they themselves might be overcome by sadness and fall into a state of mental suffering. In the worst case, this person might even take his or her own life. But if they were able to develop compassion prior to reflecting on those sad circumstances, in addition to saving their own life, the author might be able to complete the story in a more optimistic manner. The reason for this is that, even while one is experiencing a sad state of mind, the author realizes that there is another step that they can take and therefore, can find a way of encouraging themselves mentally. Another reason is that if you have great love for other sentient beings, although you might be willing to give up your own body, you would not be able to give up your concern for others. This result comes about through being able to combine a sad mind with one that wishes to benefit others.

We Tibetans have many books that are written about suffering and difficult situations, and the number of persons who read them is also not small. After reading these books, the reader tends to lose his or her attachment for every kind of prosperity that is found in this world and develops a strong feeling of dissatisfaction toward them. In addition, this understanding causes one to seek a spiritual path that can be meditated on; it doesn't cause them to give up their life. This is because the instructions provide a series of steps that represent a path that can be followed after one has developed such feelings of sadness. The authors who write these books do so based on their own personal experience, and toward the end of their lives, they are able to abide in a state of limitless peace and joy. This also is due to their having a compassionate mind. If someone is able to develop this kind of attitude, then they will be able to benefit both themselves and others.

Similarly, if the persons who are capable of creating things that are useful for all beings in the world should develop limitless compassion, that would be ideal. But even if they are only able to achieve a form of compassion that is significantly far-reaching, they will be able to achieve more easily what all of us need. Not only is it possible for human beings to develop this kind of attitude, there are in fact persons who have actually done so. Nevertheless, I do not hold the expectation that all creative persons will be able to develop such a precious

གྲུང་གྲུབས་པས་ཤེན་དུ་ནས་རྩ་ཆེ་བའི་བསམ་པ་དེ་རྣམ་དཔྱོད་ཅན་ཆོས་མར་ཡོད་ཐུབ་
པའི་རེ་བ་རྣམ་ཡང་རྒྱག་གིས་མེད། མ་མཐར་ཡང་འཇིག་རྟེན་འདིའི་འགྲོ་བའི་བདེ་སྐྱག་ལ་
བསམ་བློ་གཏོང་ཤེས་པ་ཞིག་བྱུང་ན་དེ་ཞི་བདེའི་སྟོན་འགྲོ་ཆུགས་པ་རེད། འགྲོ་བའི་བདེ་
སྐྱག་ལ་འཇན་འཇུར་ཡིན་རྒྱུའི་བསམ་པ་ཞིག་སྐྱེ་ཐུབ་ན་དེ་ཞི་བདེའི་སྟོན་འགྲོ་ཆུགས་པ་
རེད། སྐྱེར་སེམས་རྒྱུད་དུ་གཏོང་ཐུབ་ན་དེ་ཞི་བདེའི་སྟོན་འགྲོ་ཆུགས་པ་རེད། འགྲོ་བ་མི་
སྐྱེར་སོ་སོས་རང་རྒྱུད་ཀྱི་ཆགས་སྡང་ཉུང་དུ་གཏོང་ཐུབ་ན་དེ་ཞི་བདེའི་སྟོན་འགྲོ་ཆུགས་པ་
རེད། གང་ལ་འབད་ཆོག་ཤེས་ཐུབ་ན་དེ་ཞི་བདེའི་སྟོན་འགྲོ་ཆུགས་པ་རེད།

དེ་ནི་གོང་དུ་ཞུས་པའི་འཇིག་རྟེན་འདིའི་དགོས་མཁོར་བསམ་ཞིག་གནང་མཁན་ཚོས་
འཁན་འབྱུར་ཡིན་ཐུབ་ན་ན་རྣབས་ཆེན་པོའི་བྱ་བ་ཞིག་རེད། དེ་ནི་འཇིག་རྟེན་འདིར་དཔལ་
འབྱོར་ཡོན་ཏན་སོགས་སྐྱེན་གྲུགས་ཡོད་པ་རྣམས་ནས་འབད་འབྱུར་ཡིན་ཐུབ་ན་ན་རྣབས་
ཆེན་པོའི་བྱ་བ་ཞིག་རེད། དེ་ནི་ཆོས་ལུགས་པ་དང་ཆོས་ལུགས་ལ་དད་པ་མེད་པ་ཆང་
མར་ལས་འགན་ཡོད་པ་ཞིག་རེད། འཇམ་སྐྱིད་ཞེ་བདེ་ཡོད་བར་ཆོས་ལུགས་མི་སྐྱ་ལས་
ཆན་རིག་པ་ཆོར་ནུས་པ་ཆེ་བ་ཡོད། ཆོས་ལུགས་མི་སྐྱ་ལས་སྐུ་རྩལ་ཆོར་ནུས་པ་ཆེ་བ་
ཡོད། དེ་བཞིན་ཆོས་ལུགས་མི་སྐྱ་ལས་ཆོང་ལས་པ་དང་། སློབ་གྲྭ་པ་སོགས་ལ་ནུས་པ་ཆེ་
བ་ཡོད། གང་ཡིན་ཟེར་ན། རྒྱུན་ལྡན་མི་ཆེའི་ནང་དུས་ཆོང་ཐལ་ཆེ་བ་ཁོང་རྣམ་པ་དང་
འབྲེལ་བའི་གནད་དོན་ཐོག་འགྲོ་བཞིན་ཡོད། ཡིན་ཀྱང་ཆོས་ལུགས་ཀྱི་བསྐུབ་བྱ་བཟང་པོ་
དང་ཁ་བྲལ་ཐབས་མེད་པར་འ་ཤེས་དགོས་པ་གལ་ཆེན་པོར་མཐོང་། ཆོས་ལུགས་པ་ཆོས་
གུང་བྱམས་སྙིང་རྗེ་དང་ལ་རབས་བཟང་སྤྱོད་ཀྱི་བསྐུབ་བྱ་དེ་དག་དགོན་པའི་ནང་ཙམ་མ་
ཡིན་པར་སློབ་གྲྭ་ཁག་གི་སློབ་ཆན་ནང་འཇིག་ཐུབ་པ་དང་། རྒྱལ་སྤྱིའི་ཁྲིམས་ནང་འཕོང་
ཐུབ་པའི་ཆེད་འབད་བརྩོན་གནང་དགོས་གལ་ཆེར་མཐོང་། དེ་ནི་ཆོས་ལུགས་པ་ལ་གཅིག་
པོ་ལ་དགོས་འཁོ་ཡོད་པ་དེ་འདྲ་མ་རེད། ཆང་མར་དགོས་པ་དང་ཆང་མར་ཕན་པའི་སྐྱན་
ཞིག་ཡིན།

སློབ་བརྩན་བཟོ་མཁན་ཆོས་སློག་བརྩན་ལམ་ནས་འཇམ་སྐྱིད་ཞི་བདེའི་ལམ་སྟོན་
བྱེད་ཐུབ་པ་དང་། དགེ་རྐན་ཆོས་ནས་པ་ཡང་ཐོག་ནས་འཇམ་སྐྱིད་ཞི་བདེའི་ལམ་སྟོན་བྱེད་

attitude. But I do believe that if they are able to learn how to think about the welfare of all sentient beings, this will establish the preliminary stage for bringing about peace and happiness. If we are able to develop an attitude that takes responsibility for the happiness of all sentient beings, this will establish the preliminary stage for bringing about peace and happiness. If we are able to reduce our selfish tendencies, this will establish the preliminary stage for bringing about peace and happiness. If each individual person is able to reduce his or her hatred and attachment, this will establish the preliminary stage for bringing about peace and happiness. If we develop a greater feeling of satisfaction with the things that we have, this will establish the preliminary stage for bringing about peace and happiness.

If those persons who were identified earlier as the ones that reflect upon the needs of the world could accept these responsibilities, this would be activity that could bring about very powerful results. If those individuals who are renowned for their wealth and other exceptional qualities could accept these responsibilities, this would be activity that could bring about very powerful results. This is a responsibility that everyone should accept, both religious persons and those who do not believe in any religion.

I believe that, in a certain way, scientists have more power to bring about peace in the world than those who represent the various religious traditions. Artists also have more power to bring about peace in the world than religious figures. Similarly, businesspeople, educators, and others of influence in our culture have more power than religious figures. The reason for this is that, during their lives, most people spend the majority of their time pursuing activities that have some connection with the fields in which these people occupy positions of influence. But I also believe that we must recognize the importance of not losing sight of the excellent forms of spiritual instruction that come from religion. Those individuals who represent religious traditions should not limit their practice of the teachings about loving-kindness, compassion, and virtuous conduct to the confines of their religious institutions. They also have an opportunity to present these values in the classrooms of secular schools and to seek to have them included within the field of international law. Therefore, I believe it is important for representatives of religious traditions to make efforts in those areas as well—which is to say, these teachings are not useful only to religious

ཕུག གནས་གཏོང་མཁན་ཚོས་སྐྱ་དབྱངས་ཀྱི་ལམ་ནས་འཇོག་སྒྲིང་ཞེ་བདེའ་ལམ་སྟོན་
བྱེད་ཕུག ཨེམ་ཆེ་ཚོས་རང་གི་ཀུན་སྤྱོད་ཐོག་ནས་འཇོག་སྒྲིང་ཞེ་བདེའ་ལམ་སྟོན་བྱེད་
ཕུག ཆོན་རིག་པ་ཚོས་ཀྱང་རྫས་དང་སེམས་ཁམས་བར་ཞིབ་འཇུག་བཀྱུད་འཇོག་སྒྲིང་ཞེ་
བདེའ་ལམ་སྟོན་བྱེད་ཕུག དཔལ་འབྱོར་ཡོད་མཁན་ཚོས་རྒྱུ་ནོར་ལམ་ནས་འཇོག་སྒྲིང་ཞེ་
བདེའ་ལམ་སྟོན་བྱེད་ཕུག དེ་བཞིན་རོལ་ཆ་འབུད་སྤྱིང་དགོལ་གསུམ་དང་རི་མོ་མཁན་
སོགས་ཆན་མས་སོ་སོའ་ཆེད་ལམ་ཀྱི་ལམ་ནས་འཇོག་སྒྲིང་ཞེ་བདེའ་ལམ་སྟོན་བྱེད་ཕུབ་ཀྱི་
རེདགལ་སྲིད་ཁྱེད་ཚོ་ལ་ཞེ་བདེར་མོས་པ་ཡོད་ན། གལ་སྲིད་ཁྱེད་ཚོ་ལ་དངལ་དངོས་དང་
མིང་གཞིག་པོའ་བསམ་བློ་རྐྱང་པ་མེད་ན། གལ་སྲིད་ཁྱེད་ཚོར་ཁབ་སེམས་ཡོད་ན། གལ་
སྲིད་ཁྱེད་ཚོར་སྙིང་རྗེའ་བསམ་པ་ཡོད་ཕུབ་ན།

འཇོག་སྒྲིང་ཞེ་བདེ་ཡོང་ཐབས་དེ་མི་སྟེར་གཅིག་གི་ཞི་བདེ་ནས་སྒྱོ་འཇུགས་དགོས།
དེ་ཡང་མིའི་མིག་ལ་མཇོས་པ་ཆག་དང་། རྣ་བར་སྒྲ་སྙན་པ་ཆག ལྕེ་ལ་བྲོ་བ་ཞིམ་པ་ཆག
གྱིས་མི་སྟེར་ཀྱི་སེམས་ལ་ཕུགས་བཀྱུད་རེང་པོའི་ཞི་བདེ་སྐྱེན་མི་ཕུག སྐྱབས་རེ་ཁོང་བྲོ་
ཡངས་བཞིན་པའི་སྐྱབས་ནས་རྒྱུན་བྲོ་བ་ཞིམ་པོ་དེ་དག་མི་ཞིམ་པར་འགྱུར་བཞིན་ཡོང་།
ཚོག་ཤེས་ཅན་ལ་ཟས་གང་ཡིན་བྲོ་བ་རྗེད་བཞིན་ཡོད། དེ་གཞིག་ཁྱད་པར་ཟས་ཀྱི་མ་ཡིན་
པར་ནང་བསམ་བློ་གཏོང་ཕྱོགས་ནས་ཡོང་བ་རེད། དེར་རྟེན་གཙོ་བོ་མིག་ལ་མཇོས་ཆ
མཐོང་བ་དེ་བཀྱུད་ནས་སྒྲུང་པའམ་སེམས་ལ་ཚོག་ཤེས། ཐུམས་སྲིང་དེ། སྟེར་སེམས་ཅུང་
བ་སོགས་ཀྱི་བཅོས་བསྒྱུར་ཐེབས་ཕུབ་པ་ཞིག་དང་། རྣ་བར་སྒྲ་སྙན་པ་ཐོས་པ་དེ་བཀྱུད་
ནས་ཀྱང་པཔམ་སེམས་ལ་བཅོས་བསྒྱུར་ཐེབས་ཕུབ་པ་ཞིག་དགོས་པ་རེད། དེ་མ་གཏོགས་
རྒྱུ་ཚོང་གཅིག་གཞིས་ཆག་དང་སྐྱར་མ་ཁ་ཤས་རིང་གི་ཞི་བདེ་ཡོང་བར་ང་ཚོའི་ལྟ་གྲུབའི་
བསམ་ཞིག་གཏོང་དགོས་པ་མི་འདུག སྐྱར་མ་ཁ་ཤས་རིང་གི་ཞི་བདེ་ཡོང་འཇོག་སྒྲིང་ཞེ་བདེ་
ལ་དེ་ཚམ་ཐན་ཐོགས་ཕུབ་ཀྱི་མ་རེད་དུན་ཀྱི་འདུག འདི་ནི་ང་བར་འཇོག་སྒྲིང་འདེན་
དུས་སྐྱབས་གཉིས་འབའ་ཞིག་བྱུང་སྟེ། ང་ཚོས་རྒྱས་མཐའ་ཆེ་བའི་དགས་འཕྱུག་གི་དུས་
སྐྱབས་ཞིག་དང་། དགས་འཕྱུག་གི་ཕྱིར་དུ་སྒྱ་སྤྱིག་བྱེད་པ་དེ་གཞིས་རྒྱན་པ་རེད། སྒྱ་སྤྱིག་
བྱེད་པའི་དུས་སྐྱབས་རེར་ང་ཚོས་ཞི་བདེར་དུ་འགྲོ་བཞིན་ཡོང་ཞེས་མི་གཅིག་གི་བརྗོད་

practitioners. They represent a kind of inner medicine that everyone needs and that is useful for everyone.

Filmmakers can use movies to teach ways of promoting world peace. Teachers can use the blackboard to teach ways of promoting world peace. Singers can use songs to teach ways of promoting world peace. Doctors can use their conduct to teach ways of promoting world peace. Scientists can use their research into the relationship between the brain and the mind to teach ways of promoting world peace. Wealthy individuals can use their wealth to teach ways of promoting world peace. Similarly, musicians can play their various musical instruments, and artists and others can use their individual skills to teach ways of promoting world peace. If you want peace, if you aren't motivated exclusively by money and fame, if you have a desire to benefit others, and if you are able to develop a compassionate mind, then the effort to bring world peace must begin with each person striving to find his or her own personal peace and happiness.

Moreover, having an object that is beautiful to the eyes, a sound that is pleasant to the ears, or tastes that are delicious to the tongue cannot produce long-term or far-reaching personal mental happiness. For example, sometimes when we are angry, those foods that we usually find delicious can take on an unpleasant taste. But a person who is easily satisfied with whatever they have will find that whatever food they eat will have a good taste. This difference is not due to the nature of the food, it comes about because of the way one thinks about these things. For this reason, the main factor that causes an object to appear attractive to the eye comes about through being able to bring about such a change in attitude in the mind in the sense of being satisfied with what one has, as well as increased feelings of compassion, loving-kindness, and a reduced sense of selfishness. So, in order for our ears to be able to hear a pleasant sound, we must first be someone who is able to bring about a change in the mind. Now it isn't necessary to think this way in order to experience happiness for a few minutes or a few hours. But I don't believe that a few minutes of happiness can contribute much to the goal of world peace.

Up until now, the world has only known two kinds of situations. One is the situation that is well-known to us, in which a war is ongoing, and the second is the situation in which we are getting ready for the next war. I heard someone say that what we call "peace" is just that period during which we are getting ready

སྐྱོང་བ་ཞིག་དགུན་གྱི་འདུག སྐྱིན་ཁ་ནི་མ་གཅིག་གཏོང་བའི་ཞི་བདེ་དེ་ཙམ་གྱི་ཏོ་མས་ཀྱིས་ ཡོད་ན་དགའ་འཕུལ་ལྦ་སྟྱོག་བྱེད་པའི་སྐབས་ཀྱི་ཞི་བདེར་འབྱོད་པ་དང་གཅིག་ལ་རེད། བཙོན་ཁང་དང་ཁྲིམས་ཁང་དེ་ཚོ་མེད་ལ་ནས་ཡོད་ལ་ཆགས་པ་དེ་ང་ཚོ་ཆོང་མར་ འགགས་ཡིན་ཡོད་ལ་དང་། རྒྱལ་ཁབ་ཕན་ཚུན་བར་མཐའ་སྤྱུང་དམག་མི་མེད་ལ་ནས་ཡོད་ པར་གྱུར་བ་དེ་ཡང་ང་ཚོ་ཆང་མར་འགགས་ཡིན་ཡོད། ཕྱིན་གྱུན་ད་ལྟ་ང་རང་ཚོའི་ཁྲིམས་ ཁང་ནས་ར་བ་ཕྱིད་སྐྱིམ་ཞིག་གིས་འགྱིགས་ནས་ཡོད་ལ་དང་། བདེ་སྐྱང་བ་མིས་བྱས་ན་ འགྱིགས་ནས་ཡོད། བཙོན་ཁང་མའི་སྐྱང་བྱས་ན་འགྱིགས་ནས་ཡོད། ཁྲིམས་ཚིག་གཏོང་ དང་གཏོང་ཕྱུག་ནས་བཏང་ན་འགྱིགས་ནས་ཡོད། ལེགས་ལེ་སྤྱུག་ཏུ་མ་སོང་སོང་སྐྱང་སྐྱི་ བ་ ཕྱུག་དགོས། འཇིག་རྟེན་འདིའི་འགྱོ་བ་ལ་ད་ལྟ་ལས་བདེ་སྐྱིང་མར་བ་སྐྱེན་ཕྱབས་གནང་ ཕྱུག་ན་ཏུ་ལས་པའི་བཟང་སྤྱོགས་ཞིག་རེད། འགྱོ་བ་སེམས་ཅན་ལ་ཉེས་པར་དགོས་པ་ དེ་རེད། ཕྱིན་གྱུན་འདི་ནི་ངས་སོང་ད་བསྐུར་སྤྱག་ཡང་སྤྱག་ཀྱིས་ཞེས་པ་བཞིན་ཆགས་ སྐྱང་མེད་པར་བཙོ་བ་ལ་རག་ལས། འདི་ནི་སྐྱེར་སེམས་ཅུན་དུ་སོང་བ་ལ་རག་ལས། གང་ ལའང་ཆོག་ཞེས་ཕྱུབ་པ་ལ་རག་ལས། འདི་ནི་སྐྱིང་རྗེའི་བསམ་པ་ཡོད་པ་ལ་རག་ལས། གུས་པར་ཡོས་པའི་ནམ་དཔྱོང་ཅན་ཚོ། གསར་བཏོང་པ་ཚོ། ཆོས་ལྦགས་མི་སྐུ་ཚོ། ང་ཚོའི་ རེ་བ་བཙལ་ས་ཚོ།

བྱར་མཆན།

སྐྱིར་བདུང་ཞི་བདེ་སྐྱོར་ལ་འཇམ་སྐྱིན་ཞི་བདེའི་དེ་དཔོན་སོགས་མཁས་པའི་དབང་པོ་ དག་གི་ནུམས་སྐྱོང་གི་ཕྱུག་པའི་བསྐུབ་བྱ་དང་། ཡིད་དབང་འཕྱོག་པའི་གསུང་ཆོ་རྣམས་ ལ་ལག་ལེན་དང་གཅེས་སྐྱང་དགོས་པ་ནི་ཞི་བདེར་སོས་པ་ཆང་མའི་ལས་འགན་རེད། འདིར་ངས་རྣམ་དཔྱོད་རྒྱལ་དང་སྐྱིང་རྗེའི་སྐྱོར་ལ་བསམ་རྒྱལ་མང་པོ་ཞུས་པ་དང་འབྱལ་ ནས་ཞི་བདེའི་སྐྱེར་ལའང་སྐྱང་ཆ་མང་པོ་ཞིག་བཏང་པ་འདི་ནི་ང་རང་སྐྱེར་གྱི་བསམ་རྒྱལ་ གང་དྲན་པ་དེ་ཞུས་པ་ཙམ་ཡིན།

for the next war. If we are satisfied with the peace that can be experienced during a one-day trip to a park, that is the same as referring to the time in which we are preparing for war as "peace."

The fact that the world has changed from a time when there were no prisons or courts to one in which prisons and courts exist is something for which we human beings are all responsible. The fact that the world has changed from a time when there were no soldiers guarding the borders between countries to one where such border guards are needed is also something for which we human beings are all responsible. However, in our courts the framework of the dock where the accused stands is usually constructed from wood. The officers who are responsible for keeping order in the court are human beings. Our prisons are mostly built on land. Legal proceedings are conducted in a way that opposing parties meet one another face-to-face. We must make sure that it does not become necessary for these conditions to become more severe than they currently are.

It would be a truly amazing accomplishment if we could bring about greater happiness for all beings of this world. This is what all sentient beings certainly want. However, as I have already stated again and again here, this will depend on our ability to eliminate attachment and hatred. It will depend on our ability to reduce our selfishness and our ability to develop a sense of being satisfied with what we have. These qualities also depend on our ability to develop compassion. This is what I have to say to the intellectuals who are deserving of our respect, to those individuals who are creative, and to those persons who are representatives of religious traditions. You are the ones to whom we direct our hopes.

Conclusion

Generally speaking, the subject of world peace is one that depends upon the recommendations that are given by those learned and experienced officials who are affiliated with organizations that are dedicated to world peace. It is the responsibility of everyone who wants peace to apply and hold in high regard the knowledge found in the wonderful writings of these individuals. The various thoughts that I have expressed here regarding the nature of creativity and compassion, as well as the opinions that I have expressed in related discussions, represent my own personal views and the ideas that I have developed for myself.

༄༅།། བསྟོད་པ།།

།སྐྱིད་ན་བདེ་བ་ཚོགས་སུ་བསྟོ། །ཐན་བདེས་ནམ་མཁའ་གང་བར་ཤོག ། སྡུག་ན་ཀུན་གྱི་སྡུག་བསྔལ་འབྱུར། །སྡུག་བསྔལ་རྒྱ་མཚོ་སྐྱེམས་པར་ཤོག །པཏ་ཆེན་ཤྐྱུ་ཕི་བྲཟང་པོ།

འདི་དཔྱིན་སྐྱང་ནང་བསྐྱུར་བ་པོ་མཁས་དབང་ Artemus B. Engle མཚོག་ལ་དམིགས་བསལ་ཕྱགས་རྗེ་ཆེ་ཞུ་རྒྱུ།

མཆན།

1. གོང་གི་ཤེས་རབ་བཞིའི་ཁྱད་པར། མཁས་དབང་དུང་དཀར་བློ་བཟང་འཕྲིན་ལས་གསུང་། ཤེས་རབ་ཆེན་པོ་ཞེས་ནི། ཡེགས་ཤེས་དང་། དགེ་སྐྱོན་གང་ཡིན་རང་སོ་སོ་རང་རྟོགས་ཀྱིས་དབྱེ་ཞིབ་བྱེད་ཕྱུབ་མཁན་དེ་ལ་ཟེར་བ་ལས་མི་ཡིས་བསྐུལབས་ནས་དབྱེ་ཞིབ་བྱས་པར་ཟེར་བ་མིན། བླང་དོར་ལ་རང་རྟོགས་ཀྱིས་དབྱེ་ཞིབ་བྱེད་ཕྱུབ་བ་དེ་ལ་ཤེས་རབ་ཆེ་བ་ཟེར། ཤེས་རབ་གསལ་བ་ནི། དགེ་སྐྱོན་གང་ཡིན་དུང་ཆང་མ་ཆེ་ཀྱང་ལ་མ་སྐྱོན་པར་ཤེས་ཕྱུབ་པ་དེ་ཡིན། ཁ་ཤས་ཀྱིས་ཆེན་པོ་ཤེས་ནའང་ཆུང་ཆུང་མི་ཤེས་པ་དེ་ལ་ཤེས་རབ་མི་གསལ་བ་ཟེར། ཤེས་རབ་གསལ་བ་ནི་དགེ་སྐྱོན་གང་ཡིན་དུང་ཆ་ལྷུ་མོ་ཞིག་ཡིན་ནའང་མ་འདྲེས་པར་དབྱེ་ཞིབ་བྱེད་ཕྱུབ་པ་དེ་ལ་ཟེར། ཤེས་རབ་ཟབ་པ་ནི། གནད་དོན་གཅིག་ལ་བསམ་བློ་བཏང་བ་བརྒྱུད་ནས་གནད་དོན་མང་པོ་ཤེས་རྟོགས་བྱེད་ཕྱུབ་པ་དེ་ལ་གོ་དགོས་ཏེ། དཔེར་ན། ལོ་བསམ་བློ་ཞེ་དགག་གཏིང་ཟབ་པོ་ཡོད་ཅེས་ཤོད་དུས་མི་དེ་ས་གནད་དོན་གཅིག་བརྒྱུད་ནས་གནད་དོན་མང་པོ་བསམ་བློ་འཁོར་ཕྱུབ་པའམ་ཤེས་རྟོགས་བྱེད་ཕྱུབ་པ་དེ་ལ་ཟེར། ཤེས་རབ་རྒྱུར་བ་ནི། བསམ་བློ་བཏང་མ་ཐག་ཏུ་གནད་དོན་དེ་ལམ་སེང་དུན་ཕྱུབ་པ་དེ་ལ་ཟེར།

2. རྗེ་རིན་པོ་ཆེ་ཚོང་ཁ་པ་བློ་བཟང་གྲགས་པས་མཛད་པའི་རྒྱལ་བ་བྱམས་པ་མགོན་པོ་ལ་སྐྱེ་སྐུགས་ཀྱི་སྐོ་ནས་བསྟོད་པ་ཆེནས་པའི་ཚོད་པར་བཞུགས་སོ།

Dedication

When happy, I shall dedicate my merit to all beings,
May joy and benefit fill all extent of space!
When suffering, I shall take on the pain of all beings,
May the ocean of suffering dry up!
—*Panchen Śākyaśrībhadra*

Translated by Artemus B. Engle, PhD

Notes

1.   This description of four types of intelligence is based upon a work written by the great Tibetan scholar Dungkar Losang Trinley (*dung dkar blo bzang 'phrin las*, 1927–1997). "Great intelligence" (*shes rab chen po*) is a form of intelligence that has the ability to distinguish such things as what is correct from what is wrong and what is virtuous from what is flawed entirely on its own. It does not make such distinctions based on what a person has been taught by someone else. Thus, the ability to properly determine how to carry out a spiritual practice by relying entirely on one's own intelligence is referred to as "great intelligence." "Bright intelligence" (*shes rab gsal ba*) is a form of intelligence that recognizes all virtuous and flawed entities, no matter how great or small. Some persons can only perceive the great entities that are virtuous or flawed, but not those that are small. That kind of intelligence is one that is lacking in brightness. "Profound intelligence" (*shes rab zab pa*) should be understood to mean a form of intelligence that by reflecting on one significant point is able to realize many additional points. For example, when we say that someone has a form of understanding that is very profound, we mean that he or she is able to perceive or gain an understanding of many different things through having considered a single point. "Quick intelligence" (*shes rab myur ba*) is a form of intelligence that is able to reach an understanding of some significant point as soon as it is reflected upon.

2.   A poem in praise of Maitreya written by Rje Bla-ma Tsong-kha-pa Blo-bzang-grags-pa [T: *rgyal ba byams pa mgon po la smre sngags gi sgo nas bstod pa tshangs pa'i cod pan*].

We don't teach our children compassion anymore. We're so focused on them being successful that we don't pay attention to them actually being good human beings anymore. Our world really needs people who care about each other more than they care about their own personal success.

—Shannon Hitchcock, undergraduate, from the Creativity & Compassion conference

The Master's Question

John Briggs

Aesthetician

I n the West, creativity has long been a vital concept, with largely positive overtones. At the same time, the concept engenders considerable popular ambivalence and confusion. On the one hand, creativity is considered frivolous, such that arts programs are the first to be cut in a budget crisis. On the other hand, creativity and innovation are considered essential economic assets. Creativity is considered a healthy means of "self expression." But creativity is also associated with being willfully nonconformist and with the narcissistic aspect of personality, as in the popular expression disparaging someone for "just being creative." We depend on creativity to solve problems, and yet creativity is often thought of as a little "crazy"; people involved in sustained creative activities are regularly assumed to be psychologically unbalanced. Though this stereotype is demonstrably untrue, it is persistent and no doubt derives from the fact that creative activity breaks molds and allows people to "think outside the box." That, of course, is just what people are also urged to do, in business, for example—think outside the box and outside the routines of thought, the clichés of opinion and solution. We feel ambivalent, though. We're afraid because such thinking seems uncomfortably abnormal.

What is creativity, then? Here's a composite definition:

Creativity brings something new or *re*-newed to the world. It connects the previously unconnected or rejuvenates previous connections, injecting them with new vitality as if they had been freshly discovered. Creativity is an immensely potent human capability. It is the source of change in the world that our human consciousness has constructed. It's generally recognized that insight is a form of creativity, as in "the Buddha had the insight about the nature of reality." Examples of creativity include the invention of new technology, the discovery of new scientific truths, making works of art that express renewed spirit; creativity in nature is expressed as the evolution of new forms and behaviors, and in human thought as insights that dispel ignorance or illusion. Humans are creative animals. We invented clothing, fire, religion, mathematics, language, indeed, culture itself.

The sustained creativity that has produced the great music, visual art, and literature of the world shows the connection between creativity and compassion. Without saying it directly, these great creative works have the effect of evoking our compassion for human suffering, including the suffering of individuals we might otherwise find repugnant (such as the character Macbeth), and for stimulating our sense of identity with every thing and everyone.

What is compassion? His Holiness the Dalai Lama has said: "Compassion compels us to reach out to all living beings, including our so-called enemies, those people who upset or hurt us. Irrespective of what they do to you, if you remember that all beings like you are only trying to be happy, you will find it much easier to develop compassion towards them. Usually your sense of compassion is limited and biased. We extend such feelings only towards our family and friends or those who are helpful to us. People we perceive as enemies and others to whom we are indifferent are excluded from our concern. That is not genuine compassion. True compassion is universal in scope."[1] In another context he observed, "Marriages that last only a short time do so because of a lack of compassion; there is only emotional attachment based on projection and expectation. As soon as our projections change, the attachment disappears."[2]

During the rise of the Cold War and the atomic age, novelist William Faulkner brought creativity and compassion together in his Nobel Prize speech in 1950. The speech is a passionate artist's statement:

Our tragedy today is a general and universal physical fear so long sustained by now that we can even bear it. There are no longer problems of the spirit. There is only the question: When will I be blown up? Because of this, the young man or woman writing today has forgotten the problems of the human heart in conflict with itself which alone can make good writing because only that is worth writing about, worth the agony and the sweat.

He must learn them again. He must teach himself that the basest of all things is to be afraid; and, teaching himself that, forget it forever, leaving no room in his workshop for anything but the old verities and truths of the heart, the old universal truths lacking which any story is ephemeral and doomed—love and honor and pity and pride and compassion and sacrifice. Until he does so, he labors under a curse. He writes not of love but of lust, of defeats in which nobody loses anything of value, of victories without hope and, worst of all, without pity or compassion. His griefs grieve on no universal bones, leaving no scars. He writes not of the heart but of the glands.[3]

The creativity that engenders the arts puts us in touch with this sense of universal connection that is both passionate yet impersonal; art reveals that our deepest connection to the world is not attachment.

Zen Buddhists argue that the creative state of mind is "the beginner's mind." Zen master Shunryu Suzuki writes that "the beginner's mind is the mind of compassion. When our mind is compassionate, it is boundless."

The Jewish tradition displays creativity and compassion joined in the action of *tikkun olam*, "repairing the world," the idea that "Jews bear responsibility not only for their own moral, spiritual, and material welfare, but also for the welfare of society at large."[4] A Kabbalistic vision of this idea declares that at the moment of creation, God's vast self contracted into vessels of light to give birth to the world. When the vessels shattered, their shards became sparks of light trapped within material creation. The Kabbalah views *tikkun olam* as the act of reuniting the sparks to restore the universal wholeness.[5] Repairing the world requires both creative and compassionate action. Related to this is the idea of the *mitzvah*, the good deed.

Here's a way to think about the convergence and divergence of creativity and compassion in an historical sense. Imagine that our human creativity has followed two paths over time.

Path 1—Creativity on this path has occurred within a context that emphasizes the self for purposes of survival, dominance, pleasure, or diversion. Path 1 creativity has had positive or negative effects, often both at the same time. Examples of this creative path are: the invention of tools and weapons—the wheel, fire, stone spearheads, atomic fission, the internal combustion engine, Hollywood special effects, horror films, and so on.

Path 2—Creativity on this path has occurred within a universal context, a context beyond the focus on the ego. Here, creativity discovers and attempts to express hidden cosmic connections, elicits compassion for others who may otherwise seem alien, and links the individual self with a spirit that embraces the entire universe. Examples of Path 2 creativity include Ice Age cave art, *Hamlet*, Beethoven's last quartets, meditation and prayer, the beginner's mind, religious ritual practiced in a way that renews previous insights as if just discovered.

Creativity along this path has a positive effect on a sense of our common humanness, fosters realizations about the interconnectedness of all things, exposes to our psyches the beauty of the natural world (and our embeddedness in it), and makes evident the delusions of the ego. It may do this, as great artists have done, by using tools such as metaphor, irony, and humor to depict the conflict, absurdity, and tragedy of our ego-bound world. By doing that, art helps us break through our attachments and ego constraints into a state of mind that Irish poet William Butler Yeats called a "gaiety transfiguring all that dread." In the preface to one of his books, British novelist Joseph Conrad described the aim of art as follows:

> The changing wisdom of successive generations discards ideas, questions facts, demolishes theories. But the artist appeals to that part of our being which is not dependent on wisdom: to that in us which is a gift and not an acquisition—and, therefore, more permanently enduring. He speaks to our capacity for delight and wonder, to the sense of mystery surrounding our lives; to our sense of pity, and beauty, and pain; to the latent feeling of fellowship with all creation—and to the subtle but invincible conviction of solidarity that knits

together the loneliness of innumerable hearts, to the solidarity in dreams, in joy, in sorrow, in aspirations, in illusions, in hope, in fear, which binds men to each other, which binds together all humanity—the dead to the living and the living to the unborn.

Note that although artistic creators following Path 2 may themselves be caught up in ambition, vanity, and the stickiness of the ego, ultimately it is not possible to produce art in that ego-bound state. At least for a time, the creator lets go of self-absorption and attunes to the larger, ultimately mysterious, cosmos.

In the West, self-focused creativity (Path 1) became the primary path for human creative expression, except in the arts. But even in the arts, creative expression became (after the Middle Ages) associated with the ego (which we can see in the Enlightenment idea of "genius," for example).

Now that East and West are in an intense conversation, it seems time to consider joining the two paths in order to address the conflict and destruction that Path 1 human creativity has magnified with its inventions. Path 1 creativity has created climate change, for example. It may be that only a combined Path 1 and Path 2 creativity can resolve such a problem. Or, to frame the matter somewhat ironically, perhaps by joining these two paths, we can put our narcissism to work for the good of all humanity and nature.

A combination of Path 1 and Path 2—linking compassion and creativity—could provide us with new and profound ways to reach out across the many barriers of thought and culture that humans have erected with the effect of creating barriers that separate us from each other, from our fellow creatures, from the earth itself. In this way, creativity might provide a means to access and to exercise authentic compassion. In a Zen Buddhist story, an enthusiastic student inquires of his teacher, "Master, what can I do to help all the suffering beings in this world?" The teacher answers, "Indeed, what *can* you do?"

The question and its answer fold creativity and compassion into each other, since the master's question about compassion will require the student's creativity.

Jennifer Salkin, one of WCSU's graduate alumni, expresses the connection this way: "I feel that compassion is a creative act. When the Dalai Lama says the

Chinese are his teachers, that is a leap of creativity/imagination." A leap into the boundless.

The planet is in peril; our well-being as a species is at stake, a well-being dependent on the well-being of all other beings on the planet. It is perhaps not an accident that despite our Western and most modern image of ourselves as an animal that is ruthlessly competitive, scientists are increasingly discovering evidence of the evolutionary importance of empathy, altruism, and cooperation to our past success as a species. Indeed, the July 2012 *Scientific American* announced on its cover the issue theme, "The Evolution of Cooperation: Competition is not the only force that shaped life on earth." Martin Nowak, a biologist at Harvard who derives equations to describe natural selection, observes that "when you look at mathematical models for the evolution of cooperation, you also find that winning [creative] strategies must be generous, hopeful, and forgiving. The world's religions hit on these ideas thousands of years ago."[6]

Notes

1.   Tenzin Gyatso, His Holiness the 14th Dalai Lama. *The Spirit of Tibet: Universal Heritage.* Allied Publishers, 1995. Excerpted on SpiritSound. 16 Dec. 1998. Web. 20 Apr 2011. http://www.spiritsound.com/bhikshu.html.

2.   "Dalai Lama Teaching: The Meaning of Compassion." Tibetan Life. 2009–2011. Web. 20 Apr 2011. http://www.tibetanlife.com/dalai-lama-teachings-the-meaning-of-compassionbr. html.

3.   Faulkner, William. Nobel Prize Speech. 10 Dec 1950. Rpt. on William Faulkner on the Web. 13 March 2011. Web. 22 Apr 2011. http://www.mcsr.olemiss.edu/~egjbp/faulkner/ lib_nobel.html.

4.   Shatz, David, Chaim Isaac Waxman, and Nathan J. Diament. *Tikkun Olam: Social Responsibility in Jewish Thought and Law.* Conference Proceedings. Northvale, NJ: Jason Aronson (1997), xii, 351.

5.   Fine, Lawrence. "*Tikkun* in Lurianic Kabbalah." Reprinted from "Tikkun: A Lurianic Motif in Contemporary Jewish Thought." In *From Ancient Israel to Modern Judaism: Intellect in Quest of Understanding—Essays in Honor of Marvin Fox.* Vol. 4, ed. Jacob Neusner et al. Charleston, SC: Nabu Press (2010).

6.   Marshall, Michael. "The Mathematics of Being Nice." *New Scientist*, 19 March 2011, 34–35.

All religions are means, in principle, to help human beings become better, more refined, and more creative. While for certain religions the principal practice is to recite prayers, and for others it is mainly physical penance, in Buddhism the crucial practice is understood to be transforming and improving the mind.

—His Holiness the Dalai Lama, from *In My Own Words: An Introduction to My Teaching and Philosophy*

Compassion and Pity as Concepts

David Capps

Philosopher

I n his book *An Open Heart*, the Dalai Lama offers the following statement about compassion: "Compassion is the wish that others be free of suffering."[1] To become compassionate in this sense, a person needs to develop empathy, which the Dalai Lama elaborates as a feeling of concern for others grounded in a recognition of human kindness and the interconnectedness of human beings:

> As we look around us at the buildings we live and work in, the roads we travel, the clothes we wear, or the food we eat, we must acknowledge that all are provided by others. None of these would exist for us to enjoy and make use of were it not for the kindness of so many people unknown to us. As we contemplate in this manner, our appreciation for others grows, as does our empathy and closeness to them.[2]

Consequently, the "wish" involved in the attitude of compassion is not to be understood as a mere momentary whim. It is rather a robust desire informed by the person's overall emotional makeup, and in particular the person's capacity for empathy. We should also notice that this "wish" or "desire" is not a self-interested one. The idea is not that we should wish that others be free from suffering as a *means* to promoting our own happiness.[3] As the Dalai Lama indicates elsewhere, we should be careful not to conflate compassion with attachment:

> Usually when we are concerned about a close friend, we call this compassion. This is not compassion; it is attachment. Even in marriage, those marriages that last a long time, do so not because of attachment—although it is generally present—but because there is also compassion. Marriages that last only a short time do so because of a lack of compassion; there is only emotional attachment based on projection and expectation. When the only bond between close friends is attachment, then even a minor issue may cause one's projections to change. As soon as our projections change, the attachment disappears, because that attachment was based solely on projection and expectation.[4]

The other major feature of compassion is its object. In order to wish to relieve suffering, obviously one must be able to identify suffering. It is crucial to recognize, then, just how pervasive suffering (dukkha[5]) is in the Buddhist view. According to the first of the Four Noble Truths, suffering is a basic condition of human existence:

> This is the noble truth of dukkha: birth is dukkha, aging is dukkha, illness is dukkha, death is dukkha; sorrow, lamentation, pain, grief and despair are dukkha; union with what is displeasing is dukkha; separation from what is pleasing is dukkha; not to get what one wants is dukkha; in brief, the five aggregates subject to clinging are dukkha.[6]

The Buddhist tradition divides suffering into three layers: a) suffering due to pain, b) suffering due to impermanence, and c) suffering due to conditions.[7] Suffering due to pain is physical suffering, e.g., the sensation that one feels having a migraine or a flare-up of arthritis, an undesirable state but one that can often be relieved by external means. It is what we normally think of as "suffering."

Suffering due to impermanence is more subtle. It includes all those negative experiences which occur by virtue of the fact that each of us stands in a contingent, unstable relationship to things that we care about. According to the Buddhist doctrine of dependent origination, everything that depends on a cause will eventually cease to exist. There is no doubt that the things that we care about depend on causes and hence will cease to exist. This means that virtually all of our experiences are tinged with some degree of anxiety signaling the recognition that they will not last.

The final layer, suffering due to "conditions," amounts to suffering due to the karmic cycle of rebirth. Rebirth necessitates "re-death," which is suffering. There is also a kind of existential ennui associated with the cycle of rebirth. Would one really want to be recycled eternally? Or mightn't we liken the experience to the myth of Sisyphus, whose punishment by the gods is to roll a boulder up a hill and then watch it tumble down to its starting point?

These layers of suffering have implications for the way we think about compassion. First, since suffering due to impermanence is so pervasive, compassion is an appropriate response in virtually any interaction. It is common in contemporary America to associate compassion with clear forms of physical suffering. But from the Buddhist point of view, compassion is appropriate even where physical pain is clearly absent. The envy or admiration we might feel for the young couple who are very much in love and have moved into their first house together should be tempered by compassion based on the understanding that their happiness is fragile, sustained as it is by contingent causes. Not that it is realistic to suppose that without training one could experience compassion in every circumstance. It is also a skill that takes practice; and we should bear in mind the Buddhist recommendation for cultivating compassion—that it should begin at home, toward one's close friends, and radiate outward from there.

Second, while the capacity for empathy is a prerequisite for developing compassion, the character of the empathy involved in a compassionate response may differ depending on the causes of suffering. For example, if I am driving in heavy traffic and someone suddenly cuts me off, instead of becoming angry, a compassionate response would be to consider the perspective of the other driver: Perhaps he is late for a meeting and will be fired if he doesn't arrive on time. As the case may be, his carelessness may be reasonably pinned down to a frustrated desire that is specific enough that imagination can play a mitigating role between the perception of one's own frustration arising and a compassionate response. But where the cause of suffering is only the general fact of impermanence, it is primarily the sustained appreciation of this fact, not imagining how it might apply to a particular case, that facilitates compassion. To imagine the young couple's reaction to their house being destroyed by a tornado would not encourage empathy, it would be an exercise in morbidity.

Now that we have clarified some aspects of the Buddhist concept of compassion, let us turn to an influential Western concept of pity and examine a few key differences. In his *Poetics*, Aristotle places the cathartic effect of "pity and fear (or horror)" as the function of tragedy. Inducing an emotion of pity and fear in an audience, in other words, is essential to that highest form of artistic creativity.

In his *Rhetoric*, Aristotle offers the following definition of "pity":

> Pity may be defined as a feeling of pain caused by the sight of some evil, destructive or painful, which befalls one who does not deserve it, and which we might expect to befall ourselves or some friend of ours, and moreover to befall us soon.[8]

Accordingly, in this view of pity one needs to be able to a) judge that suffering of the kind described by the definition is occurring, b) judge that the suffering is undeserved (or in excess of what is deserved), and c) judge that one might suffer in the same way.[9] This definition is somewhat narrow, but it does seem to capture something to which we can easily relate. Most of us have had the experience of seeing footage of, or even witnessing firsthand, a car wreck or plane crash. Wincing, one thinks: that could just as easily have happened to me. (More crassly, sometimes one hears: "Sucks to be you!") That Aristotle's view of pity approximates our own is also confirmed in the fact that it is difficult to pity a criminal in proportion to the severity of his crime: the more severe the crime, the less likely we are to conclude that his punishment is undeserved.

Aristotle also offers a characterization of the suffering that occasions pity:

> All unpleasant and painful things excite pity if they tend to destroy, pain, and annihilate; and all such evils as are due to chance, if they are serious. The painful and destructive evils are: death in its various forms, bodily injuries and afflictions, old age, diseases, lack of food. The evils due to chance are:

friendlessness, scarcity of friends (it is a pitiful thing to be torn away from friends and companions), deformity, weakness, mutilation; evil coming from a source from which good ought to have come; and the frequent repetition of such misfortunes. Also the coming of good when the worst has happened: e.g., the arrival of the Great Kings' gifts for Diopeithes after his death. Also that either no good should have befallen a man at all, or that he should not be able to enjoy it when it has.[10]

Here seems to be a division of the items into those that are common to the run of human experience on the one hand, and items that are less common but whose presence is just as keenly felt—presumably due to their relation to the good life (would one really want to live without friends?). One might question the specifics of each list, but what is important for our purposes is to notice that the items that excite pity according to Aristotle's conception apparently all belong to the first layer of suffering in the Buddhist framework. The failure to stumble upon an evil of chance does nothing to lessen the Buddhist truth that all is impermanent. If this conception reflects the way we typically categorize the objects of pity, it follows that in order to pity in this sense we do not have to understand the nature of suffering from impermanence or conditions. This points to a difference in scope between compassion and pity, as we might already have suspected. It would be, after all, nonsense to pity the young couple who have just bought their first house, even if compassion is appropriate.

A second difference is that pity, in this view, unlike compassion, is self-regarding. As Aristotle makes clear:

And, generally, we feel pity whenever we are in the condition of remembering that similar misfortunes have happened to us or ours, or expecting them to happen in the future.[11]

From a Buddhist perspective, feeling this kind of pity amounts to so much projection of the "I" onto experiences of suffering. If so, to pity in this sense is counterproductive to cultivating compassion, even if both sentiments presuppose some ability to sympathize with and to recognize our common humanity with the other. If the objects that excite pity present themselves as a live danger to oneself, one might simply flee rather than responding compassion-ately. Aristotle himself notes that the experience of pity may transition to that of terror depending on how "close" one is to the one pitied:

> For this reason Amasis did not weep, they say, at the sight of his son being led to death, but did weep when he saw his friend begging: the latter sight was pitiful, the former terrible, and the terrible is different from the pitiful; it tends to cast out pity, and often helps to produce the opposite of pity.[12]

A third difference between the concepts of pity and compassion concerns depth. Compassion may be more or less deep, pity may be more or less intense, where the depth or intensity depends in large measure upon how developed each capacity is. (I would suggest that "depth" applies fundamentally to the ca-pacity for compassion, and derivatively to the feeling associated with its proper exercise. Someone surging with compassionate feelings when donating for the first time to a charity lacks the depth of compassion of the committed volunteer who happens to be experiencing compassion fatigue.) If I have gone through exactly the same experience you are going through, then, other things being equal, my pity will be more intense than if I had gone through something com-parable but dissimilar (e.g., loss of a pet vs. loss of a spouse).

The depth of compassion also depends on the existence of shared experi-ence, if only because some shared experience is necessary for empathy—period. But what reveals the difference between the intensity of pity and the depth of compassion is the role that shared experience plays in the exercise of each ca-pacity. Recall from our definition that someone who pities generally makes a judgment that relates the object that excites her pity to herself as an experience she might (or already did) encounter. This aspect of our definition introduces a limitation on how intensely pity may be experienced from the inside. For it means that to the extent that one cannot imagine what it would be like *for oneself* to have a certain kind of experience, then, to that extent, one cannot pity someone (or something) who does have that kind of experience.

For example, if one can be said in this sense to pity a lobster that has lost its tail, the intensity of one's pity will be determined in part by one's ability to imagine oneself having a tail, losing it, etc. Now it may be that one faces

42

no serious imaginative impediment in this regard. But then again, one might. This is no isolated case. The point is that the depth of compassion is unaffected by such considerations, since someone who is skilled in compassion need not route the recognition of suffering through any comparison, implicit or not, to what they might—or did—experience. In this way, while having a sympathetic imagination helps cultivate compassion, truly deep compassion is not conditional. It does not involve the same cognitive engagement that intense pity does. (Perhaps this can be seen even in the case of the lobster. Ask yourself which is easier: to imagine that the lobster is suffering, or to imagine yourself suffering like the lobster?)

The same distinction can be approached from another angle. Switching back to the "feeling" talk of compassion and pity, consider what it would mean, according to our characterization of the intensity of pity, to experience a pity of maximal intensity. Among other things, it would entail that the suffering that activates pity is identical to the experience of suffering one recollects or anticipates when one feels pity. But how could this be? They might each be a token of the same type of experience, but clearly they are distinct tokens, since they accord to distinct individuals. A line from Wallace Stevens's poem "Bantams in Pine-Woods" comes to mind: "Your world is you. I am my world." Right? But according to Buddhist metaphysics, the matter is actually not so clear. In that picture, there may be spatial or temporal factors to which one might appeal in order to distinguish tokens of experience, but any item that corresponds to a stable and unified "self" to have those experiences is no longer available.

Further, Buddhists hold in accordance with this "no-self" view that it is possible to attain a state of mind wherein experiences do not present themselves as "mine" or "yours." For one who had developed such a frame of mind, considerations that bound the intensity of pity—whether suffering is deserved and the act of making comparisons to experiences similar to one's own—would fall away as irrelevant to the visceral fact of being moved by the suffering at hand. It should be noted in this connection that the Buddhist tradition urges compassion toward all sentient beings. Deep compassion extends even to animals. There is a famous story in the *Jataka Tales* that recounts how a previous incarnation of the Buddha sacrificed himself to feed a starving lioness and her cubs. What would it be like to feel such compassion? It is hard to imagine, but

I would doubt that a judgment like, "Oh no! I might some day be reincarnated as a starving lion!" had any bearing on the experience.

It is clear from the above considerations that the concepts of compassion and pity are readily distinct. A final difference to note is that there is a sense in which pity, but not compassion, may remain inert. One might pity someone and in doing so *only* manifest the judgments characteristic of pity as we have defined it. Typically, however, a compassionate response to suffering is one that mobilizes into action. More than that, compassion seems to be subject to a norm that pity is not: Necessarily, one's compassion is defective (or at least shallow) if one fails to actively respond to suffering where an active response is possible. By contrast, it would seem that pity need not represent any personal failing if it fails to motivate. But we needn't rest only on how things seem. If compassion is subject to the requirement that it does motivate to action, it partly explains why we understand compassion in terms of the desire to relieve the suffering of *others*. For when someone is genuinely compassionate—actively—he could not then at the same time desire to remove his own suffering: He would already be doing something to that end by being compassionate. Self-compassion would be redundant. Similarly, self-pity is only pathetic.

Notes

1. Tenzin Gyatso, His Holiness the 14th Dalai Lama. *An Open Heart: Practicing Compassion in Everyday Life.* Boston: Little, Brown and Company (2001), p. 91.

2. Ibid., p. 92.

3. Even if it is reasonable to believe that our own happiness will fall into place if we live compassionately.

4. "Dalai Lama Teachings: The Meaning of Compassion." Internet resource. http://www.tibetanlife.com/dalai-lama-teachings-the-meaning-of-compassionbr.html. Cited: June 2012.

5. Literally: "dis-ease."

6. Drawn from the Buddha's first discourse, summarized at http://en.wikipedia.org/wiki/Four_noble_truths.

7. My exposition follows Mark Siderits, *Buddhism as Philosophy: An Introduction.* Indianapolis, IN: Hackett (2007), pp. 20–21.

8. Aristotle, *Rhetoric*, 2.8 136a. Available here: http://rhetoric.eserver.org/aristotle/rhet2-8.html#1386a.

9.   It is important to recognize that these judgments are the mental prerequisites for pity, and not themselves constitutive of pity; to think otherwise would be to step away from Aristotle and into the realm of the Stoics.

10.   Aristotle, *Rhetoric*, 138b.

11.   Ibid.

12.   Ibid.

Every moment has both creativity and compassion in it. One of the panels was talking about brushing your teeth. That's weird, but it is creative? Every single moment does have some aspect of creativity in it.

—Shannon Hitchcock,
undergraduate,
from the Creativity &
Compassion conference

Experiencing Compassion

Deborah Calloway

Professor of Law

When we think about the "meaning" of anything, we think in terms of concepts. We consult the dictionary or search online to clarify our understanding. However, the meaning of compassion can be understood most clearly from the perspective of experience.

Consider the experience of listening to someone you love very deeply as this person is relating an experience of suffering. Perhaps your parent, spouse, or child contracted a life-threatening illness or was badly hurt in an accident. When we encounter situations like this, we experience deep compassion and concern.

How does this experience feel? Does it make you sad? Does it make you cry? Why do we experience sadness? We want to help, but we don't have the skills required to relieve suffering we confront. We are even more uncomfortable if we realize that our loved one's pain, illness, or injury has no cure. We are sad because we feel helpless. We want to help but we don't know how. We also are sad because we fear loss. Even if our family member survives, he or she may be physically limited or depressed. We are afraid the relationship we enjoy will change for the worse. We may fear possible financial costs and losses. We may fear the burden of caring for a loved one with significant needs.

We label our sadness as *compassion* and perceive it as grounded in the relationship we label as *love*. These labels are misconceptions. Genuine love wants others to be happy. Genuine compassion wants others to be free from suffering. Our sadness is grounded in our ego-driven needs, not in our genuine love. It is grounded in our need for this relationship to remain unchanged. Even our desire to relieve our loved one's suffering is grounded in our need to fix the situation. Our sadness doesn't help our loved one. Instead of one sad person, now there are two. Lost in sadness, we are distracted and unable to see what we actually can do to help.

Genuine compassion, undistracted by feelings of helplessness and fear of loss, allows us to see how to actually help. Often, the most helpful thing we can do for someone who is suffering is simply to be there, listening with an open heart. Listening this way is helpful in itself. In addition, when we listen without distractions, we may discover many ways to help our loved one. Perhaps we can put their financial and business affairs in order, thereby relieving them of worry. Perhaps we can provide music or spiritual counseling or simply share a smile and a loving touch.

The egocentricity that fuels sadness and helplessness also leads to misunderstanding compassion in other contexts. Consider the experience of encountering an individual with a severe disability—perhaps someone who is blind, or wheelchair-bound, or even cognitively limited. If we look at our mind when we encounter severely disabled individuals, we may see pity rather than genuine compassion. Pity contains a subtle sense of pride or superiority fueled by the egocentric thought, "I am so glad I am not like that." Even the language we use to describe these circumstances is permeated with superiority: impairment, disability, limited, challenged, and abnormal.

In addition to pity, fear also interferes with our ability to interact skillfully in this context. Consider your response to reading news accounts about Stephanie Decker, the Indiana woman who shielded her children from a tornado and lost both legs as a result. Consider reading about Aimee Copeland, a grad student who had her left leg, right foot, and both hands amputated in order to save her from flesh-eating bacteria. Consider encountering someone who is paraplegic or brain-damaged as a result of a diving accident. When we encounter individuals who have suffered significant losses, we often experience fear. Coming face-to-face with the fragility of our existence causes us to fear as we considering the possibility of facing the same or similar loss. This ego-driven fear can cause us to feel uncomfortable when we interact with individuals who have endured extreme losses of what we consider to be normal functioning.

Genuine compassion is not clouded by pity or fear. Genuine compassion simply wishes others to be free from suffering. Freedom from suffering may mean returning to normal functioning, or it may mean reaching a state of contentment or even a state of appreciating life experienced from a different perspective. Genuine undistracted compassion allows us to perceive ways to actually be helpful or see that the individual who aroused our fear and pity is actually quite happy and has extraordinary qualities to offer the world.

Consider, for example, Harriet McBryde Johnson, an author, lawyer, and disability rights activist who lived in Charleston, South Carolina. Harriet wrote:

> It's not that I'm ugly. It's more that most people don't know how to look at me. The sight of me is routinely discombobulating. The power wheelchair is enough to inspire gawking, but that's the least of it. Much more impressive is the impact on my body of more than four decades of a muscle-wasting disease. At this stage of my life, I'm Karen Carpenter thin, flesh mostly vanished, a jumble of bones in a floppy bag of skin. . . . At 15, I threw away the back brace and let my spine reshape itself into a deep twisty S-curve. Now my right side is two deep canyons. To keep myself upright, I lean forward, rest my rib cage on my lap, [and] plant my elbows beside my knees. . . .
>
> I used to try to explain that in fact I enjoy my life, that it's a great sensual pleasure to zoom by power chair on these deliciously muggy streets.

Harriet, who died in 2007, didn't need our pity or fear. She was brilliant and witty, a skillful writer and orator who was an effective advocate for individuals with disabilities. At the same time, she required a full-time assistant to help her with daily life functions, including bathing and dressing. She was somewhat surprised, but totally appreciative, on the rare occasions when she encountered individuals who were *not discombobulated* by her appearance (e.g., not distracted by pity or fear), but rather recognized her actual needs, while appreciating her qualities—dealing with her as an intelligent individual with a point of view.[2] In this context, genuine compassion includes remembering to ask her how wide her powered wheelchair is if she is coming to visit your home.

Compassion and creativity from a contemplative perspective

Dictionaries provide an uncertain starting point for considering the meaning of creativity. Older editions of Webster's dictionaries simply defined creativity as "the quality of being creative or the ability to create."[3] Definitions with more substance include "artistic or intellectual inventiveness,"[4] and "the ability to transcend traditional ideas, rules, patterns, relationships, or the like and to create meaningful new ideas, forms, methods, interpretations, etc.; originality, progressiveness, or imagination."[5]

From the earlier reflections, we can see how compassion relates to creativity. Genuine compassion is free of ego-driven distractions, stereotypes, and labels. Letting go of our egocentric desires, sadness, and fear frees us to respond creatively to the challenges posed by a terminally ill or seriously injured loved one. Letting go of our pride (in the form of pity) and fear frees us to see clearly and respond appropriately to the qualities and needs of others, including individuals with seriously limiting impairments. The same is true for all the relationships in our lives—whether we are relating to a salesperson in a checkout line, negotiating a contract with a roofer, teaching a class, working on a team project, or playing games with a child. Genuine compassion lives in the moment, recognizing that each moment is fresh, new, alive with possibility, and constantly changing:

> [T]he dissolving of fleeting thoughts, the fading of vibrant emotions, the quick alternation of our perceptions—a sound, a touch is there and then gone. But at the very instant we experience the end of a moment, we experience the process of birth; a new world is born as fresh thoughts and colorful emotions arise in response to shifting perceptions. Therefore, the end of a moment is also a renewal.[6]

Every present moment of experience provides us with a fresh, open, spacious, and relaxed view that makes it possible to "transcend traditional ideas, rules, patterns, relationships, or the like and to create meaningful new ideas, forms, methods, interpretations." This is the essence of creativity.

How can we tap into this compassionate and creative space? Many contemplative practices are available to train our minds to rest in present awareness, work skillfully with emotions, and generate genuine compassion. Meditation instruction is available from many organizations throughout the United States. Many books are also available. Good starting places include *Stages of Meditation* by the Dalai Lama,[7] *The Miracle of Mindfulness* by Thich Nhat Hanh,[8] and *Lovingkindness: The Revolutionary Art of Happiness* by Sharon Salzberg.[9] In addition, numerous audio and video recordings of teachings on meditation, generating compassion, working skillfully with emotions, and transforming suffering are available online.[10]

Notes

1. Harriet McBryde Johnson, "Unspeakable Conversations," *The New York Times Magazine,* February 18, 2003. This is a wonderful article, capable of completely altering one's views of individuals with disabilities. I recommend it highly.

2. Ibid.

3. Joyce R. Robinson, M.S.Ed., "Webster's Dictionary Definitions of Creativity," *Online Journal of Workforce Education and Development* vol. III, issue 2 [Summer 2009]. http://opensiuc. lib.siu.edu/cgi/viewcontent.cgi?article=1071&context=ojwed.

4. David B. Guralnik, *Webster's New World Dictionary of the American Language.* 2nd College Edition. NY: World Pub. Co. (1976).

5. *Random House Webster's Unabridged Dictionary.* 2nd Edition. NY: Random House Reference (2001).

6. Dzogchen Ponlop Rinpoche, *Mind Beyond Death.* Ithaca: Snow Lion Publications (2007).

7. Tenzin Gyatso, His Holiness the 14th Dalai Lama, *Stages of Meditation.* Ithaca: Snow Lion Publications (2003).

8. Thich Nhat Hanh, *The Miracle of Mindfulness: A Manual on Meditation.* Boston: Beacon Press (1987).

9. Sharon Salzberg, *Lovingkindness: The Revolutionary Art of Happiness.* Boston: Shambhala Publications (1995).

10. See, for example, www.vajraechoes.com.

Breaking Habits

Roland Merullo

Writer

Be kind—for everyone you meet is fighting a great battle.

—Philo, 1st century Jewish mystic

I sometimes think that the most important book I've ever read is Martin Buber's *I and Thou*. Though I was assigned to read it during my senior year at Brown University, I did not really examine it with care until three years later in the plain-furnished upstairs room of a boarding house in Rutland, Vermont. I'd gone to Rutland to try out a solitary, ascetic routine for one winter—almost like a worldly monk—and reading a few pages of *I and Thou* every night fit into that routine perfectly. It's an extremely dense book, painfully difficult to read, filled with made-up words, sentences you can spend a year thinking about, and ideas that surface and re-surface over the course of a life and make more sense with each new appearance.

If I can risk putting Buber's philosophy into a small package, I'd say it has to do with seeing other people as full souls. In order to do this, two things have to happen. First, you have to see yourself as a full soul. You have to appreciate the miracle of your own existence. You have to believe that you are lovable and loved—by other people and by the spirit that created you. Second, you have to get past the self-absorption of the person who goes around thinking: What a miracle I am! How wonderful! How special! How unique!

If things are going badly, you have to somehow remember that you are not alone in your suffering. If things are going well, you have to learn to enjoy and appreciate your good fortune, without giving yourself all the credit for it.

All this is a kind of spiritual balancing act—keeping a full sense of the wonder of your own existence without losing sight of the wonder of others'.

In a similar kind of balancing act, the Christian monks of long ago used to say "suffering is grace." It's a strange concept, especially for people of the modern world who've developed a million ways of avoiding or lessening pain. But I think the idea behind it is that, when you suffer, when things don't go the way you want them to go, you are being given an opportunity to feel compassion for anyone and anything that suffers. You can learn to see the *I* there, in that other pair of eyes, and to feel the *You* of that other soul inside yourself. Surely this attitude finds expression in the Dalai Lama's famous statement, "My religion is kindness," and in the words of Hazrat Inayat Khan, "To the Sufi, all religions are one."

And I think this is where creativity comes into the picture, too. It seems to me that creativity should be defined in the widest possible way. What a mistake it is to consider only writers, sculptors, painters, or actors as creative people. What a limiting idea! Yes, we are born into a certain body here on earth, in certain circumstances. And, yes, those circumstances place limits on what we can and cannot do. But within those limits, we all have tremendous freedom in terms of how we respond to each second of our existence. Rather than get stuck in old patterns of anger or selfishness or coldness or greed, we can find creative ways of changing our habits, especially the habits of our thoughts. A mother can be creative in terms of how she speaks to her child. A teacher can be creative in terms of how he or she conveys information to students. A man buying coffee and doughnuts can be creative in the way he speaks to the person selling the food. This kind of thinking makes life into a continuous co-creation, an art form, and it gives our days a richness that is the opposite of boredom.

It also gives us a happy flexibility in how we relate to the world around us. I remember once, when I lived in southwestern Vermont, pulling into a gas station to fill the tank and talking with one of the attendants there. He wasn't a particularly educated young man, and he probably wouldn't have been the first person you'd pick out of a crowd and say, "Now, there's a spiritual being." He told me he'd just had an argument with his girlfriend, and we talked about that for a little while, and the last thing he said was, "I'm just trying now not to have bad thoughts about her."

What a creative and compassionate response to an everyday situation. Most of us in that situation would go over and over the argument in our minds, finding ways to justify our point of view and tear apart that of the other person. Maybe we'd make up eventually, but there would be a bruise, and it would take awhile for the blood beneath the skin to fade away. But here was an ordinary guy who'd come up with an extraordinary response to his domestic upset. What a lesson that was for me. How hard it is, even now, 30 years later, to put that lesson into practice.

Being alive in human form is a constant opportunity to be compassionate and creative. Every day, every minute, we're presented with situations good and bad, easy and difficult, mundane and exceptional. Another of my favorite writers, Thomas Merton, used the phrase "the perfection of freedom." I think what this means is that, even given the limitations we are born into, we always have perfect freedom in terms of how we respond to people and situations. We can break our habits. We can learn new ways to do old things. We can use our time creatively, in the service of reaching an I and Thou awareness, in the service of compassion.

It's not fair to expect that of ourselves in every encounter. Even Buber thought an unblemished I and Thou approach was too much to ask. It's probably not possible to be absolutely compassionate and marvelously creative in every situation. But as I once heard the great Zen master Seung Sahn say, "Try, only try."

The difference between empathy and compassion? Empathy recognizes the suffering of others, but with compassion, you have a desire to serve as a refuge from suffering for other people. It's not just recognizing that they are suffering and being sad about it, but having this whole other desire to be able to protect them from suffering. The only question is, "How do you go about doing that?" That's where the real creativity comes in.

I would also say that creativity is value neutral. You can be creative in—for lack of a better word—evil. Creating a biological weapon is creativity. There is no inherent value one way or another to the act of creativity. So it comes back to the question, "What is the motivation of creativity?"

—Paul Hackett,
from the Creativity &
Compassion conference

Creativity and Compassion on the Path to Enlightenment

Paul Hackett
Professor of Buddhist Studies

One of the luxuries of encountering the Buddhist tradition in the 21st century is the wealth of sources to draw upon when considering nearly every topic. This is abundantly clear with regard to the Tibetan tradition in particular. Although the Buddhist literary tradition consists of a canon of core religious and philosophical works comprised of thousands of texts and hundreds of thousands of words, a person encountering the tradition for the first time would be hard-pressed to identify a single aspect of the contained teachings that has not received some consideration or exegesis over the 2,500-year history of Buddhism.

Compassion, although a generally well-known concept in the West, has typically been intermingled with notions in the Western context of empathy and sympathy, though more often also with pity. While much could be said about these various uses of the word in English literature, in a Tibetan Buddhist context, the word typically translated as compassion, *nying-jé*, has a very specific definition. A very clear and succinct definition provided by one author is that compassion is "a state of mind in which one desires to serve as a refuge from suffering for others." What is nice about this definition is that in addition to isolating the precise mental state that characterizes this disposition of compassion, it also points to the central determining factor in compassion—one's motivation—while at the same time, calling attention to what is not spoken of in the definition—any specific actual instructions for fulfilling that aspiration. While the motivation is easy to state, one could argue that the aspect of engaging in actions to bring about the desired result—serving as a refuge for others from suffering—is difficult to do, since, in any situation, knowledge of the precise action to benefit others is not easy to come by. Indeed, developing the capacity for successfully and actually benefiting others could be said to constitute the entirety of the Buddhist path to enlightenment. An understanding of what this means, however, lies at the heart of understanding the transformation from an unenlightened state to an enlightened one.

When we talk about our normal state of existence (our typical "unenlightened" state), the perspective we adopt is naturally a subjective one—the point of view of one's own self wrapped up in a self-identity. If we examine our self-identity, however, we can observe certain patterns in our description of ourselves. When asked to identify ourselves, to those who know us, we give our name; it is a designation that is intended to trigger a wide range of attributes and associations in the hearer. To those who are unfamiliar with us, however, we might resort to a variety of descriptive terms: "a student," "a musician," "a doctor," "a lawyer," "a mechanic," and so on. What all of these qualifying terms have in common is the fact that they are functional descriptions, that is, they describe how one behaves in a specific functional context: When in school, one performs the functions of a student, when in a concert setting, one performs the functions of a musician, and so on as a doctor, lawyer, etc. Indeed, if we were to try to describe ourselves in any realistic terms whatsoever, we would find every description to be contextual, that is, merely describing our conduct or reactions within a certain environment and under certain circumstances.

This, in essence, is the Buddhist conception of personal identity: that we exist only in contextual relationships to our surroundings and define ourselves in terms of our responses to them. Just as significantly, the same holds true of a Buddha, and hence a Buddha is a state of existence that is simply characterized by a very particular set of responses to situations and settings of the world. In the case of a Buddha, however, these responses are described in terms of the so-called "perfections"—patience, ethics, insight, and so forth. In its simplest terms, the Buddhist path to enlightenment then, is one of cultivating a set of responses to external (and internal) conditions different from our normal, habitual, unexamined ones. Where an unenlightened being responds to anger and hatred in kind, a person on the Buddhist path ideally responds with patience, and understanding. One does not need to ground such responses in some grandiose metaphysical or religious system; from one's own experiences, it is easy to accept that hatred, abuse, and intolerance give rise only to suffering for oneself and others. Indulging in those tendencies is a habit that can easily be seen to be self-destructive. The challenge to the practitioner committed to overcoming such tendencies then, is to affect a change in personal habits in an efficient manner.

Foremost in this process is contending with the mind and its tendency toward habitual behavior. From the first moments of every day, each of us experiences sights and sounds, smells and sensations, and all impinge on our consciousness. While our mind cannot determine what we experience, it does determine how we experience it, and more importantly, how we respond to it. As the tradition repeatedly emphasizes, changing one's personal responses to stimuli and our associated habits is ultimately a matter of familiarization through repetition. The more we indulge in a certain behavior, the more accustomed to it we become, and the easier we find it to be, until it simply becomes a natural response. It is a pattern observable in both negative and positive actions: the more one drinks alcohol, the more habituated one becomes to doing so, and the easier it is to consume more and more. Similarly, the more one becomes habituated to exercising patience with difficult circumstances, the easier it becomes to do so, and one's capacity for such a response increases accordingly.

In order to bring about these sorts of changes in one's personality, the tradition speaks of different strategies for doing precisely this. The simplest approach to overcoming self-destructive behaviors (anger, violence, desirous attachment, and so on) is simply to take a vow of restaint aimed at never engaging in such actions again. While effective, such an approach takes time to affect long-term results. A more proactive approach, in addition to maintaining vows of restraint, is to commit oneself to positive actions that act in the opposite direction of the faults one wishes to overcome. For example, in addition to restraining oneself from responding to situations with anger, one can also make a commitment to actively respond with patience and understanding.

Although these basic principles are sound in general, the challenge lies in their specific application. This is often the same challenge found in many religions. It is very easy to set forth general guidelines for behavior, but all too often, these guidelines devolve into dogmatic assertions to be applied unwaveringly in all situations. While there are vows, such as the prohibitions against killing, lying, and so forth, that seem to be inviolable, even within the Buddhist canonical sources there are stories of them being broken—a famous example being the story of the Buddha in one of his previous lives, in which he killed a would-be mass-murderer (though despite his good intentions, the earlier incarnation of the Buddha was still reborn in a hell realm as a consequence of his action). Thus, guides to behavior exist throughout Buddhist literature, giving examples of incidents and experiences and providing reasoned responses in accordance with the teachings, although one would be hard-pressed to find absolutely proscriptive statements.

Far from providing definitive proclamations concerning one's actions in every circumstance, Buddhist scriptures call on individuals to familiarize themselves with the fundamental principles underlying them. In this way, every individual is encouraged to take responsibility for their own actions and their own decisions in constructively engaging every situation on its own terms. Such a principle of self-reflection in all circumstances applies on all levels of the path, from beginners, and teachers, up to full enlightenment itself—a final state in which there is no doubt regarding the best course of action to benefit others.

Consequently, one finds texts such as Śāntideva's *Guide to the Bodhisattva's Way of Life* speaking at length about the perils of destructive activity and unhealthy responses to life in the world, while at the same time offering advice and guidance on adopting a constructive attitude toward life and its difficulties. As one proceeds on the path, one develops facility with appropriate responses to the vagaries of life and even to the various insecurities and concerns of one's own mind. At the same time, however, even greater responsibilities become incumbent upon a would-be teacher and guide to others and this topic also receives extensive treatment in Buddhist literature. Some texts discuss the attitude of respect that a student should take toward a spiritual teacher who has dedicated themselves to the well-being of their students. Far more importantly, however, such texts make the point that a great burden is assumed by the teacher in his or her conduct in all regards. A far cry from the cult-like attitude that might be assumed to surround a spiritual teacher (or "a guru"), in the Buddhist tradition, the point is made repeatedly that it is not the students who must strictly adapt to the will of the teacher, but rather the teacher who must creatively adapt to the needs of the students. It is, in this sense, a far greater burden assumed by the teacher in being a teacher, than by a student in being a student.

Hence, the Buddhist path to enlightenment necessitates great responsibility for one's actions with regard to others, especially those under one's guidance and care. Thus, it is the responsibility of both a practitioner and a teacher to carefully engage in non-dogmatic, creative responses to each and every situation, motivated by compassionate concern for others, and grounded in one's own studies and experiences, while at the same time cultivating the capacity for insight into proper actions. It is in this manner that true creativity—not as self-expression, but as insightful response—manifests within Buddhism.

Thus, the Buddhist presentation of the path to enlightenment, like many other religious systems, can be presented as the opposite of artistic creativity, where artistic creativity is equated with self-expression, and the Buddhist path is seen as a precisely specified sequence of meditations and religious proscriptions. But Buddhism is actually a far more "open" system of conduct in terms of its repudiation of rigid dogmatic assertions. Because of being grounded in an ethic of compassion, this overriding concern necessitates a flexible response to ever-changing circumstances. It is the ability to recognize these circumstances and respond in the most constructive manner possible that is the hallmark of advancement along the spiritual path. In this way, the Buddhist path challenges the would-be student to overcome rigid patterns of thought both in terms of one's perceived identity and the limits of one's own capacity for response in any situation, and thereby "create" a constantly adapting self-identity, an enlightened self-identity that is capable of transcending self-imposed limits to one's capacity for compassion and compassionate responses.

Although people work in order to be happy,
It is uncertain whether or not they will find it;
But how can those whose work itself is joy
Find happiness unless they do it?

—*Udānavarga* 7:64

གལ་ཏེ་བདག་ལ་དགའ་བྱེད་ན། །
ཉེས་པར་བྱེད་པས་བདེ་བ་དག །
བདེ་སྐྱག་ཁ་ན་མི་འཚོབ་པས། །
འདི་མི་ལྡག་ལ་གཤུག་མི་བྱ། །

2
The
Compassion
of Art

Levels of Compassion and Art

Susan Altabet

Musician

I think we would all agree that there are many problems in this world and among its inhabitants. Undoubtedly, we would like to clear away all these problems. But how can we do that? Compassion is one tool that we might agree can definitely help. I would propose that the arts can help also.

The theme of His Holiness the Dalai Lama's visit to Danbury, Connecticut, in 2012—Compassion and Creativity: Embracing the Challenges of the 21st Century—was conceived by a group of people involved in the arts. Our group was very interested to hear the wisdom of His Holiness as it related to creativity and, especially, the arts. Some years ago, when our group found out that he was scheduled in October, 2010, to participate in an event titled "The Creative Journey: Artists in Conversation with the Dalai Lama about Spirituality and Creativity," we all anxiously went down to Emory University in Atlanta, Georgia, to hear his thoughts. We were a little perplexed by his perspective. He said in effect that he wasn't really moved by art, and he didn't have anything much to say about the subject. So Richard Gere and Alice Walker, who were participating in the conversation, engaged His Holiness in a fantastically creative discussion on another topic that was, of course, wonderful. But what about the arts, what about the creative journey?

The Dalai Lama's wisdom about how compassion can help the world seems quite boundless. And since compassion and the arts have so many similarities, perhaps his wisdom could enlighten our thinking about using art along with compassion as a means to "embrace the challenges of the 21st century." Such a huge portion of Westerners connects with the arts either as participants or observers. In the West, the arts are present in everyone's daily life in movies, TV, iPods, radio, advertising, magazines, books, paintings, museums, concerts, interior decorations at home or work, music in shops, sculptures in banks, ads in trains and subways, movies in planes, etc., etc. Because audiovisual technology is now widely pervasive, there are so many mediums for the arts, and virtually everyone in the West is experiencing some version of the arts all day long. Therefore, the opportunity to use the mind-transforming capabilities of the arts to help heal the world's problems has tremendous potential.

There are so many levels of compassion, from having a simple feeling of pity for some poor inferior creature to a mother's compassion for her own child; the emotion can encompass compassion for our family and relatives, for our pets and animals, for our community and country, and can extend all the way out to having infinite compassion for all sentient beings. If we look around us for examples of all these levels of compassion, we can see that the more expansive a person's compassion is, the less selfish and self-centered that person is. An example: I love my own child with so much compassion that I sacrifice my life, time, possessions, and wealth for that child, but I don't feel that way about my neighbor's children. A second scenario: I feel sorry for someone because they are less fortunate than "me" but I don't necessarily go out of my way to help them. In contrast, the altruistic ideal is embodied by the Buddha or Jesus, who both had infinite compassion and love for absolutely everyone.

Western art similarly has many levels of scope: An artist can make a work with the intention of expressing personal feelings, creating an entertaining diversion, crafting a captivating emotional experience, or even fashioning a creation that can transform the mind and spirit for the benefit of all. These levels of art parallel the different levels of compassion in their range, from complete self-involvement to selflessness. From the point of view of both the artist and the observer, for example, art is used in advertising to penetrate into our minds and get lodged in our subconscious; art can provide addictive gratification that we can experience anywhere, at all times, thanks to our numerous technological devices; art in the form of entertainment is used to distract us from our daily worries; but art is also used to enhance spiritual worship and as a highly sophisticated method of transforming the mind and transcending the self, allowing us to touch the world of the infinite.

Unlike the disciplines of science, finance, building, sports, and many other areas that are focused in the outer material world, both genuine compassion and the purest arts are mainly generated by and affect the inner world of the heart and mind. (In Eastern cultures, the mind and heart are considered to be the same.) Compassion involves using a crystal clear wisdom that considers the good of the whole and all of its parts. Genuine compassion transcends the blinding obstacles presented by the needs of the personal self and always takes into account the needs of the whole. It follows then that this kind of compassionate mind can only be cultivated through going inside the heart and letting go of our powerful attachment to always looking after "dear me and mine." Needless to say, this can be a very long, long process that involves a path of extensive study, contemplation, and meditation.

Similarly, the purest arts in the West are devoted to finding a universal, aesthetic value in sounds, shapes, colors, forms, words, etc., that takes the artist and the observer deep inside the heart-mind, way beyond any sense of self. At this level of creative activity, the search for perfect artistic expression through refinement of artistic mastery transcends the search for self-satisfaction and gratification of the base senses. For these kinds of artistic seekers, there is also a long journey that requires much practice, training, and letting go of the temptations of praise, fame, pride, and the like that can be the greatest stumbling blocks to pure artistic expression.

Creativity is an integral part of both compassion and art. When you have genuine compassion, you are driven to creatively use spontaneous, universal vision in order to react wisely and selflessly to respond to any given situation. Similarly, the most refined forms of the arts tap into the creative imagination to give rise to universal, selfless, mind-transforming works of art.

In cultivating both compassion and art, you need to foster sensitivity to others and merge your own self into the greater whole. In developing compassion, you need to learn to be aware of others in order to give them what they need, not influenced by your own needs, desires, or limitations. When playing music, you often need to blend melody, harmony, rhythm, and musical motivation with the other musicians to create a unique collective musical experience that can transform both the players and the listeners. Even if you are playing by yourself, you are developing sensitivity to rhythm, harmony, sound forms, and how these blend together to express beauty through music.

Both compassion and art ultimately can touch the universal and the innermost essence, the ephemeral and the eternal. Because they are both ineffable, it's difficult to explain why and how this happens. But we can learn the techniques for developing both from great masters. For example, His Holiness the Dalai Lama is a great master of compassion, and he teaches us how to increase and cultivate compassion if we do various practices and meditations daily. Through constant, consistent effort in this way, we can all learn to increase our ability to bring a more compassionate presence to all our activities. And by being more compassionate, thinking more of others and focusing less on "me" all the time, we actually become happier and thereby can make others happier, too. In music, you also often go to a great teacher and study various skills, techniques, theories, and musical forms for many years. Then, through consistent effort and daily practice, you can gain an awareness of musical expression that enables you to appreciate the deeper meanings of music—and benefit from them—by becoming a more sensitive, humanistic individual.

The worldview of both artists and compassion practitioners is quite different from our usual perception of the world as full of things that are independent and permanent. In order to create their artistic expressions, artists play in their minds with a world full of various shapes, colors, sounds, fragrances, and sensations, all with infinite possible pliant reformations. Compassion practitioners see a world where all is interconnected and quite impermanent. Through an awareness of the interconnectedness of all things, the self is recognized as the whole. Therefore there is no longer any need of seeing "me" as more important than "you." Because of an awareness of interconnectedness, one doesn't become alarmed, defensive, afraid, sad, happy, or proud when something changes. Things are always changing, and our attachment to the notion that things are permanent causes our own suffering and is blinding to our ability to think wisely and act compassionately.

On the other hand, art energy can also be used in many destructive ways. It can increase self-centeredness, create more distractions, and take us further and further away from compassionate thinking into problems and suffering. Many performers and other artists are motivated solely by a wish to be in the limelight. We have producers who make films to satisfy the basest of human drives so that they can make the most money for themselves. We have artists who seek fame and fortune at any expense. We have artists in all forms of art expressing and promoting hate, anger, and violence without any concern for the effects these produce in the minds of observers. We have commercial art promoting desire and attachment to objects that make us momentarily happy and then leave us wanting something else new. We have the arts that create constant distractions and leave us with no thought of what is real, who we really are, or how to help our neighbor.

There is a great deal of self-serving energy found in so many of the arts in the West today. If artists could take responsibility to find ways to infuse more compassion and virtue into the arts—since there are so many connecting similarities between the arts and compassion—it makes sense that they could easily build a bridge between these two. This way, compassion can flow into the arts and have far-reaching effects, since just about everybody is connected with the arts to some extent. Therefore some amount of compassion could reach just about everybody.

As an example of how this can happen, I can share my own personal story. I was a musician my whole life, and about 15 years ago, I became involved in Tibetan Buddhist compassion meditation practices for purifying the mind. The goal of these practices is to be freed from all the obstructions that cause me to think about me first and others second, cause me to be interested in fulfilling my own desires, cause me to become angry at truly unimportant things, and cause me to think that my self-centered view of life will make me happy. I won't go into all the details here, but I can say that my music-making and teaching changed significantly as a result of the integration of compassion practices into my mind. Music training was like the bridge to compassion training for me, and then compassion transformed my music.

There are so many possible ways to infuse the arts with compassion, and that is what we have been exploring at the Creativity and Compassion Conference.

This research into compassion and creativity has such great potential to help the world because of the vast size of the arts audiences and the deep scope of compassionate solutions that could arise through the arts.

Therefore, the arts can be used to greatly benefit humanity and the planet or completely destroy them. Since compassion and art are similar in so many ways, it would make sense that we should investigate further how to combine the arts with compassion, harnessing the compassion of art in our efforts to embrace the challenges of the 21st century and beyond.

When I create, I like to improvise. In writing, my best process comes when I'm—I don't even know how to describe it, but it's some place other than me. And it sort of comes through . . . slipping through another awareness.

—Janet Kathleen Ettele,
from the Creativity &
Compassion conference

Natural Connections

Stephen Dydo
Composer and Musician

During our ongoing organizational talks arranging the details of His Holiness the Dalai Lama's visit to Connecticut, one of the questions that loomed larger and larger was this: Although His Holiness has been involved in discussions relating many other disciplines to Buddhism, especially the sciences, he has never been much involved in the relationship of Buddhism to the arts. This became a focal point for us. The original core group developing "The Visit," as it came to be called, was heavily represented by people working in the arts and aesthetics. (In this essay, "the arts" and "art" can be generally understood to mean *all* the arts.) So we decided to make our focus "Compassion and Creativity." It seemed clear to us that the tradition of the arts in the West came out of, and even possibly came into being at the same time as the traditions of spirituality. But the further we got into it, the clearer it became that this was not something that made a lot of sense to the Tibetans involved in our conversation, and it seemed that we were running into a dead end. At one point, it came up that there is not even a word in Tibetan that corresponds to "creativity" as we use it in the artistic sense. Yet it is abundantly clear to Western outsiders that artistic creativity is alive and well in Tibetan culture. Our first conference, preceding The Visit by seven months, was developed primarily to address this seeming anomaly from a number of points of view.

Sometimes listening to various seemingly disparate threads of thought about a theme can help pull together the loose ones in one's own mind. In the opening panel of our conference, we had discussions about the nature of compassion, the role of intentionality in art, Laozi's construction of a parallel model of the world, and many other things. The breadth of these topics helped to coalesce some of the thoughts about the relationship—or lack of it—between real compassion and the creative process.

Let's start out with Laozi, the near-mythical Chinese philosopher working around the 6th century BC. His legacy is often a bit murky to Westerners, with its mixture of mysticism and naturalism. But the part that seems clearest to us, and perhaps the most essential part of his thinking, is that man must be intimately connected to the natural world to be fully developed, to be fully human. In chapter 43 of his one surviving work, *Dao De Jing*, we read, "The softest thing in the world dashes against and overcomes the hardest; that which has no (substantial) existence enters where there is no crevice. I know hereby what advantage belongs to doing nothing (with a purpose). There are few in the world who attain to the teaching without words, and the advantage arising from non-action."[1] This is an essential statement of the concept of *wu wei* (no action), which may be loosely translated as "go with the flow." That is, the superior action is the one that follows nature.

The essential focus on natural connections carries through to the world of art and music in classical Chinese culture. Of course, there is a tradition of excellence in the creation of *artificial* art, just as there is in the West. But there is also a very ancient strain of *natural* art, as well. For instance, let's look at the scholar's rock, seen in gardens and even on writing desks of the literati. This would ideally be a large stone, even an immense boulder, which had been shaped by wind or water into an elaborately cratered shape. Often there is a helping hand from man involved in the creation of such a thing; holes are drilled or chiseled and the rock is then left to weather for a period to seem more natural. But such artificially weathered rocks are less valued because of the tooling involved; the natural creation is the most prized.

Another pertinent example of the relationship between art and nature in Chinese aesthetics is the scholar's instrument, *guqin*. This is a seven-string zither with a notated performing tradition extending back about 1,500 years. The ideal place for playing music on the instrument is in a grove, or by a river, or on a mountain, where the music is blended with the surrounding sounds of nature. In such an environment, the delicate vibrations of the strings are almost inaudible, even to the player. In extreme instances, a scholar will leave his instrument hanging on the wall, preferring the soft rustlings of the strings created by the occasional breeze instead of his own "artificial" plucking. (However, it has been said of some that they are really just trying to avoid practicing!)

So, then, from a Western point of view, is there any artistic creativity involved in these examples of high art? The issue of intentionality is worth examining here. We are talking about found rocks, unplayed instruments. Where exactly is the intention? Is it possible to have creativity without the intention? Is the creativity in the beholder and not in the creator?

Returning to Laozi, there's another notion that may be of help to our understanding—that's the concept of *qi* (气), meaning energy, life force, vitality. Laozi tells us that *qi* is universal, everywhere. It is generally regarded as positive, but may also be negative, such as the *qi* in a tomb. In the world of art, *qi* is fundamental. A certain type of brush stroke may be full of *qi*, another lacking; the balance between the two creates the harmony and movement of a painting. Similarly, in the musical domain, a certain way of playing will have a lot of *qi*; another will have little. An example from the music of the *guqin* demonstrates a difference between Chinese and Western aesthetics: In the West, string players—particularly guitarists—take pains to avoid making a squeaking or brushing sound when moving the left hand along the strings; but among *guqin* players, this is regarded as a part of the music, and if it isn't there, the playing lacks *qi*.

These examples from Chinese art and music demonstrate a level of connectedness with the environment *through the art form itself*. The scholar with the water-formed rock sculpture, the painter allowing the water from the brush to spread chaotically into the paper, the *guqin* making random sounds on the wall—all represent an attempt to remove the self from the creative process, or to blend oneself into the environment, or both.

How this might relate to a compassionate way of artistic expression can be made clear if we examine the nature of compassion from a Buddhist perspective. Of course, we don't maintain that Buddhists have a corner on compassion!

Nonetheless, there is a particular perspective that Buddhism, and particularly Mahayana Buddhism, brings to bear that is important to examine in our search. At the same time, that perspective can give some insights into the nature of compassion itself.

What has often seemed self-evident to artists is that there must be an element of compassion in the very best of their art—that in order to make an art that truly addresses the human condition, one must have some deep well of compassion driving the art. So why is it, when His Holiness is occasionally cornered on this issue of the arts and its place in a compassionate world, his response is generally that he doesn't know anything about the arts except that a lot of people seem to like them, and they have some entertainment value that people find important? What is missing in this sort of dialogue that makes something so obvious to us—the depthless spirituality inherent in the highest of our high arts—appear to be of so little interest to this great spiritual leader? This is the core of our conundrum.

One answer may be in our assumptions about spirituality and compassion. For example, are we always clear in the difference between compassion and empathy? An example of this potential confusion was evident in a dialogue between His Holiness and one of our more thoughtful musicians, Dave Matthews. The musician maintained that his concert experience was often colored by compassion; while performing, he frequently felt a deep connection with his audience and responded to the feelings aroused in this connection. Yet such a connection, even if deeply shared, is actually a form of shared empathy. That is, the sharing of feelings, even of some spiritual vision, is not by itself an instance of compassion.

To be sure, this sort of empathy is a powerful connection that must be a prerequisite of compassion; however, one additional element in compassion that is not a prerequisite of empathy: universal connectedness. This is more than the empathy we feel when observing the suffering of a child or loved one. That involves a local connection only, and does not spread significantly from one's own community. The universal connection, on the other hand, extends not only beyond one's community but even beyond what one specifically knows. Using the bodhisattva[2] as an example, we have a being with a commitment to the welfare of *all sentient beings*, even including species unknown to her.

How this might look from a Western point of view was expressed by the Anglican priest Henry Melvill (1798–1871): "Ye live not for yourselves, ye cannot live for yourselves; a thousand fibres connect you with your fellow-men, and along those fibres, as along sympathetic threads, run your actions as causes, and return to you as effects."[3] This statement is interesting for a number of reasons. For one thing, it's usually ascribed to Herman Melville, who, although he heard Melvill speak and admired him greatly, did not write those words. But, more interestingly, the imagery of the connection by threads echoes the notion of Indra's net, in which an infinitely large net has a single jewel at each node, with each jewel reflecting each of the other jewels.[4] Additionally, and most surprisingly, it serves as a concise definition of the law of karma. Was Melvill knowledgeable about Indian philosophy? Whether he was or not, it's clear that some key elements of universal connectedness were known to him.

Aside from that, however, there is one additional element in compassion that is not a prerequisite of empathy: concern for the welfare of all others. From this point of view, compassion involves a universal connection with all others; but it also involves a commitment to their welfare. The compassionate being will not only share in the feelings of the other in the shared moment, but also at all other times. The bodhisattva is the most complete example of this. As a fully enlightened being, she can get out of the endless cycle of birth, suffering, and death; however, because of the commitment to the welfare of others—all others—she returns continuously to assist in the complete enlightenment of all sentient beings. This view of enlightenment suggests that other great sages have had the same stance, especially including Jesus Christ.

A dictionary definition of compassion would be, for instance, "sympathetic consciousness of others' distress together with a desire to alleviate it." Or: "a feeling of deep sympathy and sorrow for another who is stricken by misfortune, accompanied by a strong desire to alleviate the suffering." His Holiness the Dalai Lama has spoken and written about compassion many, many times; this is one of his definitions: "Often people think of compassion as a feeling of pity, and regard the person who is the object of compassion as somewhat inferior. . . . Genuine compassion must arise from recognizing that other beings—just like ourselves—desire happiness and wish to overcome suffering. Based on this, a genuine empathy or connectedness arises when we encounter others' suffering.

This is genuine compassion. We feel responsible toward the other and a deep concern for the other's welfare. There is therefore an underlying recognition of utter equality between ourselves and others."[5]

If we accept the notion that compassion consists of (at least) empathy toward all living beings coupled with a universal connectivity and commitment to universal welfare, we can see where there could be a bit of a culture clash around this issue. We in Western culture generally don't have a commonly accepted notion of universal connectivity such as is seen in the Chinese Daoist tradition. Nor do we have an embedded idea of living for the betterment of all beings, as in Mahayana Buddhism. In fact, there is in the United States a very different model that is known to all of us—the rugged individualist, the self-made man, the self-achiever, the master of self-expression. Of course, even here, our greatest artists in their greatest works completely transcend such ideas in their reach for universal expression; but they must swim against the tide of our culture to do so. Therefore, we shouldn't be surprised when the Dalai Lama finds it difficult to engage with much of Western art. The potential of humanity that he cares most about—the possibility of compassion that is directed toward universal enlightenment—finds expression as the exception to the rule.

Yet as an artist, I have to wonder if my own tradition might yet succeed in this area. That tradition in fact probably extends back at least 50,000 years, since man first created musical instruments and paintings and sculptures. It is generally thought that the prehistoric art we know about was created for spiritual experience. We now have evidence of the arts in the period *preceding* the last Ice Age. Artworks and musical instruments have been found in Europe dating back 40,000 years or more. Until the age of humanism, most of the musical and visual arts were oriented toward religious expression. That is an extremely significant period! The few hundred years in which the arts have been moving more toward being entertainment during leisure time are, at this point in our history, a mere blip. As it turns out, people working in the arts may become more acutely aware of the power of spiritual expression in the near future. The last century has seen a number of existential threats to humanity (global warfare, nuclear weapons, and now climate change). These have had the effect of focusing mass attention onto the fragility of our existence, often with a fearful result. At the same time, there has been a great deal of searching inward, of looking for some meaning to our seemingly ephemeral presence on this planet.

There is one more thread from the conference panel that I want to pick up. Western art always presumes some kind of intention in its creation; the activity of the artist could be anything from portraying a spiritually significant moment in the life of Christ to developing a sales image for cupcakes. The Western focus of intention is true even for artists specializing in found art, or ecological art; perhaps especially so in such cases. But it doesn't necessarily have to be that way. The observer may be as much the artist as the creator. Once we acknowledge the act of viewing art, of reading poetry, of hearing music, as active participation in the creation of great art, we have moved a step further toward a universal art, and possibly an art of compassion.

Two further examples from Chinese culture come to mind. One is the story of Boya. "Zhong Ziqi . . . was a friend of Boya. When Boya played the *qin*, Zhong Ziqi was a good listener. When Boya was focused on Mount Tai, Ziqi said, 'Wonderful, as grand as Mount Tai.' When Boya's focus was flowing streams, Ziqi said, 'Vast and swelling, like flowing streams.' Whatever Boya described Ziqi attained. When Boya traveled on the north side of Mount Tai and met heavy rain, he stopped below a cliff, took out his *qin* and played it. First it was 'Continuous Rain Lament,' then it was 'Crashing Mountains Melody.' Each time he played, Ziqi completely understood. Boya then set aside his *qin* and sighed, saying, 'Wonderful. When you listen it is like our hearts are resonating together. How can my thoughts escape like this?' When Ziqi died, Boya split apart his *qin*, broke his strings, and never played again, because at that time there could never be another person who could understand his music."[6]

The other example is of a good friend of mine and an excellent *pipa* (Chinese lute) virtuosa. While visiting me at my home one sunny day, she grabbed my arm excitedly and said, "Music!" I said, "What? What music?" She pointed to the pair of wind chimes, one wooden and the other metal, doing their own duet in the breeze. I have never heard them the same way since. Perhaps one day I will be able to hear everything as music and view everything as art and hear all words as poetry, and in that way become a universal artist. That could be the beginning of expressing compassion in art. Of course, that "beginning" is precisely the moment when we don't know where the music or the images or the words are coming from, when we are just channeling them as if we were awestruck observers taking dictation. But that's another story . . .

Notes

1. *The Tao Teh King, or the Tao and its Characteristics*, translated by James Legge, 1891. The original is 天下之至柔，馳騁天下之至堅，無有入無間，吾是以知無為之有益，不言 之 教，無為之益，天下希及之.

2. Buddhist Sanskrit term referring to someone who has dedicated his or her life to the welfare of all sentient beings; that is, all living things with consciousness and the potential to achieve Buddhahood.

3. "Partaking in Other Men's Sins," an address at St. Margaret's Church, Lothbury, England (12 June 1855), printed in *Golden Lectures* (1855).

4. One excellent description of this interconnectivity: "Far away in the heavenly abode of the great god Indra, there is a wonderful net which has been hung by some cunning artificer in such a manner that it stretches out infinitely in all directions. In accordance with the extravagant tastes of deities, the artificer has hung a single glittering jewel in each 'eye' of the net, and since the net itself is infinite in dimension, the jewels are infinite in number. There hang the jewels, glittering like stars in the first magnitude, a wonderful sight to behold. If we now arbitrarily select one of these jewels for inspection and look closely at it, we will discover that in its polished surface there are reflected all the other jewels in the net, infinite in number. Not only that, but each of the jewels reflected in this one jewel is also reflecting all the other jewels, so that there is an infinite reflecting process occurring." Francis H. Cook, *Hua-Yen Buddhism: The Jewel Net of Indra*, Princeton: Penn State University Press (1977), p. 11.

5. Tenzin Gyatso, His Holiness the 14th Dalai Lama, *Practicing Wisdom*. Boston: Wisdom Publications (2005), p. 95.

6. Liezi, quoted in *Qin Shi (History of the Qin)*.

Children and Genocide

Jane M. Gangi

Educator

For the past several years, I have been studying children's and young adult literature written in English about genocides since the Holocaust of World War II. Those genocides have occurred in Cambodia, Guatemala, Iraq, Bosnia, Kosovo, Rwanda, and Darfur. The authors, who come from both the cultures about which they write as well as outside of them, seem to, in the Dalai Lama's words, "experience a vivid sense of altruism." The authors who write responsibly and authentically have developed, as the Dalai Lama says, "genuine sympathy for others' suffering and the will to remove their pain."

It is unlikely that anyone can remove the pain of having lost loved ones in a genocide. But it is an act of compassion toward victims and survivors when empathetic and creative authors acknowledge the trauma of genocide through poetry, plays, fiction, biography, photography, visual arts, and informational texts.

There are authors who seem not to have cared enough about genocide victims and survivors to include in their writings the voices of those most affected by the actual histories; an author in 2008 wrote, twice, that the Rwandans are largely "over" the 1994 genocide. No one would say the Holocaust survivors are "over" the Holocaust. Those books written without the authentic voices of the victims are "artificial" books, and there are such works for children and young adults on the genocides, but those will not be my focus here.

Given the limits of space, I share here a few examples of compassion and creativity relationg to three genocides: Cambodia, Bosnia, and Rwanda.

Cambodia

In *Alive in the Killing Fields: Surviving the Khmer Rouge Genocide*, Nawuth Keat of Cambodia and Martha E. Kendall of California worked together to create a testimony of the Cambodian genocide. The Khmer Rouge, led by Pol Pot, closed the Cambodian borders in 1975 and began a genocide that killed at least two million people. The Khmer Rouge came to Keat's village when he was a child, forced his family into a ditch, and shot them all. Although he was shot three times, Keat survived. He found his way to a married sister. He and her family were forced to work in labor camps, and almost died of starvation. From a Thai refugee camp, he made his way to Oregon, then to California, where he became a student in Kendall's World Literature class in San Jose City College, California. Something in Martha Kendall made Keat ask, in his soft-spoken way during the last class, if he could share his story. Upon hearing Keat's story, Kendall and the rest of the class wept. Kendall worked with Keat to shape his story into a manuscript for publication. This creative collaboration resulted in an insightful book, giving voice to a survivor's experience.

Michelle Lord and Shino Arihara created the first picture book on the Cambodian genocide. Lord and Arihara write and illustrate the story of the boy Arn Pond. The Khmer Rouge separated him from his family, whom he never saw again. Pond had always loved music, and it was music that sustained him during his long ordeal. His Khmer Rouge captors grew to miss music, and asked for volunteers to learn to play the traditional Cambodian *khim*, a stringed instrument. Pond volunteered. As is possible with all the arts, the music momentarily took not only him, but those who listened, out of the brutal world they inhabited into a kinder, more beautiful one. Eventually Pond escaped to a Thai refugee camp where Reverend Peter Pond saved his life, adopted him, and brought him to America. In an afterword, Lord explains that as an adult Pond went back to Cambodia to save its music, which had "saved his life." Creative compassion imbues this picture book, from Lord's finely crafted narrative conveying Pond's engagement with music, which soothed and encouraged others, to Arihara's evocative illustrations.

Bosnia

Led by the Serbian president, Slobodan Milosevic, who stirred up destructive nationalism and recruited thugs from the Belgrade underworld to carry out his plans, a genocide began in Bosnia in 1992 that killed a quarter of a million Bosnian Muslims. This genocide was not inevitable; Orthodox Christian Serbs, Roman Catholic Croats, Sephardic Jews, and Bosnian Muslims had lived side-by-side for centuries, often peacefully, especially in cosmopolitan Sarajevo. Yet where multicultural tolerance had long prevailed, Serb nationalists kept Sarajevo under siege for three years—the longest siege in modern history.

Nadja Halilbegovich was a child during the siege and kept a diary that she described as her "only place of peace amid the chaos." In *My Childhood under Fire: A Sarajevo Diary*, Halilbegovich, now an adult, revisits her childhood diary in an unusual format, interspersing adult reflections on her childhood writings. She tells of watching her parents, in their despair, trying to keep their courage up, and of the way arts and crafts provided momentary safe havens from their awful reality. Halilbegovich shares the source of her compassion:

> I often ask myself why I stayed alive when thousands of children were brutally killed. There is no answer. I know that nothing can bring them back, but only forgetting would make them truly dead. They will live in my heart and in the following pages as long as I live and share their stories.

This decision to bear witness through remembering is consummate compassion.

Savo Heleta's *Not My Turn to Die: Memoirs of a Broken Childhood in Bosnia* is the only book I am aware of written from a Serbian perspective. Heleta and his family lived in Goražde, a primarily Muslim city. They were Christians, and when the war broke out, Heleta's parents made a conscious decision to remain, based on their friendly relations with their neighbors. Yet because they were Serbs, they became objects of suspicion, and some of their Muslim neighbors betrayed them. The Heletas had to go into hiding. Heleta writes:

For a long time after the war, I considered reconciliation as a weakness. I saw revenge as the only way, the "manly" way to move on with my life. But with the help of my family, and after my life changed for the better and I got exposed to education and traveled all over the world, I realized that was wrong. I realized that only brave and strong people can put years of suffering behind them, reconcile with the past, and move on with life. I wanted to be one of them.

Heleta's compassion begins with himself—by letting go and moving on. It is often said forgiveness is the gift we give ourselves; Heleta gives this gift to himself and others.

At our Creativity and Compassion Conference at Western Connecticut State University in April, 2012, the concept of courage was explored in its relation to creativity and compassion. I shared the story of the young man, who I will call Ahmed, who ran the hotel where I stayed in Sarajevo, Bosnia and Herzegovina, during the summer of 2011. Ahmed told us of growing up mostly in basements because of the constant shelling and of how, during those rare moments when the electricity came on, he and his family scrambled to take showers, wash clothes, and prepare what little food there was. Now in his mid-20s, Ahmed is a cheerful, gregarious young man who is hopeful for his future. A Muslim, he had even gone to Belgrade, Serbia, on a recent vacation, and intends to go back. But Ahmed also told of his sister, who became mute and bedridden during the siege of Sarajevo. There was nothing physically wrong with her; it was the only way she could respond to the horror surrounding her. Could one say Ahmed's sister was any less brave than he? Her muteness and listlessness was her "creative" response to an uncompassionate world. During our conference, Peter Elbow, professor emeritus at the University of Massachusetts, attributed to Ahmed's sister the "courage to feel a strong feeling."

Rwanda

In 1994, radical Hutus, some of whom had studied Hitler and Nazism, carried out a genocide against Tutsis and moderate Hutus that killed close to a million people in one hundred days. International forces contributed to the slaughter.

The French and Chinese had made Rwanda, one of the smallest countries in Africa, one of the most armed countries on earth; the Belgian colonialists had required Hutus and Tutsis to carry identity cards beginning in 1933. These identity cards promoted a racist ideology based on European pseudoscience with the theory that lighter-skinned humans are somehow smarter than darker-skinned humans. Unarmed Tutsis and moderate Hutus—close to a million people—had no idea on April 6, 1994, what was about to be unleashed upon them.

One Tutsi girl, Jeanne, watched the slaughter of her family in what they thought was a safe haven. Jeanne eventually immigrated to Germany, where Hanna Jansen adopted her. Over time, Jeanne told Jansen her story, which was published in the book, *Over a Thousand Hills I Walk with You.* That her adoptive mother "walked" with her through her traumatic experiences brought some healing to Jeanne's life. When the Dalai Lama speaks of compassion, I think of Jansen and Jeanne—that Jeanne trusted her adoptive mother enough to explore the worst experiences of inhumanity with her, and that Jansen loved her adoptive daughter enough to listen for an interplay that Alan Schoen might call "connecting heart-to-heart in the moment." The Dalai Lama says, "You should take good care of others, be concerned for their welfare, help them, [and] serve them." Both Jeanne and Jansen exemplify this.

Broken Memory, a novel by Élisabeth Combres, is based on true stories of Hutu women who risked their own lives to take in orphaned Tutsi children. One example of these young orphans is Emma, who hid behind a sofa when the killers came for her family, and who eventually found Mukecuru, a Hutu woman who risks her life to give her a home. Demonstrating the interdependence of which the Dalai Lama speaks, Emma's friendship with others, as well as with Mukecuru, helps her begin to heal.

The Dalai Lama says, "From my own limited experience, I have found that the greatest degree of inner tranquility comes from the development of love and compassion." I don't personally know the authors and illustrators of these books, but I hope that, having cared for others more than for themselves, they are finding the great wealth of inner tranquility.

Thank you to Mary Ellen Levin for her generous reading of this essay.

Works Cited

Combres, Élisabeth. *Broken Memory: A Novel of Rwanda.* (Trans. Shelley Tanaka) Toronto, Canada: Groundwood (2009).

Tenzin Gyatso, His Holiness the 14th Dalai Lama. "Compassion and the Individual." http://www.dalailama.com/messages/compassion, cited June 2012.

Halilbegovich, Nadja. *My Childhood under Fire: A Sarajevo Diary.* Tonawanda, NY: Kids Can Press (2006).

Heleta, Savo. *Not My Turn to Die: Memoirs of a Broken Childhood in Sarajevo.* New York: Amacom (2008).

Jansen, Hanna. *Over a Thousand Hills I Walk with You.* (Trans. Elizabeth D. Crawford) Minneapolis, MN: Carolrhoda (2002).

Keat, Nawuth, with Martha E. Kendall. *Alive in the Killing Fields: Surviving the Khmer Rouge Genocide.* Washington, D.C.: National Geographic Children's Books (2009).

Lord, Michelle, and Shino Arihara (Illus.). *A Song for Cambodia.* New York, NY: Lee & Low Books (2008).

A principal practice for developing this awakening mind is the practice of exchanging oneself with others.

—His Holiness the Dalai Lama, from *In My Own Words: An Introduction to My Teaching and Philosophy*

Artists Helping Our Species Survive

Eric Lewis

Composer and Musician

T he protagonists in this age of anxiety, a high-tech age wallowing in the creativity of making things through "better chemistry," aided by religious zealots and venture capitalists and philosophers promoting the virtue of selfishness, have generated a toxic brew that cannot solve the problems of this over-populated planet of seven billion human beings. Is there any hope? What will "hope" look like in the 21st century? How will it be manifested? Who will or what will be the agent of hope? Where do seven billion people turn for deliverance from worldwide suffering amplified by these protagonists? My answer is radical: the reeducation of our society along the lines of the "Artist-Poet-Musician." This reeducation would promote universal creativity and compassion for human beings. These were in fact the stated aims of the Manhattan School of Music, which I attended during the 1960s.

The Manhattan School of Music on East 110th Street in East Harlem began as a Union Settlement house serving newly arrived and impoverished Italian, Polish, and Russian immigrants; it evolved into a first-rate conservatory of music under the leadership of Dr. Janet Schenck. An extraordinary activist for social causes who had ties to the international music elite (e.g., Harold Bauer and Pablo Casals), Schenck helped in the conservatory's founding, bringing her music to the poorest section of Manhattan. Her neighborhood music school developed into a national music conservatory, and by the 1960s, it was the largest international conservatory of music in the United States. During that turbulent decade, brimming with social pressures relating to war in Vietnam, protest marches, civil unrest, full-scale race riots (which occurred down the street in the school's neighborhood), political chaos, and several assassinations (John F. Kennedy, Robert F. Kennedy, Martin Luther King Jr., Malcolm X), I moved into the Manhattan School neighborhood to study works of the great classical composers so I could become a concert violinist.

The school infused its students with a deep sense of caring for people who were in dire stress because of poverty, political oppression, abuse, and social injustice. Janet Schenck's spirit and vision have lived on in the many generations of musicians fortunate enough to have attended the Manhattan School of Music. Ethnomusicologist John Blacking, in his 1967 study of South Africa's Venda children's songs, articulates Schenck's vision well:

> Music is a primary modeling system of human thought and part of the infrastructure of human life. "Music-making" is a special kind of social action, which can have important consequences for other kinds of social action.

Blacking's theory locates music as central to human behavior. In the context of the school and its legacy, Schenck's social action plan became our mission: the regeneration of hope and creation of an alternate survival paradigm. She encouraged us to promote the compassionate world without the distractions of hyper-careerism and its attendant goals of wealth and fame. We were to do so by fostering an atmosphere of empathy and integrity. We had to remain faithful to the principles of music-making in its most inspiring form: to encode a connective element for sharing the "good nutrient" for its audience in the tones of our creation.

Détente through music

The Russian composer Peter Ilyich Tchaikovsky's visit to the United States for the opening of Carnegie Hall in 1891 introduced his music to an American audience for the first time—a music of pure emotion, empathy, passion, and compassion. It is a music on the human plane of existence, filled with the fascinations of human experience: love, tragedy, conflict, simple living, hatred, anger, confusion of religion, and transcendence. Tchaikovsky's music demonstrates the ancient Greek philosophers' important principle of human empathy in the arts; his music provokes a cathartic response. To find oneself in the shoes of the character on stage experiencing in empathy his or her joys and sorrows is the supreme experience of art. Such should be the overarching structure of the artist's inspiration. Does our encounter with a great work of art move us? And what are the recognizable constituent elements of that state of excitement (chills, warmth, a deep sense of satisfaction, revelation, weeping from grief or joy, touching of the soul, setting vibrations in motion at fractal levels of being)?

The concentration of compassion-energy is a powerful tool for "peacemakers" in our society. And so I come to my own choice of focusing the compassion-energy: chamber music.

Chamber musicians are, by the discipline of their art, innately trained diplomats, because they employ a form of interaction among themselves that I call "the chamber music principle." The string quartet form is the ultimate vehicle of "the chamber music principle" because Western civilization's greatest composers have lavished their most inspirational, intimate musical secrets on its development. It is part of the chamber musician's education to learn how to apply this chamber music principle in creating a performance that bonds the audience together in compassion. To accomplish this in our intense collaborations (four instruments interacting as a single organism), we have to adhere to strict rules of conduct in the discussions and "rehearsal" that lead up to a performance. These rules for preparation of the performance include: banishment of cynicism and generalization; confessional trust; postponing judgment to avoid self-righteousness; avoiding angry outbursts at all costs; and working to create a holographic image of the composer's inner mind so as to reveal the composer's hidden intentions. This approach for achieving the highest performance goals requires a mutual respect akin to brotherly or sisterly love. Encouraging support for each member of the ensemble to find self-fulfillment and individual empowerment creates a healthy community of seeking minds.

"The chamber music principle" can be applied to any small, leaderless group of musicians, scientists, politicians, clergymen, statesmen, diplomats, and others, engaged in endeavors aimed toward the common good. Chamber musicians are not surprised when they discover that our 18th-century Founding Fathers gathered at the Monticello home of Thomas Jefferson in Virginia to play the string quartets of Haydn and Mozart. The playing readied them to launch the most far-reaching altruistic experiment in the history of the human species: the United States of America.

Music diplomacy in the "glasnost" era

I had the rare opportunity to apply the chamber music principle at an actual moment in the history of diplomacy, the years from 1985 to 1989 when the Cold War was at its height. During this period, called "glasnost," when the gradual breakup of the Soviet empire began, I was traveling in the Soviet Union with the Manhattan String Quartet. The United States ambassador to the Soviet Union, Arthur Hartman, later credited the quartet with a key role in the process of glasnost. Knowing the Russian history of cultural diplomacy in great detail, Ambassador Hartman very wisely used our young American string quartet for the purpose of image-altering (the "ugly American" imagery was quite prevalent in international circles at the time) to promote trust and respect between the negotiating parties and help seal a successful and historic agreement on nuclear disarmament. Hartman wrote a letter dated March 22, 1995, that describes the quartet's role in this highly charged atmosphere:

> My friendship with the Manhattan String Quartet goes back to my years as U.S. Ambassador to the Soviet Union, 1981–1987, when I invited the group . . . in 1985 to participate in the preparatory activities for the first Reagan-Gorbachev summit meeting in Geneva . . . [using] their ability to relate musically and personally with that evolving society. They played many of the Shostakovich quartets (they have recorded all of them) and Schubert's "Death and the Maiden." They thrilled music-loving Moscow. Their ability particularly to work with young people was noted. They gave a kind, loving, human face to the American artist and won the hearts of all who heard them. This was a demonstration of musical power in the diplomatic arena, for it helped smooth the nuts and bolts of the government negotiations. I am especially proud to present these artists who were born and trained in the U.S. and are now highly acclaimed on the international scene.

We used encoded music from their own country to "move" the Soviets, touching their diplomats with the sincerity of our approach, to give hope for a collaborative diplomatic breakthrough. In a time of crisis, one charged with our mutual need for survival in a nuclear age, music provided the trust and respect needed for these delicate and nuanced negotiations. Using the "chamber music principle," the name I gave to our code of behavior, the Manhattan String Quartet collaborated as artists to recreate, measure by measure, in a cathartic musical performance a humanistic musical picture of Russia's Stalin-era holocaust and its resultant psychic trauma. Dmitri Shostakovich (1906–1975), the great 20th-century Russian composer, wrote 15 string quartets that are known for their storybook quality and the intimate nature of Shostakovich's composing style. The quartets are encoded with musical allusions pointing to specific moments in his biography. These moments, because of his celebrity and his forced involvement in political culture for the purposes of advancing Stalinist propaganda, not only tells his story in detail but that of the vast Russian 20th-century tableau of Stalinist repression and war. For our musical re-creation of this story, it was entirely appropriate that we picked his most autobiographical work, the String Quartet No. 8 in C minor, and filled this vessel with as much of our empathy and compassion as we could understand from a distance. Imagine a group of young musicians from the "alien" United States playing music of Russian sensibilities with Russian nationalistic overtones. The ambition to undertake such a monumental effort was conceived decades ago and passed to us, teachers to students, at the Manhattan School of Music.

Shostakovich's string quartet gem was created in the artistic crucible of the Russian revolution and its aftermath. The composer wrote the quartet during a visit in 1960 to the devastated German city of Dresden, which the Allies (over Russian protests) had firebombed at the end of World War II, creating the historic man-made firestorm that consumed it in a genocidal experiment of revenge and rage. The String Quartet No. 8 in C minor reads like a Russian novel highlighting Shostakovich's themes in flashbacks of his past compositions, which probe betrayal, grief, and oppression. He accomplishes this effect in the first movement of the work with his own musical signature of unremitting grief; with searing iconic musical images of flames and mechanistic burlesque in movements two and three; and in the fourth and fifth movements an evocation of the KGB "knock on the door" that heralds the fear, torture, oppression, and betrayal of the Russian people. At the center of this matrix (the composition's golden mean) is an ancient Jewish folk song sung to me by my father, who learned it as part of the infinite chain of melody passed from generation to generation of Russian children over millennia. Shostakovich, expressing deep sorrow for the millions killed in the 20th-century catastrophe, held up this rescued folk song fragment, called "Tormented by Heavy Bondage," as a reminder of the atrocities perpetrated under Hitlerism *and* Stalinism.

The closing measures leave one in stunned silence, weeping. Our performance portrayed these thoughts in detail and was received by our Russian audience as something they had never heard before. A music critic explained it to me, after he heard us play the quartet. He felt our interpretative focus of empathy for the Russian people's plight, even with Shostakovich's very prominent dedication—"to the victims of war and fascism"—was absent in Soviet quartet performances of the piece because the contemporary Russian quartets were not bringing out the empathy and compassion encoded in the work. Soviet musicians were always very mindful of the ever-present censor and as a result were not free to express such a controversial view of Soviet society. He said, "You have held up a mirror of our suffering to us. It is quite extraordinary that it had to come to us in this way from America."

We envisioned Shostakovich's musical life story as an experience of immensely crushing sorrow that would touch the core of the listener's musical soul with no differentiation between Russian or American sensibilities. We were playing to an international audience in the tones of Shostakovich and asking, "Do you not hear the lessons of this history, feeling their anguish, in hopes of a newly created philosophy of life to rise from this epitaph to the victims?"

The artist's work for the 21st century

We stand at the precipice looking into a chasm, a black hole of annihilation for our children. It will not be a single leader, political system, or religion that will rescue the human race from extinction. It will be an artistic process understood by all people. The human species has evolved a great capacity to create and remember patterning. This awareness will become a crucial survival technique as we pivot from our habituated patterns of destruction to the use of the improvisational skills for creating "expectation violation" (the violation of our expected patterns)—to find new variations for survival. Artists learn and teach this technique in the arts. It is most easily discerned in the practice of music-making. In the patterns of the artistic mind lie the universal secret: "The cosmos is us—the people with their separate lives are inseparable from the landscape."

I propose we waste no more time, energy, and wealth on weapons of war. They are obsolete, and it is time to establish a newly energized diplomatic corps in which artists engage in the art of compassion to civilize our world dialogue for the collaboration now necessary. The challenges of the 21st century will depend on a new activism of the young artist-intellectual class ready to educate the world's children in the new creative paradigm, one encoded with compassion. We cannot survive these crises alone. No thought conceived by genius is produced in a vacuum. We are all connected in this lifeboat of a water planet. While we are here, let us work together. Let's make the best of it and talk . . . and listen, really listen to each other in our "otherness." We human primates are the masters of adaptation. The dynamic of "natural selection" that involved murdering the "other," the "enemy," is at an end. Human warfare has never been a solution for billions of human souls. We create our new hope through the adaptation of our minds to collaboration (the chamber music principle) for engagement in a new thrust of creativity and compassion for the "other," recognizing that enemy "other" is us.

As a psychotherapist, I have a view of compassion that I want to share here. Compassion requires a capacity to see oneself in a compassionate way and to understand one's own humanity, one's flaws, and one's vulnerability, and in that way see every person as an extension of oneself.

—Peter Jampel,
from the Creativity &
Compassion conference

Universal Talent

Peter Jampel
Arts Therapist

> *Talent is not a gift given to only a few; it is universal. Talent comes out of openness, integrity, simplicity, and the courage to feel and take risks.*
>
> —Michele Cassou and Stewart Cubley,
> *Life, Paint and Passion*[1]

Talent is not just an inherent gift but instead issues forth from candor, authenticity, and emotional honesty. As a music therapist, this belief underlies my work with all lovers of music, particularly with people who have serious mental health issues. Music should not be the sole province of a select few but should offer an opportunity for anyone to be a performer. It should reduce the divisions between those who perform and those who witness it. It should promote the unification of people, not their further separation. The performance process has the capacity to empower the creative self while simultaneously connecting the self to others. These special dynamics, which help us to acknowledge individual achievement while connecting to the universal spirit of creativity, exemplifies, I believe, compassionate action. It makes possible the integration of Western and Eastern ideals of individual and collective activity, developing our individual ability to attach to personal goals while still valuing the benefits of non-attaching group behavior.

However, too often, performance becomes an isolating process. Performing music is often fraught with inhibitions. It can be frightening, intimidating, and anxiety-inducing. The casualties are numerous among trained musicians, music therapy students, and people with mental illness. Performance is frequently experienced as an ordeal, a competition, or something that others do.

The repeated experience of being judged (by self and others) and endlessly compared to relative degrees of skill (or beauty) can corrupt the notion that anyone can be a performer, replacing it with the idea that the only ones who can be a performer are those who receive great recognition and approval. No longer does performing have intrinsic meaning but it becomes instead an association to extrinsic measurements. That is what I refer to as "performance pathology." Many musicians suffer from it, and some are completely paralyzed by it.

Creativity and performance pathology

Abraham Maslow's 1968 study of psychological health was revealing in terms of the way creative people approached situations fearlessly, experiencing high levels of satisfaction and meaning.[2] These individuals almost invariably felt secure in their primary relationship attachments and experienced social intimacy as a rewarding constant in their lives. In psychoanalytical theory, the "object relations" approach posits that stable object constancy—a consistent and loving relationship with one's parents and parental figures—as a child promotes sufficient confidence to be able to gradually venture off into increasingly autonomous and individuated pursuits. Confidence in the love and approval of empowering parental figures encourages the fledgling creator to take risks in an increasingly discerning manner. The result is risk-taking that calculates in more accurate ways which risks are best worth pursuing, thus further refining and self-perpetuating the creative process. Conversely, risk-taking that is burdened by parental anxiety or over-control can result in overly cautious creative approaches. Others become threats, potential competitors, or adversaries. Audiences can become projections of the performer's inner emotional state. The performers can become pathologically attached to these projections.

From this perspective, healthy attachments are a necessary condition not only for creative action but also from a spiritual/psychological dimension, as a precondition for non-attaching, autonomous behavior. Over-identification with outcome reflects a need for external validation. It can smother the creative process in layers of clinging behavior characterized by a need to be seen and acknowledged. Achievement then becomes a defensive activity that wards off the fear that the self will dissolve in the absence of perceived accomplishments.

Performance pathology manifests itself in a number of ways: hypersensitivity to criticism, approval-seeking behavior, a brittle and fragile sense of self-worth, or the narcissism of an excessive and bloated sense of self-worth; it is also evidenced in a tyrannical drive to produce, obsessive-compulsive behavior, manic-depressive cycles, hyper-sexuality, obsession with physical appearance, panic attacks, self-destructive use of drugs or alcohol, chronic fears of failure, an inability to manage intimacy, and a failure to connect deeply to music-making or through it to others.[3] These symptoms reflect the collapse of creativity into an empty and hollow pursuit of personal glory. But does this necessarily imply that performing music is vapid? Can there be some other way to fulfill the desire to play and to share one's music with others that integrates the self with the "all other"? In fact, can performance itself be a pathway through this dilemma?

Connection and the five dimensions of musical performance

Culture can influence how performers view themselves, each other, are how they are viewed through the eyes of their audiences and by the society in which they operate. Cross-cultural differences from the clinical perspective of a music therapist should shift when considering what performance psychopathology looks like in different cultures. It is my contention that the prevailing Western view of music and the arts all too often promotes too great an emphasis on the attitude of individual, egocentric accomplishment. The obsessive quest for the perfect musician is an ideal that leaves most everyone wanting, envying, or never even trying to perform. Cultures that see performance as an activity that is not just devoted to a talent elite but as a medium of coming together, celebrating, remembering, and acknowledging, tend to promote a universal spirit rather than the glorification of individual achievement.

Yet Western culture has also developed a tradition of artistic accomplishment that has produced an enduring legacy of brilliant individual creative invention through which universal identification has been fostered. Such achievement has produced works of profound human understanding and compassion. So given the different cultural traditions in musical performance, can we somehow amalgamate the best of both approaches by bringing together self-focused and universally focused creativity? I would suggest that the two paths are not inherently incompatible and can be fused by the nature of performance itself.

Public music-making is a complex set of simultaneous and overlapping experiences or dimensions.[4] The most immediate experience takes place within the performer as the degree of connection one has to the music that is being made. If I cannot connect to the music that I am making, I feel my disconnect and others see it. Another dimension of connection involves the relationship among performers through the act of making music together. This can be incredibly intimate on one end of the spectrum or totally out of sync on the other. Both of these dimensions can be perceived by the audience. This important connection among the performers can either cause the listeners to connect or to be distanced from the performers, creating a synergistic or enervating reciprocal loop between musicians and audience.

The fourth dimension is unseen by the audience but is very much a part of the performer's consciousness. This dimension involves what is going on in the mind of the musician. I call this dimension the "inner audience."[4] This aspect of the experience can range from random distracting thoughts ("I'm hungry") to powerful sensations of fear, anxiety, or anticipation of a difficult musical passage. Past or present figures from one's life—such as expectant parents, critical teachers, or alienated life partners—may take center stage in the performer's mind.

All of these dimensions produce the totality of the felt experience of the performer, the fifth dimension. If there is a significant disturbance in any one or more of the four previous aspects of experience, the fifth dimension suffers. When all dimensions are operating in maximum synchronicity with each other, the fifth dimension soars.

Self-understanding is an instrument for creative action. Greater insight leads to enhanced mindfulness and compassionate action, and thus the balance between the individual and the group becomes more finely attuned. The process of striving for musical harmony offsets the potential struggle of attaching to personal creations. Achievement is recognized and supported as a reflection of the accomplishments of the individual but within the context of the group. Tolerances for differences in skill and motivation are not threats to the fabric of the whole but can knit together a collective that inspires each performer toward greater effort. The more distinct each person becomes, the more they can feel secure in a collective state of belonging.

Notes

1. Cassou, M. and S. Cubley. *Life, Paint and Passion: Reclaiming the Magic of Spontaneous Expression.* Los Angeles, CA: J. P. Tarcher (1995).

2. Maslow, A. *The Farthest Reaches of Human Nature.* NY: The Viking Press (1968).

3. Jampel, Peter. "Performance in Music Therapy with Mentally Ill Adults." PhD dissertation. New York University (2006).

4. —. "Performance in Music Therapy: Experiences in Five Dimensions," *Voices: A World Forum for Music Therapy*, 11 [2011] (1):(11(*1*).

Aesthetic Distance

Norman Carey

Musician

he finest art reveals its secrets by engendering an inner state of detachment known technically as "aesthetic distance." The central component of the aesthetic experience is awareness. In the highest form of aesthetic experience, powerful emotions do not sweep us away, but rather fuse into a singularity. They become "happy/sad," as my precocious daughter put it at age four.

An experience that I had playing piano at 16 years of age had a highly significant impact that illustrates this point. As a student in Manhattan School of Music's preparatory division, I was sitting, along with my fellow young musical acolytes, in the front seats of a large room with a tapestry on the front wall and a grand piano before it. We were getting ready to perform at the annual Maytime recital. I was to play the Schubert *Impromptu* in A-flat, op. 90, no. 4. As one of the older students, my piece was slotted near the end of the program. When it was my time to play, I got up, went to the piano bench, and, with a little nervous excitement, began to play the cascading arpeggios of the first section. It was all going quite well until an extraordinary sensation overtook me as I began to play the third and final section. It was as if I could see the entire rest of the piece—the entire rest of the performance—laid out in front of me. It was so completely clear: I knew that all I needed to do was to rest in this absolutely still awareness, and, if I did, there was *no possibility* except that the rest would go flawlessly. I had only to remain aware and inwardly unmoving.

The realization was terrifyingly simple. All strategizing could stop. All sense of concern could dissolve. Everything was there. So, rather than focusing my attention on playing, I focused rather on remaining still. It required a kind of skill, but a rather negative one—the skill of doing nothing. It is the same skill one finally latches onto when one learns to ride a bike by surrendering the desperate jerky micro-efforts to remain upright. By daring to fall, one paradoxically balances.

At another time, my brother and I were walking past a playground in Central Park. Although we were in our twenties, a nostalgic echo of childhood pulled us inside. There was a rope dangling between two platforms, but, standing on one, the other seemed too far away for any would-be Tarzan to swing to. Sure enough, as each of us traded tries, we found ourselves a few tantalizing inches from the goal. Each attempt was accompanied by stronger and stronger propulsive pushes off of the starting platform. Each fell short. All of a sudden I looked up and there was my brother, standing on the other platform. How did you do it?" I asked. He was nonchalant: "I didn't try."

I remember reading about Philippe Petit, the French aerialist who walked on a wire strung between the two towers of the World Trade Center in 1974. He was asked, "Aren't you ever afraid up there?" His answer has always stayed with me: "No, I know my craft too well, I am never afraid in that sense. However, I am so completely alive on the wire that it is easy to be overwhelmed by waves of euphoria, and about this I must be very careful."

The expression "aesthetic distance" has a number of meanings, but the one that resonates with me is the one that derives from its originator, Edward Bullough, who wrote that aesthetic distance "is obtained by separating the object and its appeal from one's own self, by putting it out of gear with practical needs and ends. Thereby the 'contemplation' of the object becomes alone possible."[1]

The story of Odysseus and the sirens helps to illustrate. When Odysseus was on his long journey home to Ithaca after the Trojan War, he and his crew had to sail past the rocky coast of the island of the Sirens. The Sirens lured sailors to shipwrecked doom through the enchanting power of their song. The clever

Odysseus devised a way to hear their song and yet pass safely by the island's rocks. He told his men to stop up their ears with wax and had them tie him up to the mast. This is a powerful image of detachment, even if it encompasses extreme measures. In the nonattached state—through a powerful ability to resist temptation—the observer may stay with the object of contemplation without getting carried away. The lower senses, symbolized by the men, are detached, so that the higher sense, depicted by Odysseus, may hear the song.

By deciding to remain inwardly still during that performance of the Schubert *Impromptu* back when I was 16, this state of contemplation magically opened. It kept its promise: The performance was flawless.

Notes

1.   Bullough, Edward (1912–1989). "'Psychical Distance' as a Factor in Art and as an Aesthetic Principle." Reprinted in *Aesthetics: A Critical Anthology*. 2nd ed. Dickie, G., R. Sclafani, and R. Roblin, eds. New York: St. Martin's Press, (1989) p. 322.

Don't think, "The little virtues that I did
Will make no difference afterwards."
Just as the single water drops
Fill up the vase,
So steadfast ones are filled
With virtue collected little by little.

—*Udānavarga* 15:6

དགེ་བ་ཆུང་ངུས་བདག་ཉིད་ཀྱི། །
ཕྱི་བཞིན་མི་འོང་མ་སེམས་ཤིག །
ཆུ་ཡི་ཐིགས་པ་ལྷུང་བ་ཡིས། །
བུམ་ཆེན་གང་བ་ཇི་བཞིན་དུ། །
ཆུང་ཟད་ཆུང་ཟད་བསགས་པ་ཡི། །
དགེ་བས་བརྟན་པ་གང་བར་འགྱུར། །

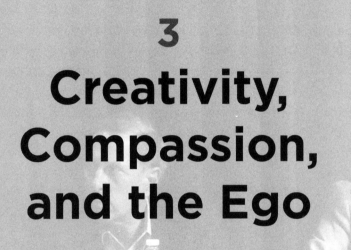

3
Creativity, Compassion, and the Ego

The Untamed Mind

Janet Kathleen Ettele
Writer and Musician

Even those who wish to find happiness and overcome misery
Will wander with no aim nor meaning
If they do not comprehend the secret of the mind—
The paramount significance of Dharma.

This being so,
I shall hold and guard my mind well.
Without the discipline of guarding the mind,
What use are many other disciplines?

—Master Śāntideva, *Guide to the Bodhisattva's Way of Life*,
chapter 5, "Guarding Alertness," verses 17–18

The trials of the ego in creativity and compassion

Challenge the ego's significance or function, and egos quickly make themselves manifest to engage in debate. Many spiritual systems agree that the ego is a mental construct that arises along with the condition of being human. It is something we unconsciously create in the process of adapting to our lives, and while we cannot pinpoint where it exists, we cling to it fervently as if it is who and what we truly are. This is different from the psychoanalytic definition of ego that considers it to be the organizing part of the personality.

After only a few years of studying the Buddhist teachings and more than a few decades of living with an ego, my understanding of the ego is that it is the *untamed mind*. In other words, it is the mind that lacks awareness, mindfulness, or true wisdom. The ego claims its existence as separate and independent, creating a world of "us" and "them," or "good guys" and "bad guys." It over-inflates our significance, feels the need to compete rather than to cooperate, or maybe even wishes to bring harm to another. It is frighteningly vulnerable to desire. Frighteningly so, because the objects of desire are simply unable to deliver any lasting happiness. The desire for these ultimately impotent objects can be so strong that many will forfeit true happiness in the pursuit of a desired object. Unable to know the experience of a peaceful mind, these seekers persist in chasing an illusion, believing it will eventually deliver satisfaction.

Mind is the reservoir of both creativity and compassion. And the ego or *untamed mind* is not only *experiencing* the trials, it is *causing* the trials. When creativity is engaged with ego, the flow of the creative process is distorted. Desire for approval, fame, material gain, or power and influence are just a few things the ego is both seduced by and empowered by. Conversely, when creativity is engaged with altruism, the creative process is unencumbered and flows with an energy that feels transcendent.

One's motivation will determine the experience and outcome of creative and compassionate acts. Therefore, all art forms have the capacity to express and inspire thoughts of love, awe, and gratitude just as readily as hatred or violence.

Whether or not we consider ourselves to be artists, we need to recognize that even in the apparent little things like random conversations, or random thoughts, we *are* creating. Our thoughts, falling under the law of karma, or cause and effect, always set something in motion to *create* our future experience. This is why mindfulness is so important. Whether we are picking up a paintbrush to apply strokes to a canvas or opening our mouths to speak, we must be vigilantly mindful that we are in fact creating our next moment, and the next, and the next.

Is compassion a creative process?

Life itself is a creative process, so, of course, compassion is a creative process as well. All of life and all that is creative combine into a dance of moments that continually changes from one experience into another. When compassion is brought into this dance, it infuses all experiences with peace and love. Whether we are mindful of it or not, every moment presents us with a choice: a choice to either engage from a compassionate view or from the perspective of intolerance, anger, or hatred. These moments of choice are no less creative than choosing to add red or blue to a painting. Whatever thought or action we select will bring about change for the next moment along with an increasing energy or momentum of a similar nature.

There is also an element of surprise in creativity. For example, the creative process in art includes incorporating something one might view as a "mistake" into the art itself. And experiences we might consider to be unfortunate mistakes can be creatively woven into our lives to add beautiful and rich textures to our overall life experience. In Buddhism, we hear the teaching that we should turn all suffering into the path. The path is one of compassion and wisdom. So, with the *tamed mind*—the mind that is *not the ego mind*—we will *always* respond compassionately.

Creativity, compassion, and wisdom can be cultivated and nurtured. They can also be ignored. While beneficial for all, it seems especially vital for educators and parents who guide young people to ensure that all three are cultivated and nurtured. If we can usher in a generation that has been nurtured by compassion and wisdom to creatively participate in the dance of life, then the potential for positive change will be vastly increased.

I've studied creativity and worked with it for many years, but I never actually put compassion and creativity together until I was forced to think about it in this process. It's definitely worth thinking about.

—John Z. Amoroso, from the Creativity & Compassion conference

The Ego's Complexes

John Z. Amoroso

Transpersonal Psychotherapist

W e can think of the ego as the central core of the individual, which harbors all of the behavioral patterns, perspectives, and accumulated life experiences as well as the awareness of the talents, skills, and defenses that define who we are as individuals—that sense of "I," or self. The ego is that sense of identity that is unique for each of us. To simplify this definition, we can think of the ego as composed of all the positive and negative themes or complexes that evolve in the process of life.

These positive and negative complexes or themes play out as specific reactive behaviors and are grounded in feelings of either adequacy or inadequacy associated with specific talents, skills, and ways of being in the world. Someone who grew up with positive reinforcement, training, and success as a musician can reach adulthood with a positive complex around the "good musician." A positive complex can coalesce around the theme of the good student, the good listener, the committed friend, or any other talent or way of being in the world. A young child who grows up in a family where being helpful to others or being of service to others was a primary ethic can evolve into an adult who thrives on that same positive complex. That complex forms around a feeling of adequacy regarding one's sense of self and service to others, which can become a primary factor in one's sense of purpose in life.

The problem is that negative complexes invariably form as well, carrying with them some feeling of inadequacy about the self. The child who grows up with parents who tend to be critical and negative can become an adult with a negative complex associated with a lack of self-confidence. Themes of abandonment, betrayal, inadequacy associated with a particular ability, or simply a sense of self-loathing are just a few of the possibilities for a person who's been shaped by such conditions. It's not hard to see how these negative aspects of the ego can form into dysfunctional behaviors and disrupt the course of one's life.

Compassion, on the other hand, is defined as "a sympathetic pity and concern for the suffering or misfortunes of others." This involves empathy or, as the word's Latin origins suggest, a "co-suffering." The act of selfless compassion commonly gives rise to an active desire to alleviate another's suffering and the inspiration to take action. But it does not necessitate action. As Buddha said, compassion is the desire to "shelter and embrace the distressed." It amounts to a genuine wish for the well-being of others.

The first step in the process of clearing the channel to engage in selfless compassion for others is to experience and fully appreciate one's own suffering and to have compassion for oneself. In other words, the real challenge is to learn to deal with one's own problems—or negative complexes—and to move to higher consciousness and liberation from those negative themes and ego attachments. This is where the psychological implications of the influence of the ego on compassion come into play.

Let's look more specifically at how the trials of the ego influence our expression of compassion during the course of life. On the positive side, one's sense of ego can enliven and be the foundation of interaction with the outside world. For example, if my sense of "I" as manifested in a positive complex has to do with being of service to others—what one might call the "All else"—then my ego can enliven the practice of compassion in a natural and authentic way. Compassion in this sense helps to fulfill a sense of purpose in the process of life that has to do with who I am.

However, very few of us are without our problems, blind spots, psychological issues, or negative complexes. That insecure sense of self, the lack of self-esteem, that fear of abandonment or betrayal are just a few of the themes that can interfere with one's authentic practice of compassion. Issues like these will inevitably influence how we engage compassion in our lives. For example, that lack of self-esteem may "engage" the act of compassion to simply remedy that personal feeling of inadequacy that comes with the complex. In this way, the ego or sense of inadequacy stored in the ego will affect the authentic act of compassion in a dysfunctional way. In this case, compassion is not engaged in a selfless way—as the Buddha advocated—but in a way so as to satisfy a failing in the ego and to achieve self-gratification. This is just one example of how one's damaged or wounded sense of self can distort or interfere with the expression of compassion—especially as it is defined in the Buddhist tradition.

As the Buddhist teachings indicate, the first order of business as we become conscious of and engage compassion in our lives is to arrive at compassion for ourselves. This does not necessarily require a deep and extended process of psychotherapy. It does, however, require a critical process of self-reflection and evaluation to bring to awareness those positive and negative complexes that are harbored in the ego. Only then, in relation to the negative themes, can one activate a "sympathetic pity" and empathy for one's self on the path to higher consciousness and release from the self. Then one can clear the channel to authentic compassion. This is what the Buddha and His Holiness are referring to in teachings when they bring up the issue of compassion for oneself.

How does creativity come into the picture? We must first consider that creativity—as well as compassion—is an inherent primal drive that we all share. And we all have the potential to engage these two forces in the process of life. In simple terms, we can define creativity as the act of making something new that has value to the individual and the world. This can involve making new objects or inventions as well as creating meaningful new ideas, interpretations, methods of thinking or working, or new communications with others that are useful. The act of creation then, draws on the ego or that sense of "I"—with all of its complexes—in the process of making something new and useful. In this respect, we can think of creativity as an expression of "I" to the outside world or the "All else." With this framework, we can see how creativity and compassion are driven by the same sense of purpose in the desire for the well-being of self and others.

It's important to note that creativity does not only relate to artists, inventors, and entrepreneurs. The creative impulse is engaged in all the normal and mundane activities of life—from making a piece of art, to cooking a nutritious meal, developing a new lesson plan, brushing our teeth in the morning, and solving any problem in the normal course of life.

How does the ego influence the act of creativity in our lives? It's not hard to see how a sense of inadequacy or a negative complex can stifle one from engaging creativity. Internal scripts that we replay like "I'm not good enough," or "If I express myself, I'll be betrayed by others," represent just a few of the themes that can easily interfere with that inherent impulse to be innovative, to solve problems, and to be novel. These complexes can interfere not only with the activity of the artist/inventor but of anyone engaged in the normal activities of life. That individual with a self-esteem complex might be overly cautious about engaging the creative impulse to solve a routine problem or make a decision, all due to a lack of self-confidence. The individual with an abandonment complex might feel self-restricted about expressing a new idea, for fear of being abandoned by others. The talented musician might feel restricted about performing in public for fear of "not being good enough." The possibilities are endless as to how a negative aspect of one's sense of self can block creativity just as it can interfere with a selfless expression of compassion. On the other hand, we mustn't forget how the presence of a positive complex can influence the process of engaging creativity. That good musician, good student, good artist, good problem-solver, and good helper can find him- or herself liberated to make the most out of that inherent drive to be innovative and produce something of value.

Creativity can be optimized and fully engaged first by recognizing the surprising fact that our ego itself—our self—is a creative product: like a sculpture that the mind, in interaction with its environment, has created. But the sculpture is in motion, still being created, and we are engaged in that creation when we work to understand how the ego and the positive and negative complexes come into play to interfere with or enliven that primal drive to create.

Here again, the first order of business is to recognize that we all have the same potential for engaging in creativity throughout the process of life. And, in order to optimize creativity, we must work to uncover and de-energize those complexes that get in the way, even as we enliven those aspects of the self that are positive.

One final thought. Considering that compassion does focus on empathy for others and the desire to "shelter and embrace the distressed" and also recognizing that creativity is about doing something that is innovative and valued by self and others, it should be clear that creativity cannot only be initiated but enlivened by engaging in selfless compassion.

For one, compassion enhances our sensitivity to the suffering or discomfort of those living beings around us. This, in turn, will make us more aware of our own suffering. In this way, one is more conscious of the process and the experience of oneself and others in the outside world. This sensitivity is bound to influence one's creative output and problem-solving process in a very powerful way, whether the project involves an artistic production, the impetus for or result of scientific research, or simply a method of communicating with others. In this manner, the practice of compassion can open the door to more meaningful and valued creative results and a much deeper sense of purpose and satisfaction to the creator. In simple terms, the compassionate creator is more creative. I think that His Holiness would agree that engaging in compassion for self and selfless compassion in the process of living the creative life would qualify as an honorable spiritual practice.

ཕྱོགས་རྣམས་ཀུན་ཏུ་སེམས་ཀྱིས་ཡོངས་བཏགས་ཀྱང་། །

བདག་ལས་ཆེས་སྡུག་འགའ་ཡང་མ་མཐོང་བ། །

དེ་ལྟར་བོ་སོར་གཞན་ལའང་རང་ལྡུག་པས། །

དེ་ཕྱིར་བདག་དགས་གཞན་ལ་གནོད་མི་བྱ། །

Through searching all directions
with my mind
[It seems that] I find none with more
beauty than myself.
Since others also see themselves
this way,
Liking themselves, do not cause
harm to others.

—*Udānavarga* 5:19

I think it's vital to remember that compassion doesn't differentiate between a friend and a stranger. I was confronted with this a lot when I lived in New York City for a few years. At one moment I nearly tripped over a homeless woman. I could have been angry at her for getting in my way; I could have walked by and dismissed her as if she wasn't there. I chose to sit down with her. We talked for over an hour as if we were old friends, and I realized in that moment that in another life, if she had chosen a different path, or I had, we could have been very dear to each other. So why treat her any differently than if we were in that other life?

—Isabel "Belle" Lopes,
from the Creativity &
Compassion conference

Ego and Self

Fredrica R. Halligan
Clinical Psychologist

t all begins when I put a dot on my paper, waiting to see how the Spirit will move me in creative directions. The dream memory comes back then:

> A woman mentions "the Program" and I know she means
> A.A. In the dream I have to lift my son into the car. Even
> though he's young he is very heavy. He's curled in a fetal
> position and I lift him using a cardboard box as a stretcher.

I reflect on this dream, recalling first the shame of "the alcohol years" when my adolescent son experimented with drugs and became an alcoholic. Then I also recall a nurse in my Health Psychology class who wrote a paper about "Creativity and Compassion in Battlefield Nursing." She had experienced the acute challenges of caring for wounded soldiers when supplies were unavailable. For nurses in the midst of war, a string could be used as a tourniquet; a sheet wrapped around poles could become a stretcher. Creative compassion indeed! Then I recognized the connection to my dream: a cardboard box could be used to carry a young alcoholic. I too had been faced with the challenges of battlefield caregiving. My battle had been the alcoholic years. My "wounded youth" had been a son who was indeed "very heavy to carry." My shame lies still buried deep within; and my gratitude lies in the healing powers of Alcoholics Anonymous (A.A.). Dare I put this personal experience out for public view? The dream this morning suggests that I must.

This dream arose just two days after participating in a panel discussion entitled "The trials of the ego in creativity and compassion. Is compassion a creative process?" Dreams are of course powerful—if not always clear—messages from the creative unconscious.[1, 2] So it's not unexpected that a discussion of creativity would elicit a dream in response.

But first, what is ego? According to Western psychology, ego is the organizing principle of the mind; ego strength is needed for such functions as reality testing, judgment, anticipation, assessment of danger, and impulse control, as well as management of anxiety, frustration, and disappointment. Ego is involved in differentiation of oneself from others.[3] From the layman's perspective, ego is identification with one's body, name, history, and so on. Here in the West, ego is considered positive (unless it is excessive, as in narcissism). Ego identity is fostered by creative people in order to receive funding, fame, and affirmation. But in the East, transcendence of ego identity is seen as a prerequisite to spiritual progress (enlightenment, liberation, *moksha*, etc.). How can we reconcile the two: The ego identity of the creative person that allows the individual to survive in Western culture—and the ego transcendence for the sake of spiritual progress?

In answer to these questions, we might consider the outlook of Jack Hawley, a Western writer and scholar of Eastern religions. He tells us: We must first understand the mind, then tame the mind, train the mind, and finally transcend the mind (what Hawley refers to as "mind" is roughly equivalent to what Western psychologists call "ego"). It seems that some degree of humility is desirable (even necessary) to transcend ego. This is evident in Hawley's translation of the *Bhagavad Gītā*:

"The Secret of Selfless Action [is] . . . when one's actions are not based on desire for personal reward . . . [one] should not crave the fruits of [them]. [Rather] refuse to be attached to or affected by the results, whether favorable or unfavorable. . . . The Illumined Ones subdue their senses and hold them in check by keeping their minds ever intent on achieving the overarching goal of union with God. They get in the habit of substituting divine thoughts for attractions of the senses. . . . The ideal . . . is to be intensely active and at the same time have no selfish motives, no thoughts of personal gain or loss. Duty uncontaminated by desire leads to inner peacefulness and increased effectiveness. *This* is the secret of living a life of real achievement![4]

The *Gītā* is thus suggesting that one must transcend one's own desires and ego investment. Or, as Carl Jung would put it, the ego must surrender to the Self or the God-life within.[5]

Recall that in the dream I encountered my sense of *shame* over having raised an alcoholic offspring. Had I failed as a mother? (Shame, like pride, its opposite, is often a sign of an overactive ego.) Just as in the *Bhagavad Gītā*, A.A. advises us to let go of our ego investments. A favorite 12-step slogan is: "Let go and let God"; in other words, do the best you can and leave the results in God's hands. How many times have I, as a psychotherapist, suggested the same approach! Compassion and healing interventions often require letting go of the results; coercion is never effective in therapeutic work.

Psychotherapy is an exemplar of a compassionate process; so, too, it is often creative. In reflecting on my therapeutic work, it seems to me that compassion and creativity overlap. They are, I think, related to one another like a Venn diagram (i.e., two intersecting circles with an area of overlap between them). This notion suggests that not all compassion is creative, and not all creativity is compassionate; but there is a large area in life where creativity and compassion coexist and are synergistic (e.g., in the work of battlefield nurses who exemplify caregivers, creatively solving problems so that their compassionate work can be accomplished).

In his small booklet, *Compassion and the Individual,* His Holiness the Dalia Lama tells us that true compassion involves a kinship with all beings, due to our "profound interdependence." We can agree that empathic consciousness is universal: One can celebrate with the happiness of all others, and feel sorrow with the suffering of all others. Thus, a truly compassionate person realizes our essential human oneness.

In my field of psychotherapy, we are taught that empathy is our core attitude, and that, in order to be compassionate with others, one must first be compassionate with oneself! Ego, we know, is centered in itself. "I," "me," and "mine" are the main concerns of ego. But we must also reflect on how compassion relates to ego identity or ego transcendence. Are ego identity and ego transcendence both necessary?

There is usually much ego involvement in one's creative work, whatever it may be. Ego identity demands it. ("This is *my* painting; *my* music; *my* writing," etc.) All the skill training required to be proficient in any artistic or creative endeavor is based on the work and development of ego strengths. Yet once basic proficiency is gained, there also seems to be a yearning for something more. That "more" may be the influx of divine energies. Ultimately, the ego aspires for transcendence of itself.

Can we learn from Eastern spirituality that our very *best* work may arise when we let our ego identity go? When the wounded soldier is not *my* son, nor *my* patient, but rather is the archetypal wounded youth, then we are in touch with the unity of humankind. As caretakers, we can act from the archetypal level, becoming among those who serve and care compassionately for others. As creative artists, we can also tune into Divine energies—the creative energy of the universe—to express what we all hold dear.

Think of visual masterpieces such as Picasso's *Guernica* (a painting that expresses the horror and pain of war) or Rodin's *The Burghers of Calais* (a sculpture showing so poignantly the self-sacrifice of six men about to give their lives for their city). Creative, yes; compassionate, yes. These pieces speak of universal pain. They exemplify the intersection of creativity and compassion. Likewise, much of the world's greatest music and literature comprise compassionate works, and therein one senses the profound source of creativity. The pathos of Shakespeare's *Romeo and Juliet*; the warlike thunder we hear in Tchaikovsky's *1812 Overture (Finale)* or in the opening to the third act of Wagner's opera, *Die Walküre*, called the "Ride of The Valkyrie;" and, in contrast, the humble gratitude that uplifts us in the song "Amazing Grace"; these too touch us emotionally. We recognize empathically both the deep compassion in these creative works, and their acceptance of flawed humanity.

So is ego transcendence necessary in the creative process? Perhaps not necessary, but it is certainly beneficial! The greatest of creative works appear to be grounded in compassion for the human condition. The great artist, it seems, has gone far beyond the individual concerns for I, me, and mine. What begins with an expression of personal experience reaches beyond the individual to something larger. Therein lies greatness, wholeness, unity, spirituality, and happiness. As His Holiness so eloquently put it:

> [I]nner tranquility comes from the development of love and compassion. The more we care for the happiness of others, the greater our own sense of well-being becomes. Cultivating a close, warm-hearted feeling for others automatically puts the mind at ease. This helps remove whatever fears or insecurities we may have and gives us the strength to cope with any obstacles we encounter. It is the ultimate source of success in life. . . . The need for love lies at the very foundation of human experience. It results from the profound interdependence we all share with one another.[6]

In Vedic tradition, the Sanskrit syllable *oṁ* denotes the creative source and foundation of all interdependent life. While ego may fear its own transcendence, the wisdom of the East recognizes the benefits. Heightened creativity might be added to the beneficial results of ego transcendence (which also include spiritual growth and power, wisdom, and even enlightenment). So if we follow the directives attributed to Krishna in the *Bhagavad Gītā*, we will work to the best of our abilities, producing our maximum efforts in terms of both creative skill and compassion for human suffering—life just as it is. We will, however, offer our works for the welfare of the whole, relinquishing personal desire for praise and moving beyond our fear of censure. Thus, equanimity becomes our goal, being alike in conditions of "success" or "failure." This is a tall order for those of us who are steeped in Western culture. Our materialism, narcissism, judgmentalism, and hierarchical values are at risk! But as Eckhart Tolle recently reminded us:

> When you yield internally, when you surrender [the ego], a new dimension of consciousness opens up. . . . You realize your true identity as consciousness itself. . . . That's the peace of God. The ultimate truth of who you are is not I am this or I am that, but I Am.[7]

In summary, we can see that while ego strengths are necessary for development of skills, and ego is itself necessary for our very survival in this world, at some point we find ourselves yearning for more. At that point, surrender—transcendence of the ego—is prioritized for spiritual growth as well as for deeper compassion and heightened creativity alike.

In the West, we tend to characterize "God" as both creative and compassionate. When we expand our capacities for both these characteristics, we become more godlike and in tune with the One Who Is.

Throughout the East, *oṁ* points to unity, connectedness, creativity, and compassion. Thus we end with the mantra, *oṁ śhāntiḥ śhāntiḥ śhāntiḥ:* To all beings, peace, peace, peace.

Notes

1.   Arieti, S. *Creativity: The Magic Synthesis.* New York: Harper/Basic Books (1976).

2.   Stein, M. *Jung's Map of the Soul.* Chicago: Open Court (1998).

3.   Blank, G., and R. Blank. *Ego Psychology II: Psychoanalytic Developmental Psychology.* New York: Columbia University Press (1979).

4.   Hawley, J. *The Bhagavad Gītā: A Walkthrough for Westerners.* Novato, CA: New World Library (2001), pp. 18–24.

5.   Stein, M. *Jung's Map of the Soul.*

6.   Tenzin Gyatso, His Holiness the 14th Dalai Lama, *Compassion and the Individual.* Boston: Wisdom Publications (1991), p. 4.

7.   Tolle, E. *A New Earth: Awakening to Your Life's Purpose.* New York: Penguin/Plume (2006), p. 57f.

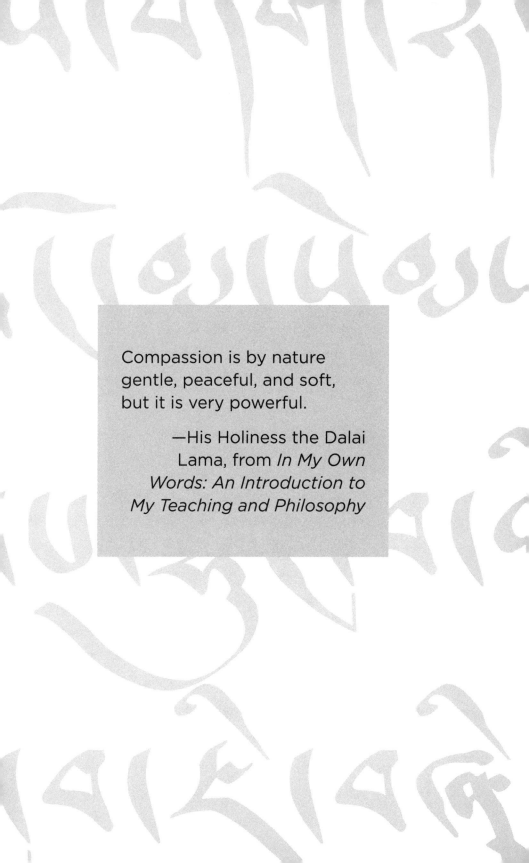

Compassion is by nature gentle, peaceful, and soft, but it is very powerful.

—His Holiness the Dalai Lama, from *In My Own Words: An Introduction to My Teaching and Philosophy*

Music for Compassionate Action

Barbara Hesser
Music Therapist

Music has played a central role in the lives of people throughout time, and in every culture there have been musicians dedicated to the use of music for transformation and healing. Today, we are called music therapists. We all come from diverse cultural, educational, and musical backgrounds to music therapy, but we come with a similar intention. We are performers, improvisers, and composers who are brought together into the profession of music therapy by our mutual love of music and our belief that music can contribute to the health and well-being of individuals and society. Music therapy is a unique profession and much more than a job for many of us. It is a life dedicated to compassionate action through the intentional and creative use of music.

My intention as a professor of music therapy is to help students who enter our graduate program to develop the ability to use their music to serve people struggling with mental, physical, and emotional challenges. The musicians who apply to our program in music therapy come with the belief that music can be beneficial to others, and they are dedicated to the idea of using their music for helping others. All our students are musicians who enter the profession of music therapy from a life in music (performance, teaching, music business, etc.). Many are motivated to change professions by the fact that they have found the music world an unsatisfying and even unhealthy experience. Unfortunately, the music milieu has become rife with competition, judgment, and criticism, causing musicians a great deal of anxiety. This is a world that has become focused on talent and the success of the most skilled. Musicians often find themselves competing to get into the best music conservatories and universities, to earn a chair in the orchestra or band, to foster their careers by winning a solo competition or signing a music recording contract. The very popular TV show, *American Idol,* where selected contestants compete for a national reputation and entrée to the music business, is a good example of this dynamic. The judges' critique of the contestants' performances can be quite scathing. It's clear that this kind of culture can have damaging consequences on musicians and their view of music.

We are forgetting that all people are musicians and are born with sensitivity to music, and that all people are capable of music-making. Though some indigenous cultures still have music as a central and integral part of their community life, somewhere along the way, the spontaneous, creative, and joyful participation in music in our families and communities has been lost. I often hear people saying, "I am not a musician," "I cannot sing," or "I am not talented in music." We are forgetting that music-making is for everyone. Many musicians have developed crippling performance anxiety, physical injuries from playing too much, and other problems. I have worked with people who have performance anxiety and are unable to enjoy sharing even the simplest song with others.

Musical creativity

No matter how musically talented or skilled our students are at the beginning of their training, part of the journey that they will go through is to look at and overcome the wounding that has occurred from living in the world of music. At the same time, students are offered experiential opportunities to deal with other mental, physical, and emotional difficulties through music. It is difficult to truly help others through music until you can help yourself. The students are also attending classes where they are helped to understand why it is so important to work on themselves and their relationship to music. They begin to understand and open themselves to how music can transform their own lives. If a student is not willing or able to work through these issues, their capacity to use music to help clients will be limited.

As they begin to face and work through their own musical and personal blocks to their creativity, they begin to use their music more creatively, expressively, and spontaneously with others. They develop a new kind of musicianship, one that now focuses on creative freedom, expressive spontaneity, intuition, and the ability to connect deeply with others.

True compassion

Although all our students are undertaking their studies because of a desire to help, service to others is often seen at the beginning in a limited way—as a way to help those less fortunate than ourselves. One of the goals of our program is to help students deepen their understanding of what true compassionate action can be. The training is oriented to expand their understanding that we are all interconnected and that there is a kinship and unity with all beings.

This path to helping others requires us to first learn to help ourselves. Students learn to face unknown and unwanted parts of themselves that have been ignored and that they've sought to run away from. They come to understand that only to the degree that we know ourselves and our own pain will we be able to be fearless enough to feel the pain of others. And music therapists come in contact with the pain of others every day. When we can face our own difficulties and problems, develop compassion for ourselves, accept ourselves, and relate directly with our own suffering, we will generate the ability to relate to others compassionately, open-heartedly, and without attachment.

Interconnections

In my approach to training music therapists, I am nurturing a student's creativity and compassion throughout the whole training program. This orientation toward the field of music therapy is only made possible by my commitment to my own musical, creative, and spiritual journey throughout the years. As my journey has deepened, I can see the reflection of that journey in how my students respond to the training. I have seen in other music therapy training programs that the emphasis is different, depending on the path and belief system of the person who heads the program.

In weaving the two concepts of creativity and compassion together throughout the training, it is easy to see that they complement and enhance each other.

It is clear that there is a connection between the two aspects of our work. From the beginning and throughout the program, students are placed in supervised internships in hospitals, clinics, schools, and other settings with patients of all ages and with a wide assortment of problems. Their understanding of clients and their needs and issues becomes more real; they become aware of how their perception of music as they have known it in the past will need to change. The reality of having to use the music with a patient in the moment brings a dedication to working on the blocks to their own creativity and developing their ability to use music more intuitively, skillfully, improvisationally, and flexibly.

The students become more compassionate as they come to the understanding that we are all wounded. As they begin to comprehend how they can heal themselves through music, they become able to offer this more authentically to others. This then helps them respond more creatively and with more expressive freedom to the needs of others.

These aspiring therapists develop the ability to see music in their lives in a deeper and more expanded way. Through this process, they recognize our common humanity.

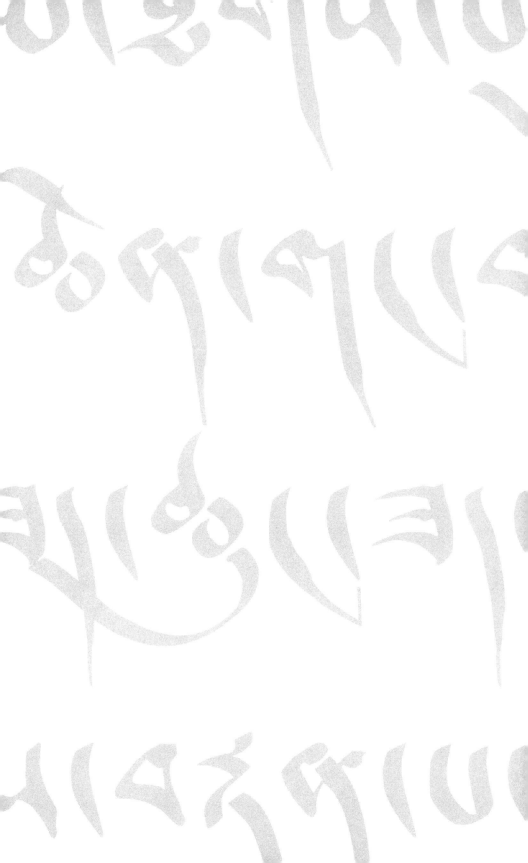

For me, compassion has to do with really hearing another person. For me, that's the most profound form of compassion. To hear somebody and say, "Yes, I understand what you are saying," or "Yes, I know this," or "I feel this," or "I can connect to what you're doing." I think the worst fear that we all struggle with is the sense that we're weird and we're the only people who feel a certain way. Then somebody else says to me, "Yeah. I get that. Oh, yeah."

—Robert K. C. Forman,
from the Creativity &
Compassion conference

Creativity, Compassion, and Mysticism

Robert K. C. Forman
Consciousness Researcher

I would like to connect a few dots between creativity, compassion, and mysticism. I do so humbly, being painfully aware that though I have studied mysticism a bit, I am a scholar of neither creativity nor compassion. So I offer the following reflections, based primarily on a few experiences, in hopes that I can contribute a little to the rich conversation reflected in this book.

I have been a daily practitioner of Transcendental Meditation for 42 years. For me, meditations are sometimes heartbeatingly active, with my mind going over to-do lists and plans as if I was at my office desk. But often meditations are like a tender caress, where increasingly slow, languorous thoughts find their way into a roundness of warmth and softness inside, like a purring feline on a warm evening's bed. A gentle kindliness wafts into my forearms and calves, like a waking sleep, and I become very soft with myself, fighting nothing, seeking nothing, but just letting my mind drift and be simply awake for all the vague, dreamy, half-seen thoughts and felt sounds. Sometimes I drop into a vast and pleasant quiet, a sense of open spaciousness that, though wide awake, is without any thinking. It is a silent space, the merest being present.

This sense of silence has, over the years, quietly permeated my everyday experience. Sometimes underneath what I am doing, I experience a sense of silence, an expanse, a bottomless emptiness that is again wide open and without visible end. This silence carries a sense of spaciousness that extends in every direction. This is why my favorite term for this is "the vastness." It is not something I have to remember to be or hold; it takes absolutely no work to maintain it. It is as effortless to be this as it is to have a right hand. I don't experience it as amazing or ecstatic, for it has become normal and everyday, though it is peacefully pleasant. When I am aware of this silence, my sense is that it is what or who I am. This silence, this vastness, *is* me. Not the me that does dishes, that worries when I have to write an article, or the me that feels alone or scared or happy. Rather this vastness is the me that watches and lives and holds all that I see, think, or do. When this is present, I am it, and thus I am, strange to say, phenomenologically infinite. But, unlike how others like to think of this "universal self," even when it is with me, the old ego-laden me—nervous or happy or scared or proud—is here as well. The Hindu tradition distinguishes this sense of the self from our ordinary self, the *jīva*. The *Muṇḍaka Upaniṣad* describes these two selves as "two birds":

> Two birds,
>> Inseparable companions,
>> Perch on the same tree.
> One eats the fruit,
>> The other looks on.
>
> The first bird is our individual self,
>> Feeding on the pleasures and pains of this world;
> The other is the universal Self,
>> Silently witnessing all.

Notice, the one bird, the *jīva* side of ourselves, is said to be the "individual self." It goes about its business, feels pleasure, pain, wants, dislikes, and on and on. But the other bird, the quiet and witnessing bird, is the "universal self." Just as in my own experience of this vast whatever-it-is, this "universal self" is not personal, not me or mine but a more abstract sense of what we are. This bird, as I understand it, is the merest consciousness, the merest sense of being awake.

The *Muṇḍaka Upaniṣad* calls this vastness "universal," suggesting that we all share a similar or identical consciousness. It relates no doubt to the Upanishadic notion of Brahman, the energy or "stuff" that is at the core of all things. And, in conversation after conversation, live and cyber, since beginning to give talks about my experiences, I have gained a certainty that others experience and describe something quite similar to what I experience as a silent expanse.

On being creative

I have had, as most people do I'm sure, moments of creativity. One snowy day, I was in my hermitage and reflecting on something that had happened to me some 40 years prior. I wrote:

> As I'm thinking back to those days, I'm looking out the bay window at a wintery scene, watching a flock of birds float by, legs dangling awkwardly beneath, the orange beam of the sunrise pointing straight up behind them. Watching them, I am entirely unaware of the surface of my skin. But I am aware how settled I feel as I watch them, how focused and welcoming I am of this moment. It makes me wonder if just a little of the focus I feel doesn't have something to do with the experiences in my past and whether without them I would be just that much more distracted for reasons I could not never know. I cannot be sure what of today connects to a shift that began back then. But I am settled with the snowfall and the sunrise and the birds and grateful for the ability to welcome them on this crystalline winter's morn.

Just a short paragraph, but it was entirely different in tone and quality than *anything* I had ever written. It was novelistic or even poetic—evocative; in the present tense but using the present to reflect on the past and what I'd become. It was a true breakthrough in writing for me. Not only was it the first novelistic writing I had ever done, but it was the moment that I found a new "voice" that I had been looking for. If I was to describe what it was like to write this, and other somewhat evocative passages since, I would say that not only did I write in a new, more emotionally connected way, but something else happened. While I was writing it, I had gone into a space that was quite similar to that space into which I drop during the deeper times of meditation and which I had come to know in moments of my everyday life.

When these creative moments happen, it is as if I become more "spread out." I drop into that sense of openness. But this is different from meditative silence, in that in it there is a clear sense that my thoughts are just flowing through my writing especially easily. Somehow, what I write taps into that very spacious quiet, as if the silence itself gives birth to the words—as a characterless cloud seems to form itself into a horse's head or a face. And the silence does this almost without any trying or thinking from my side; the writing almost writes itself. The clear sense is that something higher, not quite me, not quite disconnected from me, is doing the writing; I am but its hand and pen. To give another example:

> I'm looking out over the snowy hills this morning. The sun is peering meekly through the graying cloud layer; it looks like it might snow. I'm not thinking as I'm writing these words. I'm *feeling* as opposed to *planning* what I need to write. A phrase, "I'm looking out over the snowy hills," comes to mind and with it comes a vague but directional feeling. That means, I know, that it's time to start jotting down.

Writing for me is more like listening than creating. What I feel is a kind of poise. I pause, listening for the presence of what seems to be real. In such a space, I seem to be able to remain connected with the quietness that is nudging me. I think a sentence, but stop—it's too clever—and I wait for what is truer to waft up. Mostly, I find myself settled in a kind of alert patience, largely without words. So I sit, the clouds grey and the day chilly, my pen in hand, patiently waiting.

The thing that strikes me is that the quality of such alert patience, the openness I feel as I enter into that space of creativity and invention, is *just the same* sense of openness I feel in those moments of openness that occasionally come through meditation. I think that in creative moments, in other words, we often experience something parallel to the openness we can find in meditation or that the mystics so extol, and we seem to tap into something more universal and expansive.

These experiences suggest to me that creativity may be tapping into the very same "openness" as does meditation. But it is different in one important way. This one, unlike the quiescence of the meditative silence or the mystical of the everyday, *expresses itself in words.* Writing in this way is not just sitting in the silence. Rather, it is sitting in that spaciousness *and writing,* allowing the spaciousness to express itself in words.

But I want to be careful here. The words I write down bear much of my own perceptions, my own thoughts, my own longings and cares. They are expressions of the silence *as well as* expressions of my perceptions and my feelings. The very language in which I write, modern English, is the language in which *I've* been trained. The writing is a skill *I've* been honing.

But even more to the point, when I wrote that passage, I was looking for the book's *voice.* Looking for it because I knew I hadn't found it, yet wanted to. And this I sought because I wanted the book to be good and also—if I am honest in telling the full truth—because I wanted it to sell, to do well, to have an impact, and to maybe even make money. These thoughts and wishes were not dominant in my mind. Mostly, I was attending to the nudges of the silence. But nor were the thoughts entirely absent. Yes, even though the moment was pregnant with listening and inscribing the words of the silence, beneath or behind that openness was a vaguely conscious set of wishes and hopes. To put this more sharply, I am, even at my most creative and open moments, both spirit and ego, needless and needy, absolute and relative, not me and me.

I doubt ego ever goes entirely away—for anyone—in the act of creation. One of the mistakes many of us make is to think that ego disappears completely in any act of creativity. When we write a book, give a lecture, play some music, we have our personal reasons for doing so. And those reasons, hopefully, are that we want to help others, and yet also that we want to personally do well.

When I was younger, I was *very* worried about success, much more concerned for my own reputation and fame than I am now. Over the years, however, those concerns have faded a good extent. As they have, there has been more space, as it were, for creativity and openness. I sense something like an inverse relationship; as the worries about my reputation or income have faded, my ability to "listen in" to the whispers of the sacred has found more room. Thus when my egocentric concerns are pretty quiet, it is easier to enter into that open space of creativity and "listening."

I believe that good art touches, as William Faulkner puts it, "universal bones," deep principles that perhaps all of us human beings must confront: joys, sorrows, births, and griefs. Wishes and hopes, and strivings and sorrows—all connected with what we call "ego"—are all part of the human situation. What allows us to write, sing, or dance at such depth has to do with touching into and harnessing the matters of ego. And so creation—healthy creation—sometimes touches the concerns of the self, as well as responds to the nudges of the sacred.

Creativity and compassion

I used to think that compassion had to do with acts of pity, donations of money or of time, and other altruistic endeavors. But I believe this is a superficial understanding, one that describes a particular kind of "good deed." I have come to believe that it is not the only form, and perhaps not even the best form, of compassion. The primary problem that we humans face, I believe, is the sense of being alone, misunderstood, weird, or different. We all struggle with a sense of being different and lonely. In the face of such issues, a truly compassionate act has to do with helping another know that he or she is heard—really heard and understood—and connected with. To hear in such a way that the speaker knows they have been heard and understood, and, for the listener, to really connect with what someone is, is a rich form of connection and love. In the face of loneliness, this is all we really want to hear.

In Faulkner's 1949 Nobel Prize acceptance speech, he bemoaned writing that focuses on ephemeral and faddish themes. When it does, he said, when writers focus on current issues or fears, they miss the real and universal issues of the human heart and life. Because of this, he observed:

[T]he young man or woman writing today has forgotten the problems of the human heart in conflict with itself which alone can make good writing because only that is worth writing about, worth the agony and the sweat.

The kind of creativity expressed in great art that puts us in touch with this sense of universal connection that is impersonal but passionate is what he calls in his speech "the universal bones." Artistic creativity reveals our deepest connections to the world and to each other.

What Faulkner sees is that acts of creation touch deep into the human situation, touch the universal bones on which all of our lives are structured. And when they do, we, the reader or listener, can see ourselves in them, hear our own struggles, and sense that we are not alone. It is deeply reassuring to recognize our own issues and discoveries in a work of fiction or a piece of music. We feel connected and human. In this sense, an act of creativity is an act of deep compassion. The deeper the act of creation, the less alone we viewers feel. That someone understands, really knows, and can say it in a way so that we can all, more or less, get it, is a gift to us all. In this way, an act of creativity is a generous act of compassion.

In other words, what Faulkner saw is that if you are really good at something like music or writing, you may be able to touch other people's hearts with your art. When you touch into your own depths, I believe, you are touching into human truths, verities we all can sense, even if we cannot say them.

Like fish inside a shallow pool,
With the passing of each day and night
This life becomes so very short—
How can it be enjoyable?

—*Udānavarga* 1:34

ཆུ་ཆུང་རན་གི་ཉ་ལྟ་བུར། །
གང་ཞིག་ཉིན་མཚན་འདའ་བ་ཡིས། །
ཚེ་འདི་ཉིན་ཏུ་ཐུང་འགྱུར་ན། །
དེ་ལ་དགའ་བར་བྱར་ཅི་ཡོད། །

4
The Art of Compassion

Fueling Creative Energy with Compassion and Emptiness

Tenzin Bhuchung
Tibetan Translator

n Buddhism, we try to make contact with the creative spirit through different forms of meditation. Once the creative spirit is developed or cultivated, it is more than an occasional outburst. Qualities like compassion, the very essence of the dharma, can unleash various creative activities that are beneficial for everyone. When one has compassion, clouds of creative thoughts unceasingly stir in the sky of one's mind, causing a downpour of rain that gently nourishes fields of sentient beings below.

Karuṇā, a Sanskrit term meaning "compassion," is one such quality that a practitioner cultivates in meditation. It refers to our ability to genuinely empathize with others. Meditation on compassion, one can argue, is both an art and science, requiring one's imagination as well as logic. On the one hand, one uses one's creativity to imagine the range of existential sufferings, going deeply into them to the point of being moved to tears. It is not uncommon that when great masters like His Holiness the Dalai Lama speak on compassion, they often burst into tears. Based on our ability to creatively consider and even feel the suffering of others, we generate the wish to help them be free from those sufferings. Yet it's difficult to conceive that process of imagining all forms of existential sufferings in their deepest intensity and then generating the thought of freeing all beings from such sufferings. Śāntideva, a 9th-century Indian Buddhist scholar/

saint, wrote that, in fact, we have not even dreamt of such a compassion for ourselves, let alone actually felt it for others.

Through creative imagination within the state of one's meditation, one gives birth to compassion. Compassion may then proliferate in various creative activities and art. Compassion can give rise to a way of being and an art of living filled with a desire to innovate ways to make a difference in the world for oneself and others. In our modern times, the lives and works of His Holiness and Mother Teresa, among many others, come easily to mind when we think of the link between compassion and creativity.

Compassion as a creative inspiration is the culmination of a process marked by many distinctive stages. The first stage is connecting and developing intimacy with all other sentient beings. We begin this stage by considering the Buddhist notion of rebirth and how there is no beginning point to our many lives. Then we reason that it is certain that all sentient beings had a close relationship with us during those countless lifetimes, sometimes as mothers, sometimes as spouses, and so forth. Then we reflect on the kindness of our own mothers during this life or observe how even animals take care of their babies. It is said that such a sequential meditation finally gives rise to seeing others as extremely close and loving. From there, it is said that it is easy and, in fact, natural to proceed to the next step, the generation of compassion for all beings.

For those who may find it difficult to believe that all other sentient beings have been our mothers in various lifetimes, there is still the possibility to see them as extremely beloved and precious. To do this, we look at how we are so dependent on the kindness of others for our survival, education, happiness, and success. Śāntideva teaches us how there is no difference between ourselves and others, in that we all want happiness and do not want suffering. He also reminds us to recognize how self-cherishing actually causes suffering, while cherishing others brings about happiness, further reinforcing the necessity, even from the perspective of "enlightened self interest," of the practice of compassion. Once sufficient loving thoughts and compassion are generated toward others, we can enhance it by reflecting on the various existential sufferings that others have to undergo. Detailed instructions for cultivating compassion are found in the two distinct meditation systems referred to as "the sevenfold cause and effect instructions" and "the tradition of equalizing and exchanging oneself and others."

But how is it possible to overcome deeply ingrained habits and personality traits that go against the spirit of compassion? Moreover, how is it possible to go into the deepest pit of existential suffering and not get emotionally wounded? The answer lies in the Buddhist concept and practice of "emptiness wisdom."

The Buddha used the term "emptiness" (*śūnyatā*) to describe the ultimate nature of all phenomena. Emptiness is the idea that things do not have any intrinsic reality apart from what we impute to them. There is the bare perception of things, which is fresh and free from any intrinsic value or character, but then thought comes and interprets that perception as "this" or "that" based on one's grasping at an intrinsic reality that is present in an object, person, or experience; that grasping is further reinforced by our cultural and personal conditioning. Thought or conceptual interpretation gives rise to discrimination, the assessment we make about whether something is good or bad, attractive or unattractive. Discrimination brings about aversion or craving. Repeated aversion or craving gives rise to full-blown anger or desire. Our life is thus at the mercy of habits formed by the dual forces of craving and ignorance, and propelled by ignorance. These three existential qualities—craving, aversion, and ignorance—are referred to as the "three roots of the afflictive emotions." They are the impulses that give rise to our conditioned existence in the endless world of suffering (*saṃsāra*).

Modern psychologists say the ability to be receptive and listen openly is a necessary step for being able to creatively solve problems. Yet it is difficult not to be fixated and attached to our usual way of reacting and solving problems. Psychologists have termed this "functional fixedness," and Buddhism maintains that such "fixedness" comes from grasping to the concept of an "intrinsic reality" to phenomena. Another powerful barrier to creative energy is our own ego and self-consciousness that give rise to an inner self-censorship that confines the creative energy within the bounds of what we consider acceptable. It is one's own inner voice that says, "I cannot think in this way or do this because others might think I am crazy or they will judge me adversely."

From a Buddhist perspective, problems of "functional fixedness" and inner "self-censorship" arise from grasping at the self and phenomena as if they had qualities that were independent of our own mental labeling and, as a result, clinging to both. When we cling to things with such fixed ideas about their qualities, thinking that they have an identity independent of our perception, that clinging gives rise to the negative emotions of aversion, craving, and ignorance. Buddhists view "self-grasping" (*ātma-grāha*)—the way in which we attribute a fixed, substantial identity to both ourselves and to external phenomena—as a wrong conception, a state of ignorance that confines us to our fixed habitual tendencies that must be eradicated with the wisdom of emptiness. When we are able to do so, then our creative imagination can soar in the sky of emptiness, unfettered by any fixated grasping.

Emptiness wisdom teaches us that what we call "self" is nothing but our mind imputing such a "self" to what is actually a matrix of many causes and conditions coming together in a state of constant flux. We have a material body that is constantly changing, and a mind or consciousness that also continuously changes. No part of the body is the self. Likewise, any moment of the mind is not the self. Yet our mind has imputed a notion of an eternal self, separate from our body and mind. This, according to Buddhism, is the most fundamental ignorance that gives rise to all other confused thoughts and negative emotions. Emptiness wisdom is nothing more than seeing that this self is an imputed concept and exists as such in a relational sense. The self *does* exist in that relational sense, but is "empty" of independent or intrinsic existence.

How do we sustain this understanding or wisdom of emptiness in our meditation? There are many techniques or approaches of meditation in Buddhism, although they all come to one point of practice—eradicating our grasping at this imagined "intrinsic and independent self." Let's go through one such approach here to get a glimpse of it:

We bring our mind to a settled state, mindfully aware of this naked fresh moment of awareness. With attentiveness, we ensure that we are not carried away by our thoughts, losing ourselves in our own projections of thoughts. We try to remain in this present moment of awareness, pure, fresh, and free from any judgment, without getting lost in past thoughts or anticipating future events. When we are settled in this present moment of awareness, if thoughts arise, we watch them objectively. When we remain in such a state of "choiceless awareness," as J. Krishnamurti phrased it, then we may be able to observe that our own thoughts produce or impute identities to external phenomena, characterizing them as good or bad. Our thoughts also produce our sense of an independent intrinsic self, one that we think is not dependent on our thoughts or conceptual imputation.

Our own thoughts also produce the sense of the dualism of a self, one that exists separately and independently from other external phenomena in the form of various thoughts or appearances of the mind. This fundamental confusion of an independent self experiencing various external thoughts is generated, when in fact, as we can observe in our choiceless awareness meditation, it is the thought that produced the sense of self. Krishnamurti described this revelation by saying that "the observer is not different from the observed." Practitioners of the sutra-level Middle Way (*madhyamaka*) philosophy describe this truth of ultimate reality by saying that things exist as mere mental imputations. The tantric *Mahāmudrā* teachings describe this by stating that all phenomena within the round of birth and death (*saṁsāra*) and the cessation of that endless round (in other words, achieving *nirvāṇa*) are nothing but manifestations or expressions of the innate mind of clear light. In the Dzogchen tradition, it is taught that all phenomena are nothing but the dynamic display of primal intrinsic awareness.

Such an experience of this in an actual meditative state, as opposed to a mere intellectual understanding of it, is supposed to free us from fixated self-grasping, which is the cause of all the other destructive emotions confining us in the cage of deeply formed habitual tendencies. Such a freedom from the "self," coupled with cultivation of compassion, produces a constructive and inspired creative energy that can accomplish the well-being of oneself and others. When there is ceaseless compassion radiating toward all beings within the state of emptiness—without the fixation on the self or others as intrinsically existing—this powerful creative force is referred to as the union of emptiness and compassion. One can also appreciate that in Buddhism, the birth of creative spirit entails both conscious training of the mind's focus on emptiness and compassion and sustaining this in single-pointed meditation so that their natural qualities express themselves effortlessly or in an "unconscious" manner.

In my own humble view, His Holiness is a living embodiment of someone who practices the union of compassion and emptiness wisdom and hence his creative energy is bringing peace, well-being, and joy to millions of people across the globe. The late Dilgo Khyentse Rinpoche, one the grand Buddhist masters of our times, offered this long life prayer to His Holiness, describing him as the one who spreads the teachings on the union of compassion and emptiness:

> The path that is the union of emptiness and compassion,
> You proclaim it extensively, Lord of dharma and beings of the snowy land!
> I pay homage to Tenzin Gyatso, the holder of the lotus flower—
> May your intents be spontaneously accomplished!

In Buddhism, when one achieves the state of enlightenment, the highest state of realization, great universal compassion is described as the only remaining creative potency of the enlightened mind. In the absence of an egoistic self, the only driving force, the only creative energy that stirs within the state of the absolute state of *dharmakāya* is the energy of universal compassion itself. The state of enlightenment has three dimensions called the three *kāyas*, or three bodies. *Dharmakāya*, the natural truth body, refers to the space-like emptiness of the enlightened mind. The clarity of the mind, which expresses itself as a divine body, is referred to as the *sambhogakāya,* or the divine enjoyment body. The unceasing potency of the mind (whose nature is compassion) is referred to as the *nirmāṇakāya,* or the emanation body, and it expresses itself in diverse forms throughout the universe to help sentient beings. According to Buddhism, all beings have a "Buddha nature"—that is, the potential to become a Buddha. Like all other phenomena, the nature of our mind is empty, like space, without any center or periphery, and is free of any conceptual elaboration. This is the basis for beings to attain the state of *dharmakāya*. Yet the emptiness of the mind is not a dark, cold void. There is intense clarity that becomes the foundation to achieve the divine *sambhogakāya* form. The mind's potency to unceasingly express itself in various thoughts and appearances becomes the basis to achieve the *nirmāṇakāya* body, the emanation body that is the expression of universal compassion unceasingly extending to all without any effort through various emanation bodies. Thus, according to Buddhism, every sentient being, by virtue of having a mind, has the potential to achieve the highest state of creativity through the dual practice of the altruistic intention to seek enlightenment for the benefit of others (*bodhicitta*) based on compassion, and the wisdom of emptiness.

The Believing Game

Peter Elbow

Educator

> *"I can't believe that!" said Alice.*
> *"Can't you?" the queen said in a pitying tone. "Try again, draw*
> *a long breath, and shut your eyes."*
> *Alice laughed. "There's no use trying," she said. "One can't*
> *believe impossible things."*
> *"I daresay you haven't had much practice," said the queen.*
> *"When I was your age, I always did it for half an hour a day.*
> *Why, sometimes I've believed as many as six impossible things*
> *before breakfast."*
>
> —Lewis Carroll, *Through the Looking-Glass*

Azim Khamisa forgave a young gang member who murdered his son, Tariq. A mysterious act. Yet people occasionally do this.[1]

I'm assuming that Azim must have continued to feel his own grief—even rage?—yet in addition, he came to see the humanity in a person who caused grievous harm and pain. And his transformation was not just a matter of seeing this person's humanity. Azim came to feel some goodness in that harm-doer.

It would be almost sacrilegious to try to analyze such a heroic act of compassion. But perhaps we can get a glimmer of understanding by asking, "What *kind* of mental and spiritual capacity did Azim somehow call on?" He surely managed somehow to *see around* his own grief to a different perspective and a new set of feelings. So here's the root question: How do you get past your own feelings and point of view and take on feelings you didn't have?

Everyday compassion

Most of us are not called to such heroic compassion, yet are we not invited often to some humbler and less mysterious kind of compassion? I can provide an embarrassing example. Over many years, my wife has objected that I drive too fast; she has continually insisted that she is actually afraid when I drive. This has always seemed absurd to me—just one more way for one spouse to express annoyance at the other. For it was obvious (to me!) that I *wasn't* going too fast or driving too dangerously. It took me many years, I'm chagrined to admit, to actually *believe* her—to believe that she is truly afraid, even when I drive in a way that seems to me obviously reasonable. Sad to say, this was hard; it's as though I had to give up something precious. "Just grow up," you might say, but the phrase merely papers over the operative question: What did I have to do simply to believe my own wife?

I'm not supposed to call this a heroic act—especially since my wife happens to be sensible, stable, rational, and loving. But, still, it seems mysterious, at least to me. Marriage is tricky; we get so stuck in our domestic tangles; and the stakes somehow get high.

So let me retreat even further from the realm of the mysterious and heroic and look at situations that are even more ordinary. And in taking this step, I can go on to suggest some concrete activities that help us enter into the mentality of people we find hard to believe—an entering-in that I sense is at the root of compassion.

I spend lots of time in classrooms and meetings, so I'd like to look at the common situation where someone advances a point of view or opinion and virtually everyone argues against it. Often the rest of us feel, "That's a crazy point of view." What would it take for us to begin to learn how to get past our resistance and genuinely believe or dwell in or participate in what feels at first like an alien point of view?

The psychologist Carl Rogers famously lays out the following approach. When someone says something we can't believe and want to argue against, we mustn't give our reply till we first manage to restate or summarize what they said *to their satisfaction*—i.e., no oversimplification, distortion, or sarcasm. Needless to say, this can be difficult yet enormously useful, especially if the "crazy" view seems complicated or odd. But it strikes me that this cognitive, intellectual process wouldn't have been enough to bring me to believe my wife. It would have been too simple for me to say: "You feel I am driving too fast, and it feels dangerous and frightening to you." That wouldn't have made a dent on me. I think the key ingredient needed here is not merely cognitive or intellectual; it is what the philosophers call "conative"—an act of desire or *will*. I needed to *try* to enlarge what I could imagine.

The believing game

In fact, we can learn to go farther than what Rogers asks for, valuable though that is: not just to manage to restate someone else's view to their satisfaction—which one can do through gritted teeth—but actually to *try to believe* their point of view—or *try to share their feelings*.

But does that really make sense? It doesn't seem as though we have any choice about what we believe. We laugh when the White Queen tells Alice to learn to believe impossible things. We wince at the exchange between the famous Oxford scholar/theologian Benjamin Jowett and his undergraduate student. Student: "I seem to have lost my faith in the divinity of Jesus Christ." Jowett: "I trust that you will find it by next Thursday at this time. Goodbye."

Nevertheless, I want to insist that we can get better at believing what we feel we can't believe. I'm not talking about achieving permanent committed belief; I'm talking about learning to believe it *for now*—that is, to learn to *dwell in* the alien view or feelings. The goal is genuine full faith—but knowing that we don't have to live there permanently.

The goal may seem crazy from the point of view of pure intellectual cognition, but not from the point of view of *effort* and *imagination*. The White Queen may have been onto something when she told Alice to close her eyes and take a deep breath. If the alien belief feels painful or even genuinely dangerous (think Nazism or violent racism), there's clearly an element of *imagining*—in a sense, even of *pretending*: giving oneself permission to enter into what's dangerous, knowing it's only a visit. ("In the destructive element immerse," as Joseph Conrad writes in *Lord Jim*.) For a seemingly trivial example, consider the child who *won't!* eat spinach. It can be helpful if she can be persuaded to say with great feeling, *"I love spinach."* Gales of laughter are likely and desirable, and this can be helpful as a small step on the way towards actually entering for a moment into the alien experience of enjoying spinach.

I don't know how to describe precisely the mysterious act of starting to believe what you don't want to believe, but I can throw light on it by describing some concrete activities that help us learn to do just that. Try them, and you'll start to understand what it means to dwell in beliefs that feel alien. My thanks to John Briggs for this wise clarifying point: "This imaginative and creative act is a precondition to compassion. It overcomes the separation between my beliefs and the other's beliefs—a difference that obscures our common humanity." Here are three specific guidelines that could be adopted in an organization, a classroom, a specific meeting—or even in a relationship—when someone is trying to advance a view, and you and others resist and object:

> *—The three-five minute rule*. If a member of the group feels that she is not being heard, she can make a sign and invoke the rule: No one else can talk for three or five minutes. Only her voice is heard; we listen; we cannot reply. This would have helped me in my inability to see my wife's point of view. I didn't have sense enough just to say, "Please just talk; I won't argue against you; I won't even speak. I need to hear more of what it's like for you when you are frightened of my driving."

For centuries, people have made good use of silence for in-dwelling. When someone takes a position that everyone opposes, what's needful is for *no one to say anything at all* for as little as two minutes—or better yet, five. This is not much time in a meeting or a class hour (though it can feel interminable to some participants), but even this little silence can have a powerful effect in helping people reflect, digest, think—and eventually communicate better. When we recognize the value of silence, we are usually acknowledging the limitations of language. Language itself can sometimes get in the way of trying to experience or enter into a point of view different from our own.

> *—Allies only—no objections*. Others can speak—*but only* those who are having more success believing or dwelling in or assenting to the minority view. No objections allowed.

172

— *"Testimony."* The person (or persons) who are not being heard tell stories of the experiences in their lives that led them to their point of view; and also describe what it's like having or living with this view. The rest of us must not answer, or argue, or disagree. Note how an argument invites disagreement, but there's no arguing with an *experience.*

The goal in these activities is safety—safety for the speaker, of course; most speakers feel unsafe if they sense we are just waiting to jump in with all our objections. But *we* need safety just as much for ourselves as listeners who are, after all, trying to learn to be more skilled at in-dwelling or believing. It's *difficult* for most of us to enter into a view we want to quarrel with or feel threatened by; it's safer for us to do so if we have permission simply not to talk about it at all—at all—for a while. We get a chance to let the words we resist just sink in—we don't say "no" but we also don't have to say "yes."

Few of us need to be as heroically compassionate as Azim Khamisa, but we can work at enlarging our imaginative and moral ability to enter into the views and feelings of others—to believe what we don't want to believe. These are small exercises in everyday compassion.

And I'd stress finally that there's not just a moral or spiritual value in that experience of methodological believing, but also a crucial intellectual value. When someone has an opinion or a point of view that we find crazy—in our own little group or in our general culture—it means that this person is seeing something we cannot see. Yes, they may be crazy, but they *may* be seeing something (even in their craziness) that is actually there or is true or valid. Unless we learn to actually see it—which requires trying to believe what we don't want to believe—we cannot make a trustworthy judgment as to whether the "crazy view" makes sense or not.

For an essay this short, I dare not use the word "creativity" in the title, but I can't resist visiting that topic before closing. I've argued above that we can see some roots of compassion in the ability to believe or enter into points of view that are different from our own. I suggest now that the same imaginative ability is close to the root of creativity, too. I suggest that creative people have especially large imaginations and can dwell in multiple and contradictory points of view—in a sense, they can see double or triple. They can dwell in more views and work with more ideas.

I'm not suggesting that Mozart and Beethoven went around trying to believe the points of view of all the cranky people they met; indeed, there's reason to believe that they were remarkably self-absorbed—perhaps even intolerant. I suggest only that these creative giants—in this case, in the realm of music— were able to *call on* the abilities we're talking about: the ability to look at a musical problem through contradictory lenses; to hold opposite or contradictory views at once and thus see things one way, yet also simultaneously see them in other ways; to transcend or violate existing creative conventions yet also work with those conventions.

Few of us are creative giants (or compassionate giants like Khamisa), yet people like us *can*, I suggest, enlarge our creative imaginations by trying as hard as we can to enter into the multiple and contradictory mentalities of the varied (and often difficult) people we encounter. Perhaps flexibility of mind is not enough in itself to make us deeply creative; but imaginative flexibility permits us to listen for the faint voice that others don't hear—the faint impulse that leads to new ideas.

Notes

1. For Azim's amazing story and the spiritual healing work that he went on to do in collaboration with the grandfather of the murderer, visit the Tariq Khamisa Foundation at http://www.TKF.org.

Works Cited

There's a long and venerable tradition about the uses of silence, and also for the ability to dwell in contraries (see my article on "Binary Thinking"). About the believing game itself, I know only of Wayne Booth's writing (see below), and I'm indebted to him for the phrase "dwell in." But I've been exploring the believing game for my whole career and list the main essays I've written below. The most recent one, from 2009, is the shortest and most precise.

Booth, Wayne. *Modern Dogma and the Rhetoric of Assent*. Chicago: U of Chicago Press (1974).

Elbow, Peter. "The Doubting Game and the Believing Game—An Analysis of the Intellectual Enterprise." Appendix Essay in *Writing Without Teachers*, Oxford University Press (1973), pp. 147–91.

—. "Methodological Doubting and Believing: Contraries in Inquiry." In *Embracing Contraries: Explorations in Learning and Teaching*. Oxford University Press (1986), 254–300.

—. "The Uses of Binary Thinking." *Journal of Advanced Composition* 13.1 (Winter 1993): 51–78; reprinted in *Everyone Can Write: Essays Toward a Hopeful Theory of Writing and Teaching Writing*. NY: Oxford University Press (2000).

—. "The Believing Game and How to Make Conflicting Opinions More Fruitful." In *Nurturing the Peacemakers in Our Students: A Guide to Teaching Peace, Empathy, and Understanding*. Chris Weber, editor. Portsmouth, NH: Heinemann (2006), pp. 16–25.

—. "Bringing the Rhetoric of Assent and the Believing Game Together—and into the Classroom." *College English* 67.4 (March 2005): 388–99.

—. The Believing Game, or Methodological Believing. *Journal for the Assembly for Expanded Perspectives on Learning* 14 (Winter 2009): 1–11.

When I first got to New York, one of the things I loved was riding the subway. When you study Buddhist philosophy, you study all sorts of meditations and theory, and all of a sudden I realized I had this great opportunity every time I rode the subway. When we think of meditation, we always think of sitting quiet, focusing on the mind. We don't always think of the flip side, the analytical meditations, where you do varieties of mind problems. And one of them is this attempt to break down these barriers, to break down this barrier of self and other.

One of the simplest meditations involves the idea of the equality of everyone around you. So I would sit on the subway from time to time and watch every person who got on the car with me, and I would look at them and think, "This person is just like me. This person wants happiness; they don't want suffering." And when someone gets out of the car and another person gets on, you do the same thing. You just go person by person by person down the row, and it just so changes your attitude toward everybody around you.

I remember someone else told me once— a Tibetan nun who came through town one time—she said, "Imagine that if you were on this subway car and something happened and that subway car was sealed and you had to spend the rest of your life with the 25 or 30 people who are in that car. How would that change your attitude toward them?" Whereas normally someone comes through the car, a panhandler, someone who is doing something annoying, and you can just ignore them until they leave the train, and then you created that distance of thinking, "This is someone I don't need to worry about. I'll just ignore them and they'll go away."

But if that was never the case, if you were really in this world together and that was it, how would that change your attitude toward them? Could you maintain that sense of distance and otherness and separation? I'm not so sure. And so these kinds of mind games, these thought experiments, or as I call them, "analytical meditations," for me are one of the most powerful aspects of trying to put Buddhist practice into everyday life. You could say, "Well, that would never happen." But, in a sense, it is happening, that is the world we live in. We are in this world surrounded by people who we interact with on a daily basis, who are not separate from us, and who we really do rely on. Whether it's the person who's driving the subway car, or whatever.

—Paul Hackett,
from the Creativity & Compassion conference

In the Quiet Space of Animals

Allen Schoen

Veterinarian

My life's journey pioneering integrative holistic veterinary medicine has been guided by a subconscious feeling of spacious emptiness filled with creativity and compassion. Yet throughout my life, periods of busy mind-traffic, egoic thought patterns, ignorance, fear, and doubt blinded me from sensing the depth and truth emanating from this space of compassionate emptiness.

To illustrate, I would like to share a story with you.

My intention was to be fully present for the entire two-day Creativity and Compassion Conference, as panelists were requested to attend all sessions. Yet early in the morning of the first day, I received two calls, one to see a horse and another to see a dog that needed my assistance. I felt reticent, but explained to others at the conference that I thought bringing creativity and compassion to the care of animals was one way to think about what the conference itself was about. I promised to bring back a report of my missing hours. I took leave from the afternoon session of the first day of the conference to see how I could help these two patients that were not responding to conventional medicine.

When I arrived at the horse barn one hour later, the concerned horse trainer told me how this 12-year-old gelding named Lucky had been suffering with a chronic low grade cough and seemed depressed ever since it arrived from

Europe a few months past. Despite appropriate conventional medical care, Lucky was not bouncing back as one might expect. After examining him, I felt that his immune system was still stressed from all the travel and change of environment. After an acupuncture treatment to help boost the immune system, the trainer and I discussed the modification of antimicrobial therapy as well as supplements to help rebuild the immune system and overall health.

As I was completing the examination, the trainer brought a small, grey bird with closed eyes and ruffled feathers to my attention; the bird had been found in a water bucket in the barn. He gently placed the collapsed youngster outside on a stone wall in the sun, and it just sat there in a semi-comatose state. Amidst the busyness of a horse barn, the grooms, barn managers, and trainers all took time away from their work to help this weak, debilitated bird. One barn attendant found out from a friend that it was a baby mockingbird that arrived too early and, with the unpredictable spring weather, was unable to cope. The caretakers made a container to nurse the bird back to health and feed it properly. This was a clear example of creativity and compassion in action.

Then a dear concerned client drove up with her 12-year-old male arthritic yellow Labrador retriever, Bosco. Bosco had successfully responded to acupuncture, chiropractic care, and nutritional supplements along with occasional conventional analgesics and anti-inflammatory medications in the years he had been under my care. Unfortunately, he had recently lost his footing and fell on a slippery wooden surface, injuring his back and hind legs. He was not responding as he normally would to the pain-relieving medications. Upon examination, I could palpate that his hind leg muscles had been severely strained, and I noticed that he was possibly exhibiting some sciatic nerve pain. After I made some gentle musculoskeletal adjustments and injected some homeopathic remedies for pain and inflammation into appropriate acupuncture points, he seemed greatly relieved. Yet I knew that due to the severity of the injury, he would need further care and assistance. I suggested additional approaches to help him recover and listened attentively to the fears of my caring client and empathetically shared in her concern.

Over my years in veterinary practice, I have recognized that I have tendencies toward being an animal empath and deeply feel and sense animals' pain and suffering when I am with them. I was feeling like that in relation to the depressed horse and the injured dog that afternoon.

After returning to the conference on the second day and sharing these stories during the panel discussion, one attendee asked what animals I have in my life currently. I answered that due to travel obligations, I share my life and home only with the wildlife that occupies my property, though I am the one who pays the property taxes.

I then told about the two families of deer who give birth to their fawns under my raised deck every spring. One quite predictably gives birth to a single fawn and the other, in a recent year, had twins. One morning, as I opened my front door to the garden, the mother with her single fawn were calmly munching away at the black sunflower seeds that a miscellany of birds had dropped from the bird feeders. To my surprise, the fawn saw me and immediately pranced right into my front entrance, almost bowling me over. I caught the inquisitive youngster at the front door and gently guided it back to its mother as she guardedly watched the incident. The mother demonstrated a wary, but patient trust, possibly due to the loving relationship we've developed over many years.

The two mothers and their fawns return to my bird feeder quite frequently. On one summer day, almost a year after our first encounter, last year's fawn was now maturing, with two little horn buds growing from his masculine body. He was munching away at the birdseed and saw me sitting on a chair in the garden watching him quietly from a short distance. As I sat unmoving, radiating thoughts of loving intention, he slowly, gingerly, approached me. He would look into my eyes, watch every body movement, and step-by-step come closer. I was quite surprised by how comfortable he felt and how close he came to me. Yet I would never have anticipated that he would actually come as close to me as he did. Sniffing the ground as he took further steps, he moved closer and closer until his nose was sniffing my toes. He inquisitively looked up at me, eye-to-eye, and began licking my toes. He then looked up again to see my response, and there was only pure gratitude and love in my heart and my eyes, permeating my whole being. He was so comfortable that I was certain he sensed a feeling of safety. After a few moments, he backed up, turned around, and went back to the black sunflower seeds. After a while, he left my garden, looking back at me with a sense of connection that transcends all words or descriptions. Since then, he continues to return and we commune again at such deep levels.

I am blessed to share my life in and around my retreat cabin with so many beautiful beings of varied species. I am grateful for sharing this sacred space with the pair of Anna's hummingbirds, who perch quietly on the broken tip of a fir tree, looking in my window daily. When I sit on my deck, it's not uncommon for one to come right in front of my face and look me eye-to-eye momentarily, in between receiving nourishment from the flowering Oregon grape and other nutritious flowers around me. The families of bald eagles, turkey vultures, multitudes of songbirds, seals, otters, seabirds, raccoons, squirrels, frogs, etc., all share this quiet sacred space. When we quiet our minds and our hearts, we connect with them at a profound depth of spaciousness filled with loving-kindness and compassion. These are precious moments.

After sharing these stories during the panel, one author, a dynamic speaker, approached me and inquired how I just did what I did. I asked him what he meant by that. He said that the entire audience reached such a deep space of quiet as I shared my stories about creativity and compassion with animals. I thought about his question, reflecting that there are many different levels on which I might address it. One awareness I have is that when someone connects with an experience of unconditional love from another being—in the actual moment or in the retelling of it—one can enter an inner place of silence within the heart that allows for the loving-kindness and compassion to arise and be present. It is not uncommon that connecting within the space of unconditional love with animals is sometimes easier for many than connecting to that place while thinking of or engaging with fellow humans. There seems to be less mind-traffic going on around animals. That has been my experience when facilitating workshops for deepening that connection with animal lovers as well as when I see clients and patients.

Let me suggest a guided experience of that as you contemplate this essay. Think of one animal in your life that you loved unconditionally. If there is not one in particular, think of a wild animal or any animal that brings you into a state of inner peace and joy. Close your eyes and take in a slow, deep breath and visualize the animal. How does that feel to you? Where are you feeling it? What are you feeling, sensing, or thinking, if anything?

I have heard many people say that they can feel much more compassion for animals' suffering than for people's. They almost seem to have become numb to all the human suffering in the world. Yet when one talks or sees videos about whales caught in fishing nets, hundreds of dolphins dying due to sonar blasting by the navy or oil exploration, dogs and cats suffering in overcrowded shelters or starving in impoverished countries, people may drop into their heart space and feel tremendous compassion for these creatures. These heart connections can actually be a vehicle for awakening and thereby be of benefit to *all* beings. I've learned from animals that compassion happens in the silence. That is why I feel that compassion is within emptiness or spaciousness. My experience when I am with animals is simply communing with them in a spaciousness of compassion. There are many gateways to a place of quiet spaciousness, or a place beyond all words, concepts, labels, beyond the beyond—experiencing glimpses of "enlightenment" or "liberation." I personally feel that for some of us, being with animals may be one of those gateless gateways. It certainly has been for me.

From the day we are born the need for human affection is in our very blood. Even if the affection comes from an animal or someone we would normally consider an enemy, both children and adults will naturally gravitate toward it.

—His Holiness the Dalai Lama, from *In My Own Words, An Introduction to My Teaching and Philosophy*

Educating through the Five Cs

Christopher L. Kukk

Educator

ducation is the bridge between knowledge and wisdom.[1] But just getting educated doesn't mean you have crossed that bridge to wisdom. In my view, there is a difference between an educated person and a simply knowledgeable individual.[2] The difference between the two is significant for society and the world, in that while the knowledgeable person knows facts, the wise one learns "how to make facts live."[3] An education that bridges knowledge with wisdom seeks to blend the scientist with the artist, and the philosopher with the practitioner, to create scholars who are engaged citizens. Many politicians and administrators are installing mechanized systems of education in our schools and universities based on the requirements of standardized testing (i.e., simply knowing facts) but, meanwhile, there should be a revival for schools on all levels requiring critical thinking as well as oral communication and writing skills; these schools would educate for the purpose of fostering innovation and valuing compassion. Ultimately, the value of an education comes from being far more than an experience that certifies students; it comes from providing a learning environment that fosters innovation, imagination, and concern for the well-being of others in and outside the classroom. There are five main interconnected elements, similar to the Buddhist philosophy of *godai*, that when combined together create learning environments that nurture an educated person. I call this "The Five Cs": concept, creativity, compassion, courage, and constraint. Educating through the Five Cs teaches students "how to make facts live."

To Know. The first element of the Five Cs, *concept,* is centered upon building a student's knowledge base. Educating in this first element is about constructing a foundation for learning by teaching a holistic understanding of basic concepts and ideas. It is not just about learning facts. To have a holistic understanding is to know concepts by examining and studying them from as many angles, disciplines, processes, and perspectives as possible. When it comes to understanding human-induced climate change, for instance, it is important to know the different temperature data sets that each side uses in the debate. That information is vital because one side uses ground and satellite temperature data, whereas the other uses only, in general, one set of satellite records. More specifically, while the climate change doubters use satellite data demonstrating a cooling of the stratosphere, the believers rely on both atmospheric (the troposphere is warming) and ground temperature data sets to construct their "warming" arguments. To know how temperature is defined in a debate about climate change is essential for a holistic understanding.

Similarly, the concept of time is key to understanding climate change and the related debate. The doubters are correct when they state that, in the past, the planet has experienced natural climate change similar in magnitude to that of today. However, the believers are also correct when they argue that our current change in climate is happening much faster than at any previous time in Earth's history. In other words, while the opponents of the theory of human-induced climate change are using time in a mainly historical sense, the proponents define time in a temporal fashion (i.e., historical and durational). Knowing, in this case, how the temperature data sets and temporal contexts are defined provides a clearer understanding of what informs the different perspectives on climate change; this is much more illuminating than simply being acquainted with the ideas or sides of the debate. This deeper level of insight represents the difference between being acquainted with an idea and really understanding it. In addition, interdisciplinary learning about concepts is necessary to gain a more thorough comprehension of a subject. For example, in relation to climate change, wouldn't it be beneficial to both society and Earth if policymakers actually knew the science behind the policies they were devising and voting on?

To Make. The second element, *creativity*, is focused on cultivating a creative environment by fostering innovative ways of using concepts and ideas. Students, throughout their education, should be viewed as creators as well as consumers of knowledge. Educating has become too much of a passive experience for students—their main activity seems to be taking standardized tests. Students should be allowed and should be taught to interactively explore and combine concepts and ideas in innovative ways. Innovation is valuable currency in a highly globalized and interdependent world, and those who can innovate will elevate their socioeconomic standing. In light of that, our school environments should be places where time for creative insight (i.e., exploration) is allowed and where creative work (which includes critical thinking) is instituted.[4] This is exactly what the highest standardized test scorers in the world, the Finns, do. A recent analysis of Finland's education system concluded, "In contrast [to the United States and the United Kingdom], the central aim of Finnish education is the development of each child as a thinking, active, creative person, not the attainment of higher test scores."[5] It is ironic that Finland, the country whose citizens lead the world in their knowledge of facts, does not focus its education system on learning those facts; rather, the nation educates its students primarily in the arena of how to make the facts live. In other words, by learning how to make the facts live, one learns the facts better. The process is similar to learning a language. A person learns a language better by having to actively live or use it in a foreign country, as compared to passively learning it from a book. Overall, this element of the Five Cs is about making something new (i.e., a new solution to an old problem, a new way of understanding, or even a new product) out of what we know from books and experiences.

To See. The third element, *compassion*, is concerned with being aware of how ideas, solutions, and actions may affect others. In this element, educating is devoted to alleviating the suffering of ignorance. For we all know the aphorism about where good intentions and ideas can lead when they are not informed by an understanding or consideration of their effects. "The evil that is in the world," according to Albert Camus, "almost always comes of ignorance, and good intentions may do as much harm as malevolence if they lack understanding." A lack of understanding was evident in the differences between China and South Korea's approaches to reducing traffic accidents in their respective countries. Both countries decided to use countdown clocks at traffic lights in an effort to reduce the number of accidents. Yet while South Korea experienced a dramatic decrease in accidents, China saw a significant increase. Why the difference? South Korea installed countdown clocks during red lights, showing when the light would change to green, while China set them up to show when the green lights would end. The South Korean authorities understood the difference of using a countdown clock during a red light as compared to a green light; while drivers are more patient waiting at a red light if they know its duration, they speed up to get through a green light if they know it's about to change.[6] Clearly, understanding the context in which an idea is going to be used is just as important as the idea itself. In this case, the context changed the meaning and understanding of a countdown clock.

If students have a comprehension of the effects that their ideas, solutions, and actions can possibly have in the world, they are likely to recognize the responsibilities that are attached with creating such ideas and, therefore, with an education in general. Becoming aware of how ideas and solutions can affect people makes students aware of the responsibilities they have as educated persons. And acknowledging the responsibility for our own words, thoughts, and actions is something that this world needs a little more of. His Holiness the Dalai Lama states it best: "In the present circumstances, no one can afford to assume that someone else will solve their problems. Every individual has a responsibility to help guide our global family in the right direction. Good wishes are not sufficient; we must become actively engaged."

To Act. Inspiring active engagement is the purpose of the fourth element, *courage.* Once a consensus is formed that an idea is generally heading "in the right direction," a school or university should encourage students and faculty to act on the conceptual innovation. An educated person does not simply sit on new knowledge, he or she does something with it. Universities, especially, should incorporate learning-by-doing into the curriculum. Two universities in Pakistan, the National University of Sciences and Technology (NUST) and Aga Khan University, are following a learning-by-doing methodology and doing good at the same time. Both universities have decided to incorporate practical training into traditional academic programs, such as engineering and the sciences, with a focus on disaster prevention and assistance. While NUST is formalizing its program with a plan to provide a master's degree in disaster management, Aga Khan simply requires 20 percent of a student's academic program to consist of community work. Such requirements make the students know what the world out there looks like. They have seen how great the need can be. When disaster strikes, they don't ask: What can we do? Instead, they ask: Where can we go? Exposure to extreme need breeds compassion, and Pakistani practice shows that involvement in direct, practical relief can be a potent idea. Such an approach won't get the university onto the Times Higher Education or Shanghai rankings of schools, but it actually saves people's lives and solidly cements the university into its surrounding community.[7]

Too many schools in the West have focused on the race for higher rankings and abandoned the journey that education ought to be. Education should not be a competition for higher rankings but a journey for the purpose of developing educated people.

To Challenge. The fifth element, *constraint*, is about educators establishing rules and using limitations to foster an environment where students feel safe to learn holistically and think creatively. We traditionally consider aspects of this element as "thinking outside the box." In order to think outside the box, however, students need to have knowledge of the box—knowledge of its dimensional limitations. Artists and designers have called such limitations "creative constraints." Poets use structure and forms such as haikus and sonnets to generate new ways of using words, while designers have produced everything from dresses to cars using the philosophy of "design through discipline."[8] A recent study from the University of Amsterdam found that "the frustrations of form come with a mental benefit—letting people think in a more holistic and creative fashion. . . . It's not until we encounter an unexpected hindrance—a challenge we can't easily solve—that the chains of cognition are loosened, giving us newfound access to the weird connections simmering in the imagination."[9] Innovators discover ways of generating creativity in the face of limitation. Creative constraints provide students with opportunities to gain a deeper and broader understanding of reality. Albert Einstein started within the box of Newtonian physics and then thought beyond that box in ways that changed our perception of reality. "Imagination," according to Einstein, "is more important than knowledge. Knowledge is limited. Imagination encircles the world." He called all concepts "the free inventions of the human intellect." An education that uses the free inventions of the human intellect shaped by creative constraints and intended toward compassionate ends has the real chance of constructively changing how the world defines and learns basic concepts.

Educating through the Five Cs is needed because the current bridge of education is broken. Our system is manufacturing students who know some facts but certainly do not know how the facts live in their everyday world.

Anyone can start anywhere on the "education godai" or, in other words, with any of the Five Cs. The Five Cs support and fuel each other, and an educator should try and connect each C in as many ways possible. The education godai, in essence, is a creative constraint in itself for educators. A high school in Hawaii, Kailua High School, decided to introduce compassion into its classes and ethos in an effort to reduce violence and bullying. The school has woven an approach that reflects the Dalai Lama's teachings into its schoolwide curriculum since 2004 and has seen decreases in violence and bullying while experiencing increased levels of critical thinking and students transferring into the district.[10] Other ideas for entering the education godai include developing interdisciplinary majors (fulfilling the Cs of concept and creativity), incorporating service learning into the curriculum (courage and compassion), and requiring capstone projects that are framed by respected creative limitations (constraint). Furthermore, educators at every level should be required to demonstrate how they are fostering creativity and innovation within their classes as well as between their students and the community. The strength of an education is determined by the degree to which knowledge and wisdom can become unified. The Five Cs lead to a convergence of the scientist with the artist, and the philosopher with the practitioner, to make an educated person.

Notes

1. Knowledge, according to *Webster's New Universal Unabridged Dictionary*, is "acquaintance or familiarity (with a fact, place, etc.) . . . information; the body of facts accumulated by mankind." *Webster's* defines wisdom as "the faculty of making the best use of knowledge, experience, understanding, etc.; good judgment; sagacity." *Webster's New Universal Unabridged Dictionary*, Deluxe 2nd ed.

2. The idea of the sentence was inspired by Richard L. Derr, "Education versus Developing Educated Persons," *Curriculum Inquiry* 14, no. 3 (Autumn 1984): 301–9.

3.   The idea was derived from Oliver Wendell Holmes, who said, "The main part of intellectual education is not the acquisition of facts but learning how to make facts live."

4.   Stephen Cave, "Waiting for the Muse," review of *Imagine: How Creativity Works*, by Jonah Lehrer, *Financial Times*, 14 April 2012.

5.   Diane Ravitch, "Schools We Can Envy," review of *Finnish Lessons: What Can the World Learn from Educational Change in Finland*, by Pasi Sahlberg, *The New York Review*, 8 March 2012, 19–20.

6.   Rory Sutherland, "Perspective Is Everything," *TED Talks* (December 2011), available at http://www.ted.com/talks/lang/en/rory_sutherland_perspective_is_everything.html, last viewed on 6 June 2012.

7.   Ard Jongsma, "Pakistan: A Different Twist to Learning by Doing," *University World News Global Edition* (26 June 2011), available at http://www.universityworldnews.com/article.php?story=20110626092910408, last viewed on 6 June 2012.

8.   Jonah Lehrer, "Chains that Set Us Free: From Haikus to Videogames, Obstacles Boost Performance," *Wall Street Journal* (26–27 November 2011): C12; John Reed, "Design through Discipline," *Financial Times* (25 May 2012): 10.

9.   Ibid., C12.

10.   "Dalai Lama Attends Spiritual Conference," *National Public Radio* (17 April 2012), available at http://kunc.org/post/dalia-lama-attends-spiritual-conference, last viewed on 6 June 2012.

The question of bringing compassion and creativity to daily life got me thinking about spontaneity. It's said that the Buddha spontaneously does whatever is best to help living beings. He naturally and effortlessly acts in this most beneficial way. When I heard this a few years ago, I really thought about it as like, "Oh, that's nice. I wish I could do that." Then I gave it a try and I realized it's not that easy, especially since given that if you're trying, then you're not actually doing it effortlessly. Then I was reading a book by Bruce Lee. I'm big into martial arts. It's my passion. In martial arts, you have to apply these same principles. You have to be spontaneous. You can't know what you're going to do next or your opponent will pick up on it. He'll know what you're going to do and read it. So you have to act spontaneously. And you have to act effortlessly. If you put forth too much effort, you tire out and you lose. How can you be spontaneous? How do you do that? How can we be spontaneous? It's not impulsiveness. It has that sense of awareness.

—Tim Silva,
psychology major,
from the Creativity & Compassion conference

The Ambiguity of Choice

Michael Joel Bosco and Keith Roland
Undergraduates

A baby bird is in the grass, its nest in the branches of a nearby tree. You realize this chick is helpless, so what do you do? Do you leave the bird where it lies, or lift it back into the nest?

Each choice breaks down into several possible outcomes. If you leave the bird, the mother may notice and protect it, but it is also possible the bird will die where it landed. Perhaps it will be eaten by some other creature in the area, such as a fox.

If you lift the chick into its nest, without any assurance of its survival, you're leaving the fox without a meal. Your scent will be left on the bird, and the mother may not accept it back. This may lead her to push the chick out of the nest once again, or even kill it.

What is the compassionate action that is most fitting? The answer in this instance is ambiguous. If you leave the bird, you may feed the fox and preserve a life. But in that scenario, you would have a hand (through your inaction) of sacrificing one life for another.

Our first impulse in situations like this is to look for a definitive solution. However, when life sparks our sense of compassion, we may not know what action to take is the right action, the truly compassionate action.

If the impact of the action is ambiguous, perhaps the compassion in that moment resides not in the choice itself—but in the awareness that one has a choice to make.

But the Dalai Lama advises us that true compassion requires more than an awareness of the suffering of a sentient being. It requires action. Sometimes we must take an action not knowing for certain that it is the right action, but having only the "right" attitude about easing suffering. This requires standing in the eye of our ambivalence, and from there, seeing if a creative solution will unfold.

We tend to think of problems as having one or two possible solutions, when in fact that number may be vastly greater. Our example about the chick and the fox is fundamentally flawed. We considered two possible outcomes that entailed either the fox or the bird surviving. But there are, perhaps, a great many unexpected outcomes.

For example, what if there were a "middle way" between the two extremes provided? What if we could not only feel, but *express* compassion for both the fox and the chick?

Coincidentally enough, just days after conjuring up our introductory example, one of us was faced with a very similar situation. Replace the fox with two savage puppies.

One of us had just arrived home. It was summer, mid-afternoon, and the dogs had been cooped up inside with their empty stomachs and bursting energy for what must have seemed to them an eternity. Opening the front door, the co-author was greeted not only with claws and wet tongues, but by a call from across the house: "There's a baby bird on the ground by the bushes around back!" Before he could process this information, the two dogs shot out of the just-closing storm door and raced to the backyard. The co-author ran after them, but by the time he'd reached the dogs, they'd already spotted the bird and began to violently bark and growl. Quickly, he racked his brain for the best possible plan of action. The then-emerging essay provided some inspiration: Realizing that its theme was ambiguity, he began to respond by acting on impulse. *The puppies are hungry*, he suddenly remembered.

Scrambling back to the house and into the kitchen, he sweated and stumbled as he piled dog treat upon dog treat into one puppy's round, silver bowl. Out of breath as he once more ran to the bushes, he was faced with another antagonist: his seven-year-old brother. Watching from a window above, his brother had noticed the chaos unfolding, and in his naïveté had joined the dogs in their dance of death. Matching the adrenaline level of the puppies, the co-author shouted to coerce his younger brother to run inside, which provided a momentary distraction from the horrified, high-pitched chirping of the dogs' helpless prey. As the puppies' eyes followed the seven-year-old on his return to the house, they also caught light of the glistening bowl of treats only a few yards away. They darted toward their new target, and when they got close enough, the co-author grabbed both puppies by the collar and dragged them inside—pulling the door tightly shut behind him. While they ate, he explained the reasons for his actions to his younger brother, giving him the job of informing the rest of the family about the matter at hand and about keeping the dogs inside until further notice. The bird was thus left to the whims of a rural Connecticut backyard. It probably would not be under threat from a fox, but who knows?

So, what happened here? Amidst the chaos of circumstance and rushing adrenaline, a middle way appeared in a creative flash, offering a fresh perspective on an ambiguous issue. Yes, the bird remained in the yard, but the co-author didn't simply abandon it. He protected it at least from the dogs, while finding a way to nurture the puppies in the process. These actions helped his younger brother gain a deeper understanding of the importance of compassion, and that perspective then rippled outward, fractally, into the consciousness of the entire household.

The compassionate awareness applies not only to the above examples, but to situations we are all faced with in the tribulations of daily life, whether it is helping a friend through a crumbling relationship, supporting a family member during a time of illness, or teaching a child to read; large or small, the ultimate consequences of our actions remain unknown to us. Yet, in the space between the positives and negatives lies a void, a unique, transformative space wherein rests the purest taste of truth, of genuine, unabashed compassion. "At that moment of total attention," writes J. Krishnamurti, "there is no entity who is trying to change, to modify, to become something; there is no self at all. In the moment of attention the self, the 'me,' is absent, and it is that moment of attention that is good, that is love." As Nietzsche observes, "What is done out of love always takes place beyond good and evil."

When I think of creativity as it relates to my field of crime and justice, I think of innovation. If you look at some of the posters that the students made that are around the room, those focus on a view that we call "restorative justice." The idea of restorative justice has been drawn from many places such as Native American cultures and Australian cultures. The problem we are facing is the mass incarceration that we have. One out of every 100 individuals in the U.S. is incarcerated. So in reaction to that, we can do a few things. One of those few things is to keep incarcerating people. But we are running out of money quickly. Or we can find alternate ways to deal with this. One of the alternatives is restorative justice, reaching out compassionately.

—Melissa Fenwick,
professor of justice and law,
from the Creativity &
Compassion conference

Compassionate Lawyering

David R. Kittay
Attorney

A frequent metaphor found in Buddhism is that of Buddha as a doctor, giving medicine to people to help them overcome their addictions to the three poisons of attachment, aversion, and ignorance. As Śāntideva wrote,

> May I be the doctor and the medicine
> And may I be the nurse
> For all sick beings in the world
> Until everyone is healed.[1]

We live in a world full of laws, yet it might seem strange if someone were to say, paraphrasing Śāntideva, "May I be the lawyer . . ." And yet there is good reason to think of lawyers as being more like doctors, caring professionals whose motivation is or should be to restore or create socially healthy individuals and a caring and vibrant society. Negative behavior by lawyers as well as negative views of lawyers and their role stem from our less-than-optimal state of understanding today, where clinging to and defending the "self" at all costs is seen as the remedy for a view of the world as hostile—and that often becomes a self-fulfilling prophecy. It's time for this to change.

Recently I gave a seminar in legal ethics to a large group of experienced bankruptcy lawyers and bankruptcy trustees. My theme was to advocate for a style of lawyering that went beyond civility—to compassion. Although there is a growing movement these days in favor of standards of "civility," which boils down to an attitude of politeness and avoiding the more obnoxious behavior sometimes encountered at the bar, there has been very little discussion of anything beyond civility.

Many lawyers—I certainly was one—labor under the misconception that their obligations to others they may encounter in a lawsuit or legal proceeding are subordinate to a duty to "zealously" represent their clients. While the former set of New York disciplinary rules and ethical considerations, which defines the ethics of interactions with clients and in court, did have the "zealously represent" language, most jurisdictions, including New York and Connecticut, have adopted a version of the American Bar Association's Model Rules of Professional Conduct[2] that *do not* refer to "zeal" or "zealous" or "zealously" with respect to the representation of clients.[3]

The specific provisions of the Model Rules provide for a "minimum level of conduct,"[4] and specifically provide that "the Rules do not, however, exhaust the moral and ethical considerations that should inform a lawyer, for no worthwhile human activity can be completely defined by legal rules."[5] Section 2.1 of the Model Rules says, "In rendering advice, a lawyer may refer not only to law, but to other considerations such as *moral*, economic, social, psychological and political factors . . ." So we lawyers *cannot* put difficult ethical questions out of our minds when we are giving legal advice or representing our clients.

I am not saying that financial considerations are not relevant. But if we desire happiness, money cannot be the only consideration. As Śāntideva wrote, "All those who suffer in the world do so because of their desire for their own happiness. All those happy in the world are so because of their desire for the happiness of others. Why say more? Observe this distinction: between the fool who longs for his own advantage and the sage who acts for the advantage of others."[6]

The story of Dandin in *The Sūtra of the Wise and the Foolish* shows what often occurs when we take an overly simplistic and self-centered view of disputes.

Once upon a time in that country there was a Brahmin named Dandin. He was very poor and lacked food and clothes. He borrowed a bull from a Householder's house, and, having used it for a day, he led the bull back to the Householder's house. At that time, the Householder was eating a meal. Dandin sent the bull into the house, but the bull went out of another door and strayed. The Householder finished the meal and got up, and then, not seeing the bull, said to Dandin,

"Where is the bull?"

"I sent [him] into your house."

"You lost my bull…. Return him!"

"I didn't lose [him]!"

Then the two of them agreed to go to the King, saying, "He will decide which of us is right and not right," and then they went.

Another man's mare was running away, and he said to Dandin, "Don't let the mare escape!" So he picked up a stone and threw it, and it hit the horse's leg and broke it. [The man] said, "You killed my horse; give me a horse!"

"Why should I give you a horse?"

"Come here," [the man] said, "We will go before the King, and he will judge us," and so they went.

But Dandin tried to run away, and jumped up on top of a wall, but there was a Weaver behind it weaving some fabric and sitting there, and he fell on top of him and killed the Weaver at once. The Weaver's Wife seized Dandin and said, "You killed my husband; give me my husband back!"

"How can I give your husband back?"

"Come, we will go before the King and he will judge us."

While they were going, there was a deep river across the route. There was a Carpenter in the water, carrying an axe in his mouth. Dandin asked him, "How deep is the water?" In saying that the water was deep, he dropped the axe into the water. Not finding the axe, he seized Dandin and said, "You made me drop my axe into the water; I didn't drop it! Come, we will go before the King, and he will judge us," he said, and they went.

So they went and came before the King, and bowed their heads down at the feet of the King, and sat to one side. The King asked, "Why have you come?" They described the entire dispute involving Dandin and the Householder. The King said to Dandin,

"Did you borrow the bull?"

"I borrowed."

"Well, did you give it back so that the Householder could see it?"

"I didn't say anything."

The King said, "Dandin gave the bull back, but, because he didn't say anything, cut out his tongue. But the Householder also didn't bother to look at the bull coming, so gouge out his eyes!"

The Householder said, "On the one hand, Dandin stole my bull, but, on the other hand, it's better that Dandin be the winner than for my eyes to be gouged out!"

Then the man said, "O Lord! Dandin killed my mare!"

The King asked Dandin, "How did you kill the horse?"

"I was walking along the road, and while I was walking, this man said, 'Don't let the horse get away,' so I grabbed a rock and threw it, and killed the horse."

The King said, "Because the horse's owner said, 'Don't let the horse escape,' cut out [his] tongue! As for Dandin, because he threw the rock, cut off [his] hand!"

The man said, "On the one hand, my horse was killed, but, on the other, it's better that Dandin win than for my tongue to be cut out!"

The Weaver's Widow said, "Dandin killed my husband."

Dandin said, "Because I had many enemies, I was afraid. While I was climbing over a wall to get away, I didn't see that a man was hidden there, and he died."

The King said, "Go and marry this [woman]!"

She said, "On the one hand, my husband is dead, but, on the other, it is better that Dandin win than that he should be [my] husband!"

The Carpenter said, "Because this Dandin asked me, 'How deep is the river?' the axe that I held with my mouth fell into the river."

The King said, "It's better to carry things on the shoulder than in the mouth. Pull out two teeth from the mouth of the Carpenter! As for Dandin, for 'Is the river deep?' cut out [his] tongue!"

The Carpenter said, "On the one hand, my axe is lost, but, on the other, it is better that Dandin win than for my teeth to get pulled out!"

So each of them was judged. Dandin was absolved of all fault.[7]

Although there are no lawyers in this sutra, the principles underlying it are relevant today. Although each of the litigants viewed him- or herself as completely in the right, the King recognized that, with one possible exception, each had a role to play in the events at issue. For example, the Householder was guilty of contributory negligence in not bothering to get up from his meal to see that the bull had been returned. Then, as now, it is a rare dispute where someone involved in it is completely blameless.

Appreciating how reality breeds compassion is perhaps a deeper teaching of this sutra. When we more accurately perceive reality, we see the interconnectedness of things, which naturally—at least when it comes to people and animals—stimulates compassion. Although the King is ostensibly not acting in a compassionate manner—after all, he mainly orders the chopping off or gouging out of various body parts—the reality of accountability in the justice system shows each of the litigants that his or her situation could certainly be worse, and shows how their accusations and culpability are interrelated.

Another valuable insight in the story of Dandin is that of the importance of state of mind. In legal terms, Dandin had no *mens rea*, Latin for "guilty mind." State of mind is not only relevant to culpability, in the past and now, but is crucial to happiness. As the Buddhist text *Dhammapada* states:

All things have the nature of mind. Mind is the chief and takes the lead. If the mind is clear, whatever you do or say will bring happiness that will follow you like your shadow.

All things have the nature of mind. Mind is the chief and takes the lead. If the mind is polluted, whatever you do or say leads to suffering which will follow you, as a cart trails a horse.[8]

A litigant, like the Householder, who is thinking, "They are seeking to rob me," would be very defensive in a psychological sense, and, like the Householder, would cling to a negative view of the intentions of others, just like the Householder thought of Dandin. Captive to his own negative view of his opponent, such a litigant leads himself and others to suffering, as the Buddha said, "as a cart trails a horse." Thus, in their anger and lack of perspective, today's litigants often miss chances to settle disputes, and only do so as a last resort, when the pain of the process (nowadays, of paying their lawyers) exceeds their perception of the injury they have suffered—exactly what happened at the end of the story of Dandin!

How much better would it have been, if the Householder had a lawyer, who could have advised him of the "moral, economic, social, psychological, and political factors" that were relevant here. Perhaps, given Dandin's poverty and simple character, and the Householder's wealth and interest in cuisine, the parties could have settled on some kind of arrangement instead of going to the King (the equivalent of the justice system at that time), with unpredictable results.

Often, the parties involved in a dispute have a very narrow view of their relationship and potential relationship. This is where creativity comes in. One of the first questions a potential litigant or potential litigant's lawyer should ask the putative opponent is, "How may I help you?" While there may be instances where the parties would refuse assistance on principle, or out of anger, it would be the rare case where nothing can be done. Dandin killed the Weaver, albeit by accident. Could he have done nothing for the Weaver's Wife?

Thinking in this way is certainly different from what we're used to. But it holds tremendous promise, both for those who would give and those who would receive. Here, some might say, "Are you kidding? We are all trying to survive in a grim world, and you folks are saying we should love our enemies?!!" This is where it's important to have some compassion for ourselves. Only then can we allow ourselves to experience the joy of even something so potentially negative as litigation. This is why in his *Lamp for the Path to Enlightenment*, the great Indian teacher Atiśa ends his description of the Buddhist path with those practices that can help generate an ever-joyful attitude and increased energy that can then be used to benefit others and, ultimately, one's self as well.

In this spirit, I told the assembled audience of bankruptcy practitioners that what we were all doing together was in fact just like a hospital, and that all of us should, every day, remember that, and give ourselves a little jolt of joy or pat on the back. The financially suffering, the debtors, are like the patients. They come to the bankruptcy lawyers saying, "Doc, it hurts—what can I do?" The lawyers apply the medicine of a bankruptcy filing and send them to the surgeons, the Bankruptcy Trustees. The Judges are like the Deans of Medicine; the Clerks of the Court are like the medical records department. Together, we are enabling these deserving yet unfortunate people—the vast majority of debtors—to live again. And, generalizing to most or all lawyers, we can take joy in the work that we are doing when it is in the spirit of "right livelihood": helping those who are injured, confused, and downtrodden to live good lives, and, where necessary, counseling those who are more fortunate to do the right thing, for the benefit of all.

Notes

1. Śāntideva, *A Guide to the Bodhisattva's Way of Life*, Ch. 10, v. 8. Dharamsala: Library of Tibetan Works & Archives (1979).

2. In New York State, the former Disciplinary Rules were replaced by the Model Rules, effective as of April 1, 2009, as Part 1200 of the New York State Unified Court System.

3. The former New York Code's section relating to "zealously" was replaced with Model Rule 1.3 providing simply that, "(a) A lawyer shall act with reasonable diligence and promptness in representing a client, " and "(b) A lawyer shall not neglect a legal matter entrusted to the lawyer." See P. Saunders, "Whatever Happened to 'Zealous Advocacy'?" 245 N.Y.L.J. No. 47 (March 11, 2011).

4. Ibid., Preamble, Para. 6.

5. Ibid., Preamble, Para. 8.

6. Śāntideva, *The Bodhicaryāvatāra*. Oxford: Oxford U. Pr. (1995), 99.

7. *The Sūtra of the Wise and the Foolish*, translation by Dr. Lozang Jamspal and the author from the Tibetan.

8. *Dhammapada*. Berkeley: Dharma Publishing (1985), 3.

May all beings everywhere,
Plagued with sufferings of body and mind,
Obtain an ocean of happiness and joy
By virtue of my merits.

—Śāntideva, *Guide to the Bodhisattva's Way of Life* 10:2

ཕྱོགས་རྣམས་ཀུན་ན་ལུས་དང་སེམས། །
སྡུག་བསྔལ་ནད་པ་ཇི་སྙེད་པ། །
དེ་དག་བདག་གི་བསོད་ནམས་ཀྱིས། །
བདེ་དགའ་རྒྱ་མཚོ་ཐོབ་པར་ཤོག །

5

Embracing the Challenges of the 21st Century

Compassion, Please, Not Niceness

Edward A. Hagan

Professor of Writing and Irish Studies

Compassion is hard work. So is creativity.

Yet it's probably the case that the work required is not readily imagined even by people who are "normally" compassionate. The Dalai Lama has argued that compassion is an innate human quality. If it's innate—a biological imperative even, it would not seem to take much work, although we readily accept that a great athlete must work hard to develop her talent. And the "lightning strike" theory of creativity usually glosses over all the hard work that created the moment when inspiration struck.

In his memoir, *The Gatekeeper*, the prominent literary critic Terry Eagleton recalls his childhood interactions with a convent of cloistered Carmelite nuns. Eagleton writes: "These women deliberately threw their lives away, a gesture which requires the defiant absurdism of the Dadaist rather than the calculations of the actuary or the zeal of the do-gooder. In refusing the powers of this world, their existence became as pointless as a work of art."[1] Eagleton dissects their otherworldliness, and, while aware of the repressed nature of the nuns' lives, he yet admires them because they do recognize how badly the world is in need of "redemption." He writes, "These women, by contrast [with so-called hard-nosed realists], acknowledged in their own eccentric way the wretchedness of the world, and were thus the reverse of the bright-eyed liberal modernizers."[2]

He goes on: "Their role was to symbolize the kind of drastic self-abandonment which the world would need if it were to become just. They were a sign not of what was to be done, but of how much it would take."[3]

The Dalai Lama is no foolish optimist, although he is gentle and challenges us all to do the good thing. But compassion is not some species of "niceness," nor is creativity mere good fortune. We need models like the Carmelites of doing the good thing; and in the early 21st century, we probably need models as ordinary as a fish 'n' chips shop owner in Derry, Northern Ireland.

Brendan Duddy, the proprietor of such an eatery, was the key person responsible for setting up the negotiations that led to the Good Friday Agreement (GFA) of 1998, a treaty that has brought a large measure of peace to Northern Ireland. Yet hardly anyone knows who he is or what his role was in creating the conditions that made it possible for Ian Paisley, the notorious fundamentalist leader of Northern Ireland's Protestant Presbyterians, and Martin McGuiness, the reputed number two leader of the Provisional Irish Republican Army (PIRA), to lead the Northern Ireland government that has evolved from the GFA. Duddy was the secret contact between the PIRA and British intelligence for about 25 years; he relayed the message that started serious peace negotiations in 1993.

It is also true that hardly anyone knows that Duddy's activities arose out of a deep spirituality that strongly resembles the Dalai Lama's claim that people's "only antidote to . . . loneliness is . . . [an] attitude of affection, concern, and warm-heartedness toward their fellow human beings." In *Beyond Religion* the Dalai Lama lays out an argument for a secular ethics but strongly insists that a person who would promote such a code must first have "inner peace" so as to be able to "endure all kinds of adversity."[4]

On the surface, Brendan Duddy seems to have been a most unlikely candidate for the very dangerous cloak-and-dagger world of secret negotiations. Born in 1936, he opened his fish 'n' chips shop in his native Derry in Northern Ireland during the years 1952–53.[5] A devout Catholic, Duddy's business grew out of a real passion for the food he made but also the reality that a Catholic in Northern Ireland in the 1950s had to create his own economic well-being: He was unlikely to be hired by any large corporation or by the government that was dominated by Protestants, even in Derry, where Catholics outnumbered Protestants by a wide margin.[6]

Duddy's fish 'n' chips shop, located in central Derry, became a late-night hangout for the intelligentsia of the city, and late-night discussions of politics were common throughout the 1960s. The shop received its deliveries of food from a truck driver—the young Martin McGuiness. And then, in response to the pressure building for more equitable treatment of Catholics, Frank Lagan, a grade school classmate of Duddy's and also a Catholic, was appointed as the chief of the Royal Ulster Constabulary (RUC) in Derry.

Lagan talked Duddy into participating in a small business owners' group in Derry: Duddy was its only Catholic member. The relationship developed further until finally, in early 1972, Lagan asked Duddy to communicate with both branches of the IRA to ask that no guns be carried on a march for civil rights that was to reach the center of Derry. That march took place on January 30, 1972, and resulted in tragedy when British troops fired into the crowds of unarmed marchers, killing 13 people and wounding 15 others (one of whom later died)—the event came to be known as "Bloody Sunday." In 2010, an inquiry finally concluded that the British soldiers were out of control on that Sunday, and Prime Minister David Cameron apologized and called the shootings "unjustified and unjustifiable."

Duddy had succeeded in getting commitments from both the PIRA and the Official IRA that they would not bring guns into the march—and apparently they did not, although biased inquiries made soon after the march claimed that the British troops had been fired upon. Duddy was outraged, and Lagan was distraught because Lagan knew that the British Army had planned aggressive activities in response to a nonviolent march. Duddy reports that Lagan "told me that 'the Army had decided to take out two or three soft targets in the area of the High Flats with the intention of provoking a fire fight with the IRA.' These were virtually his exact words. I remember the phrase 'taking out' in particular. It sticks in my mind. I was appalled. I could not accept that a human being would kill another human being indiscriminately."[7]

Nevertheless, Duddy's career as a secret go-between was launched after Bloody Sunday, and the event plunged Northern Ireland into over 20 years of violence. During that time, Duddy developed a strong relationship with Michael Oatley, later the number three person in MI6—Britain's Secret Intelligence Service—and with other British agents who succeeded Oatley. Duddy was central to many near-miss attempts to negotiate a peace. He became good friends with Oatley, friendly enough to lecture the intelligence officer on the British politics of "niceness": "Of this I feel sure, I have had enough of the sickness of power politics. I have prayed to God that I get the strength to break through the niceness and bring peace to ordinary people." Duddy was appalled by the British claim to "civilized behavior"; their propaganda portrayed them as "nice," innocently caught between the warring neanderthal Catholics and Protestants.

Duddy is clearly an exceptional person. He was educated at St. Columb's College in Derry, a superb secondary school for Catholic boys that lists Seamus Heaney—the Nobel Laureate in Literature—and John Hume—winner of the Nobel Peace Prize—among its alumni. Other notable graduates include Seamus Deane, poet, novelist, and literary critic; Phil Coulter, songwriter; and playwright Brian Friel as well as other notable men in all walks of life. The rigor of Duddy's early academic training led him to keep voluminous records of his activities that form a remarkable archive of his involvement in Northern Ireland peace politics from the early '70s well into the '90s.[8] He clearly understood that he had an obligation to history to keep these records; many of them are handwritten notes about his state of mind.

We know from those notes and from additional interviews that Duddy is a deeply spiritual man, and that he is not conventional. Though a strong Catholic, he expresses exasperation and disgruntlement with priests and bishops (and admiration for nuns who perform acts of charity regardless of politics). He has described his practice of seeking the solace of religious places, regardless of their denomination, whenever he was hard-pressed by the very real dangers he faced in his peace-making role. His favorite place of solace was the 5,000-year-old Grianan of Aileach, an early Iron Age stone fort in county Donegal in the Irish Republic. By his own account, Duddy went there to walk the walls and settle his mind: "I run up here every single day, and it got to the stage of being a place of personal internal freedom. And it was like a spiritual re-charging. This brought you back to earth again. This brought you back to being a person—very important."

His pacifism derives from a similar foray into the countryside, a hunting trip on which he shot an animal. He recalls:

> This beautiful creature just stood up in front of me. It was at that particular point I shot it. And then I looked at this beautiful, beautiful creature that I just murdered, and I realized what violence was all about. Clashed with thoughts of men shooting at men, it was the display of the futility in that, the understanding in an instant, this is not the way to live.[9]

Duddy's perspective clearly resonates with Eastern philosophy, and he has expressed some recognition of the shortcomings of Western thought. He gained insight into this arena in 1976 when he went on a hunger strike for 30 days—a tactic with a long history in Ireland as well as in Mahatma Gandhi's India. He has described the illuminations brought on by his hunger:

> I am finding my own lack of food *not* easy, but I find my awareness of life much more full. I see western life maybe as I should—selfish.
>
> Now, we have decided that there is a lacking in spirit of the British government, that there's a lacking in generosity—this we would accept might be due, almost entirely due, to their own political problems and conditions which exist in the House of Commons or in Westminster.[10]

Being on a hunger strike helped Duddy to see the foolishness of ordinary life, but it also led him to contempt for the bureaucratic, "nice" behavior of politicians and civil servants in contemporary life. Their roles insulate them against change of any sort, and breaking through their rigidity is an exercise in creative politics. Duddy came to recognize that British officials could not change their positions even when they wanted to or when it was in their interest to do so. Change could not be contemplated without alarm even at the moment in 1993 when serious peace negotiations could finally begin. Duddy writes, with a side-jab at the Roman Catholic hierarchy:

> So in April and May [1993] the IRA offered a 2-week ceasefire to enable dialogue to start. It was the "Moment" of my life. . . . I went to London with

the ceasefire in my hand. The British Politicians began to see that things had moved too fast for them. (Very, very, like events in Rome) and the British simply didn't give an answer or acceptance, they simply delayed and delayed.[11]

Duddy understands how bureaucratic thinking creates the box that the creative politician must break out of:

And the task is to take the first step towards straightening out this 400 years of anger. The image I have is that of a small animal burrowing in circles below the surface of the earth, occasionally putting one tiny nostril above the clay and immediately retreating into its recognized life pattern.

If the present efforts are to succeed, then everything possible that can be done must be done, to enable Republicanism to emerge in an evolutionary peaceful fashion.

Failure comes instantly when the civil servant whispers into his masters [sic] ear, "Can't really accept that one sin, contravenes section 75 of such and such an act." The civil servant may be doing his job but he's killing off the prospect of change.[12]

Then Duddy goes on:

Rallying calls, parliamentary statutes, constitutional articles are the bog lands of failure. Time and the healing process are what is needed at this moment. Time without deception, time with generosity, a vision for the future of what peaceful togetherness can offer.

The most significant contribution I have heard in the last ten years is as follows: When asked by a leading Republican, "What if we enter into dialogue with good faith and after two weeks of trying we fail? What then?" And the reply was, "We will simply have to try again, because this problem must be resolved."

This reply heralds the area of hope which must be expanded. More work has got to be done.[13]

Yes, more work.

Duddy had realized in 1976 that the challenge was to break through easy wishful thinking and encrusted modes of behavior that had a long history. Cognizant of history, he recognized the moment for peace had arrived in 1993, and he inspired all the parties to spend five years in intense negotiations to work and negotiate and work some more. His work was completed when he moved the Provisional IRA, the Protestant Loyalist paramilitaries, and the British Government into a position where, at last, a role for a back-channel operator such as himself was no longer needed.

I think the Dalai Lama would approve. He might even ask Brendan Duddy to try his hand on a deal between the Tibetans and the Chinese. Apparently, Duddy has tried to work with the Palestinians and the Israelis. There is hope. Duddy has had his health problems in recent years, but I suspect that he is ready to work on peace in more places. He has observed, "I wanted to show people that, actually, the world can be changed."[14]

Notes

1. Terry Eagleton, *The Gatekeeper*. New York: St. Martin's Press (2001), 12.

2. Ibid., 14.

3. Ibid., 15–16.

4. Tenzin Gyatso, His Holiness the 14th Dalai Lama, *Beyond Religion: Ethics for a Whole World*. Boston and New York: Houghton Mifflin Harcourt (2011), 37–38.

5. The name of this city is a matter of controversy. Catholics call it "Derry"; Protestants and the British call it "Londonderry." I accept the Catholic name, in view of the fact that they are and have been the majority in the city.

6. The 2001 census of the Derry Urban Area found that 77.8 percent of the population was Catholic in background, yet Protestants, through gerrymandered districts, ruled the area for most of the 20th century.

7. Brendan Duddy Archive, National University of Ireland–Galway, Document No. POL 35/45 (8).

8. In 2009, Duddy gave his papers to the National University of Ireland–Galway, where they are now housed in the Department of Special Collections.

9. Brendan Duddy, interview by Peter Taylor, "The Secret Peacemaker," BBC Two, March 26, 2008.

10. Brendan Duddy Archive, National University of Ireland–Galway, Document No. POL 35/121 (2). (15 Jan. 76).

11. Brendan Duddy Archive, National University of Ireland–Galway, Document No. POL 35/293 (1).

12. Ibid.

13. Ibid.

14. Brendan Duddy, interview by Peter Taylor, "The Secret Peacemaker," BBC Two, March 26, 2008.

With the realization of one's own potential and self-confidence in one's ability, one can build a better world. According to my own experience, self-confidence is very important. That sort of confidence is not a blind one; it is an awareness of one's own potential. On that basis, human beings can transform themselves by increasing the good qualities and reducing the negative qualities.

—His Holiness the Dalai Lama, from *The Dalai Lama's Book of Wisdom*

Active and Passive Compassion

Daniel W. Barrett

Psychology Professor

"Ask me again in 15 or 20 years!" That was my response to the question posed by the panel moderator of the Creativity and Compassion Conference about whether Facebook would increase or decrease overall compassion in the world. Given the relatively recent explosive growth in the use of social media during the past few years, and the inherent difficulty in actually assessing whether the "mass" of compassion in the world has changed or will change, I couldn't help but delay answering the question for a decade or two!

The working title for our panel was "Making Connections: Facebook, Twitter, and Social Media: Modes for Spreading Compassion or a Wasteland of Fabricated Images and Narcissism?" Although I love the provocative nature of the title, I can't help but question its premise—that social media could fall under one or the other category. Social media—like most other social phenomena—are rich, complex, and multitudinous, and are not easily categorized, summarized, or encapsulated. Rather than placing them in one or another box, we should evaluate to what degree might these labels be useful. In the process, we need to think about the nature of compassion and its conference partner, creativity.

As an academic, I naturally want to question every assumption and carefully scrutinize every construct and claim. However, given that I am not writing for a journal, let me be a bit more impressionistic than usual, raising a few questions and issues without systematically trying to answer them. And of course I recognize the distinctly Western bias in my thinking.

First, we need to ask what creativity is—although not specifically included in our title, it is obviously relevant, given the overall conference purpose. Without being too pedantic, it seems to me that creativity involves, at minimum, the introduction of something novel. This could take many forms, ranging from coining a neologism to writing an original poem or song, or offering a radical paradigm for understanding human evolution. We can point to "small" examples of creativity, such as fixing a leaky pipe in a nontraditional way, or "larger" examples, such as painting the *Mona Lisa*. Furthermore, creativity often seems to morph into its opposite, destruction. I believe that nature—including human nature—is inherently creative at the same time that it is necessarily destructive. Creativity has a "dark" side. Perhaps there is a dialectical relationship between the two, such that destruction is necessary for creation, and creation for destruction.

Second, we should think about the nature of compassion. My intuitive sense is that compassion, at minimum, involves concern for the welfare of others, particularly with regard to unmet needs that may impair their ability to lead a healthy, fulfilling, and productive life. But to me compassion is more than just concern. In addition to this, it requires acting in ways that are consistent with that concern. Publicly acknowledging another's pain, devoting time and/ or resources to helping others in need, or raising broader awareness of the plight of others and working to channel resources toward alleviating suffering should all be considered acts of compassion. Perhaps we should differentiate *passive* compassion that is mere acknowledgment from *active* compassion that involves actually doing something.

Third, to return more pointedly to the question from our panel, how do we "know" whether compassion is spreading? What would it mean to spread compassion? As a user of both Facebook and Twitter, it seems to me that the relationship between social media and compassion is dynamic and multifaceted, and depends on how the former are used. There are relationships, but no relationship. These relationships should be seen as "local" or "contextual" rather than "global." We are no more justified in claiming that social media have generally increased or decreased active compassion and creativity than we are in asserting the same with respect to books, newspapers, and magazines. But I can speak of my own experiences.

On the one hand, I think that *passive* compassion—mere awareness and acknowledgment—has likely increased. I personally have heard about the suffering and pain of many people across the globe as a result of my online communication. Every day I see Facebook and Twitter posts depicting the struggles of others—struggles that I would probably otherwise not have known about. I can effortlessly "express" concern by clicking a button, making a comment, or reposting an item. But what are the real-world implications for such virtual activity? It is important to note that exposure to compassionate expression is largely voluntary. The "friends" who I have on Facebook and the feeds I subscribe to on Twitter are those that I have sought out. Thus I have engineered my own increased awareness by exposing myself to the postings and comments of people who are compassionate and hope to relieve the suffering of others by using social media. For instance, the Dalai Lama frequently posts compassion-related comments, and I see many of these. How many of the 950 million Facebook and 140 million Twitter users choose to do this?

On the other hand, if spreading compassion refers to *active* compassion that reduces suffering, then any inferences we draw are on less certain grounds. How do we conceptualize, let alone produce, a metric for suffering? I honestly don't know how to answer this one.

I can't say that my own active compassion has been directly affected by social media. The groups to which I give time or energy are largely unrelated to my online presence. More generally, it's clear that social media may be a tool that some deploy in an effort to spread compassion (e.g., the Dalai Lama), whereas for others it may serve the opposite goal of spreading hatred and pain (e.g., extremist groups). We are left to wonder about the nature of the real-world consequences.

One way to wrap my head around these difficult questions is to try to find an analogue that has been empirically studied in psychology, my academic discipline. One psychological construct that comes to mind is willpower, which is the ability to control one's urges, particularly with respect to delaying immediate gratification. Willpower has been the subject of a great deal of recent, fascinating research. One of the ways that psychologists have investigated will-power has entailed putting people in situations and challenging them not to engage in instant gratification, and then probing the effects of such restraint. Briefly, the research points to two intriguing conclusions. First, the exercise of willpower uses up mental energy. Second, and relatedly, willpower acts like a muscle, and therefore can be both exhausted and replenished. There may only be so much "willpower" within a person or a population.

Similarly, *active* compassion can tax one's mental and physical resources. I think this is true in situations in which an adult cares for an elderly parent, a social worker tries to improve the well-being of a neglected child, or a donor generously gives to a variety of organizations devoted to helping others. People can and do suffer from compassion fatigue; as with willpower, compassion is depleted. Therefore, they need a "break" to restore and replenish it.

Having said all of that, I'll offer a provisional, speculative answer to the question that I delayed at the outset: While *passive* compassion may in fact have increased, I doubt that social media have had a similar impact on *active* compassion. At a global level, I think that *active* compassion may be like a whack-a-mole: It can only increase in one domain of life by decreasing in another. Where does creativity enter into the discussion? Well, creativity can serve to facilitate both *passive* and *active* compassion.

Moderator, Jeffrey Schlicht (professor of exercise science): Can we actively do something on Twitter or Facebook that actively reduces someone's suffering?

Katherine Calvey (undergraduate): There's compassion with a capital C, where it's not just feeling with somebody who is suffering. There's compassion that compels you to move. I think the general movement on Facebook and social media is that you react to others in a very fleeting way. It's compassion that is not lasting. You look at a post that says, "If you click 'Like,' we'll solve world hunger." People will click Like and share the message and think, "Well, I clicked on my mouse and now I did my job." I've noticed that pattern recently with the massive sharing of this video *Kony 2012*. It's a very popular video and an issue that nobody really noticed. Now, because there is this creative video—even an awareness package that you can buy that includes a bracelet and a poster and other paraphernalia—it's already done for you. You don't have to be creative about it, which is a way of injuring creativity itself and I think is injuring compassion. Because people may for one day or one week feel sympathy, but they don't make any real moves toward changing the situation.

Sheldon Pool (undergraduate): I don't think you can make the generalization that people just re-blog things and it has no effect. I can't say that when I re-blogged Kony that my friends who saw it didn't do anything about it.

Josh Durkin (recent graduate): A lot of what we're talking about showed up even before Internet-based social networking. We've all had birthday parties with relatives who come with a gift, and there's that card on it that you read for half a second. Greeting cards are similar to what we're saying here about social networks. When you 'Like' something that you see on a person's Facebook page, it's just a fleeting thing. Maybe I'm supposed to appreciate greeting cards more than I do.

Jeffrey Schlict: So does Hallmark spread compassion? Is that what we're asking?

Josh Durkin: I think Hallmark spreads "stuff."

Galina Bakhtiarova (professor): Those are ready-mades when you don't have to add your own creativity; where you don't have to write from your heart—if we're talking about compassion and you're writing a sympathy card to somebody. You write out of your own heart and you try to concentrate and be creative, and your creativity and compassion come together or you go the easy way. Or you go to Hallmark and grab something that reflects what you were thinking, and you send that. That's the same as all those ready-mades that we have on Facebook.

Katherine Calvey: Yes, that's what I was trying to say—that there is generic compassion that is being sold. And I would love to see people making it into their own words.

from the Creativity & Compassion conference

Perspectives

Michael Holm
Middle School Teacher

I know from experience that a shift in my perspective can bring about a sea change in a person's sense of compassion. Compassion, the feeling of sympathy and urge to take positive action to ease the suffering of someone or some creature in distress, comes naturally when we see our friends and family suffering. It's harder to come by when it concerns someone we may regard as an adversary—"a difficult person," as the Buddhists say. However, changing our perspective about our adversaries can reveal new depths of compassion.

Creativity or someone else's compassion can operate powerfully as sparks for such shifts in perception. With this in mind, I offer three examples from my daily life that illustrate the relationship between compassion, creativity, and perspective.

For seven years, I worked my summers at a state park in my hometown. I had come to love the pristine landscape there, with its rolling fields and inviting lake, and I similarly enjoyed the hard work that was required to keep it in its state of natural beauty. But something changed the last summer I worked there, when new management took over. Countless heat waves had parched the land and demoralized the park's staff. Tensions ran high. Divisions cropped up between the employees and management. The park that I had loved for so many years now left a foul taste in my mouth. I brooded over the daily squabbles. People who I once respected were now my enemies. My last day of work that summer couldn't have come soon enough, and the season was wrought with enough drama to make me despise the park as a whole. *Good riddance*, I thought, as I sped away on my bicycle at the end of my final shift.

That night I drove to my girlfriend's house (she is now my wife) feeling negative about the park and my coworkers. Unbeknownst to me, she had arranged a creative end-of-the-summer celebration, complete with homemade decorations and a cake made from scratch. Through the course of the night, I got to talking with her about how awful I felt about the park and the people there, but no matter what I said, she always brought my attention back to the countless good memories rooted in the park's fields and the lake that I loved. I started to reflect on this, feeling my perspective change. I wasn't the only one working at the park who felt the heat and stress of the summer. I imagined how the new management must have felt, thrown into a new environment with new employees. Surely their headaches outweighed mine. And that's when it made sense—that's when compassion emerged. These people were not really my enemies; my former perspective, haggard and negative, had skewed them as such. A weight was lifted off my shoulders as my new, more compassionate perspective took shape.

Two days prior to the Compassion and Creativity Conference, I received a desperate phone call from my wife as she drove home during rush hour. She said that a cat had been hit by a car just up the road, but it was still moving. She wasn't sure what to do. I told her to pick me up so that we could retrieve the cat and bring it to the veterinarian together. I brought a towel and braced myself, knowing that what I was about to see was likely going to be intimately raw. As we neared the now motionless body, we stopped the car in order to block traffic so that I could safely retrieve the cat from the middle of the road. I took my time gently lifting the bloodied cat into my arms, realizing that it was still alive.

It was at this point that I became aware of the blaring horns coming from the growing line of cars behind my wife's car. These people were infuriated that their evening commute had hit a roadblock. Unaware of why I was impeding their drive home, many continued to honk as they negotiated their way around my wife's car. Although I will never truly know what these commuters thought, I do know that those who managed to get past my wife's car slowed down enough to observe the person standing in the middle of the road—me. And since no more than five feet of pavement separated me from the passing motorists, I know that they were able to see the wounded cat I held. Could my act of compassion have changed their perspective? Did they no longer view me as the roadblock that was preventing them from getting home in time for dinner? I'm not sure, but I do know that in my past I have been incredibly agitated while waiting in traffic, only to find myself regretting those feelings once I've driven past the mangled car wreck that caused my delay. Our daily lives are filled with nuisances that range in tenor from mild annoyance to complete frustration, but if we look for the compassion in action that surrounds us, we will be more apt to find it—and practice it ourselves.

During the last school year, I gave my students an assignment to create an original short story and take it from brainstorm to publication. My general rule of thumb had always been that the fewer confines I put on my students, the more their creativity will be able to soar. One student in particular took advantage of this laxity to the extreme. To say that he had been a hardworking student throughout the year would have been a gross overstatement. I considered just getting him to write a sentence on paper a success. So when I received a six-page final draft of the paper—it was even typed—I was taken completely by surprise.

Then I started to read it, and in about three sentences, I began wondering what kind of monster I had let loose. Through intentionally transparent innuendoes, my student had written what could be termed a teenager's guide to sex, drugs, and rap music. Despite this content, it was incredibly well-written, full of vivid imagery, and the grammar was up to par; he had incorporated a year's worth of learning into one short story. More than anything, though, I could tell that he had enjoyed crafting it. Even though he was trying to test me with the subject matter, he had gone above and beyond the writing expectations of the assignment, which thrilled me.

Few of my colleagues shared in my excitement, however. They pointed to his brazen choice of four-letter words and the overall crassness of the subject. Nevertheless, I marveled at his use of sensory details and transitional language. Here was a kid who hadn't done much of anything all year, but, given the opportunity to expand his creativity in a manner of his choosing, he ran with it. My fellow teachers, holding on to a limited perspective of the student, weren't able to see the magnitude of this accomplishment. For some of them, this student's story only further tainted their view of him. My perspective had changed after seeing a creative side of him that had been previously hidden.

After I had handed back the assignment, he explained to me his difficulties with formal writing, which was very much the opposite of this assignment. Uninspired by the formal style—which dominates our curriculum—coupled with his problems at home, this was the first time all year that he had gotten caught up in an assignment. His creativity on this piece had shifted my perspective of him. Not only was I now more understanding of his circumstances, but I felt a greater sense of compassion in regards to his previous lack of motivation. My only wish was that this short story had been assigned at the beginning rather than the end of the year.

In each of the above instances, my perspective was significantly altered because of an unexpected incident. But it is these types of incidents that make up what we call our daily lives. Life is not always predictable; even well-thought-out plans go awry. Because of this, it is best to keep in mind that our perspectives are very limited. We don't ever really know someone else's motives or the truth behind every speed bump we encounter. However, by allowing creativity and compassion to share the driver's seat, we will be better able to adapt our perspectives appropriately for the benefit of ourselves and others.

The real test of compassion is not what we say in abstract discussions, but how we conduct ourselves in daily life. Still, certain fundamental views are basic to the practice of altruism. . . . Democracy is the only stable foundation upon which a global political structure can be built. To work as one, we must respect the right of all peoples and nations to maintain their own distinctive character and values.

—His Holiness the Dalai Lama, from *In My Own Words: An Introduction to My Teaching and Philosophy*

Since periods of great change such as the present one come so rarely in human history, it is up to each of us to make the best use of our time to help create a happier world.

—His Holiness the Dalai Lama, from *In My Own Words: An Introduction to My Teaching and Philosophy*

Creativity and Society

Bill Spontak

Philosophy Teacher

Compassion and wisdom are inseparable. They are like the two wings of a bird that will lead us to enlightenment.

—Stephen Powell, *Releasing Life: An Ancient Buddhist Practice in the Modern World*

Creativity is the quintessential trait of the human species. Like the water fish swim in, creativity's all-encompassing nature is largely invisible and, as such, its centrality to our individual and collective well-being is little understood. Despite the ubiquity of creative endeavors, our culture's focus seems more and more centered upon the feats of individuals and how well they are rewarded economically. The photograph is beautiful, but what will it sell for? The invention is useful, but is it marketable? Or a more destructive variant: The invention is useful, but whose market will it encroach upon? These narrowing considerations have a fracturing effect upon society and promote a culture of individualism that is unnatural, stifles our creativity, and alienates us from one another. As a result of these narrowing perspectives, the possibility of creative influence having a positive impact on our society going forward has become ever more untenable; this is a call to reevaluate the relationship between creativity and culture.

Much of the tension between creativity and culture is a sort of straw man's game of peekaboo. On the one hand, culture warns us to be wary of the untried, the potentially dangerous, the unknown new, and the misunderstood other.

These are important considerations, but where these concerns shift into an effort to protect the status quo or generate unwarranted fear and superstition is often difficult to detect and even harder to compensate for. On the other hand, culture is where creativity finds both its food for thought and its communal rewards. Whether posthumously rewarded with fame, as Socrates and many other innovative thinkers have been, or compensated with cash in the here and now for an entertaining yet trivial app like Angry Birds, culture has always set the parameters for who, what, and how creativity is valued. It is this econo-centric influence that modern culture has had upon creativity that is the crux of so many problems facing our civilization today.

Another part of this problematic perspective is that we do not connect the way we live now with the creative past that brought it into existence. For example, we forget that a completely uncontroversial (to us) idea like *the consent of the governed* was a product of the creative mind of John Locke, and put forth at considerable risk to life and limb. We live in the aftermath without a thought of the creativity that made this life possible. For us, it's as if things have always been this way, and thus we lose the comparative wisdom that would come with an understanding of the idea's impact and place in history. We do not consider how different our world would be had Locke failed to put this idea forward, or had it arisen 100 years later. Looking back, we are contented by the notion that things are as they should and could only be this way. Could an idea that revolutionary thrive in our world today? Even if we put aside the considerable ability of entrenched power to thwart new paradigms, the fact is that ideas that elevate the well-being of all peoples rarely convert into economic gain, making them less likely to arise and very easy to dismiss. These factors do not bode well for a progressive future.

And yet we find it easy to think that whatever problems we may face, our native creativity will rise to the occasion and save the day. Out of thin air and through human ingenuity, we have created countless deities, free-market capitalism, inalienable rights, lunar landing modules, national borders, cyberspace, and indoor plumbing, to recount a mere fraction of our creative output. Our creative nature is so taken for granted that we are admonished not to worry about global warming's potential consequences because we will inevitably innovate our way to a solution that will have minimal impact upon our lifestyle.

Of course, this hubris is another example of the fractured society in which we now live.

If we want to be more truthful, we should accept what every investor-in-future-prospects knows: Past performance is no guarantee of future success. With that in mind, a reevaluation of our current cultural constructs and where they are leading us seems necessary for our collective survival. To be sure, a closer look at the relationship of culture with its progenitor, creativity, could be insightful.

To stretch an old linguistics theory: If language is the product of dead metaphor, culture is certainly the remains of dead creativity. What worked in the past is slowly codified and then perpetuated into the future. The inevitable result of this preferencing creates culture, and in turn, tension is generated as newer solutions challenge established ones; this is a clear iteration of the primal paradox promulgated by individuals that WCSU's John Briggs has put forth as a dynamic within the creative process. Indeed, this dynamic can offer the potential for an invigorating and renewable culture that in turn fosters a furthering of the Aristotelian notion of *eudaimonia,* a flourishing of our human nature.

So what went wrong on the way home from the forum? Why are there no news reports of outbreaks of human flourishing in the village square, or testimonials to the fulfilling nature of urban environments, or of days on the factory floor? Why are our creative endeavors more focused on making money than furthering happiness?

The short answer is that Western culture, and by extension, modern culture, has lost its way. That is to say, the human qualities that our institutions claim to champion have been largely abandoned. We pay these noble ideals lip service and little more. Almost one hundred and fifty years ago, Friedrich Nietzsche observed that the spirit of God was dead in man. In other words, the intentions behind our actions are more secular than spiritual, despite our insistence otherwise, even if we might attend four-hour religious services. Sixty years ago, Erich Fromm noted that while many Westerners claimed to be Christian, their way of life would be more accurately categorized as pagan-materialism. And when it comes to this day and age, our frauds are bitterly transparent. What educated person could possibly believe that unlimited, anonymous campaign contributions will be a benefit to any democracy? The working classes are not the ones supporting the notion that money is free speech. (The very concept makes "free speech" an oxymoron.) Few truly believe the lies we tell and are told, yet we keep telling them and allowing them to be told. This increasing level of alienation further perpetuates our fractured society.

Anything that reinforces the notion that we are all in this together would improve cooperation and contribute to a more egalitarian society. Imagine hedge-fund managers contemplating the suffering of the thousands of homeowners caught in the housing bubble instead of strategizing about how to get the most profitable return on their investments. Imagine a future beyond the necessity of leasing your labor to underwrite your survival. These and better ideas are within the scope of our creative natures once they are freed from our culture's economic imperative.

Of course, making the world a more compassionate place is a no-brainer, and well beyond the focus of this paper. A more tenable proposition is a plea to develop our compassionate capacities as a means of and in concert with renewing our connection to our inherent creative natures. In other words, begin the process of deprogramming and replacing the competitive, acquisitive, cog-in-the-machine mentality with independent thought and adventurous speculation. For the individual, the opportunities to exercise and expand one's creative abilities are endless, and as a society, we need to make room in our schedules and our expectations of others to promote these long undervalued yearnings. As a society, it is time to grow up.

And there is much to do. Aside from reinstituting abandoned arts programs in schools, our education systems need to replace competition with compassion and adjust classroom methodologies to include fostering creativity as it arises. This type of focus does not lend itself to systems management, but its goal is not the production of obedient cogs. Schools should not be mechanisms for enforcing conformity. Our schools should foster independent thought and compassionate mindfulness, for these qualities offer the best hope for addressing the problems our civilization faces. And, there are problems aplenty.

The need for a compassionate intervention in our society is equally pressing and important. We need to stop lying to ourselves about what our society has become and create what we need to make human flourishing a growing reality. Virtually every social system in our country is in decline, corrupt, or being dismantled for profit. Our political system has been gerrymandered and bought off. Wall Street and the banking system fleece citizens of their savings at regular intervals. Corporate citizens openly operate with the moral conscience of psychopaths and less accountability than five-year-olds. Advertisers intentionally deceive, insurance companies drop their ill policy holders, everyone is conditioned to look for loopholes, and our most reliably unbiased news is found on Comedy Central. If only these conditions were truly funny.

If we continue to believe human nature is essentially selfish and competitive, we will continue making it such by the actions these beliefs engender. If we continue believing that society's function is to protect us from each other, we will continue to create a society that isolates us and encourages our basest natures. Compassion is the means to rise above these culturally conditioned beliefs. And compassion is the necessary condition for wisdom to prevail in the face of power. It sets the stage for cooperative and creative endeavors, and it opens the door to the immense possibilities of our kind. It is time to create the future that humans deserve, not one they must be conditioned to endure. That will only happen when we start to care about all of us.

One of the most important things I learned was the idea of seeing others as an extension of ourselves. I feel that's one of the main things in creativity and compassion because underneath I feel that everyone just wants to be understood and accepted as part of a group. Because everyone is a social creature.

—Jessica Lin,
undergraduate,
from the Creativity &
Compassion conference

.

Did I Hold the Door So You Could Thank Me?

Isabel "Belle" Lopes

Recent WCSU Graduate

We all know what it's like to hold a door for someone who just walks right through without the slightest acknowledgment of our trouble. Feelings of anger and resentment stir. We're left wondering why that person didn't say "thank you," or why we even bothered to hold the door in the first place. We might even decide that we won't hold the door again for anyone else that day!

Do we want to be people who hold doors only for the "thank you" that we expect to receive? Or do we want to be people who hold doors because we genuinely care for others? It's easy to engage in these sorts of activities when we get recognition for what we do; it becomes more of a challenge when our efforts are overlooked. The true sign of genuineness is to be blissfully anonymous in our acts of kindness.

This line of thinking can be applied to many moments within everyday life. Would we let someone merge into traffic if we knew that she was not going to show appreciation? If the answer is "no," we should ask ourselves a very important question: Are the acts of kindness we do inspired by what we expect to receive from others or by the benefit we are providing to them? We may find that we are only looking for a payoff, that the kindness we thought we were bestowing altruistically on a stranger is nothing more than an attempt to feel good ourselves. In the end, this leads to a sense to self-righteousness and moves us away from happiness. There is hope for everyone, however, to increase compassion and to nurture peace within ourselves by extending genuine kindness toward others. We must challenge ourselves—every day if possible—to confront our intentions and aim toward selfless giving. Even in small doses, such as holding a door without the expectation of recognition, we are having a positive impact. His Holiness the 14th Dalai Lama encourages us to reflect on these activities in the context of the ultimate goal of happiness, which we all equally desire. In his own words, "Even if you searched for eons to find the best method to achieve permanent happiness, you would find that the only way is to generate love and compassion."[1]

Notes

1. Tenzin Gyatso, His Holiness the 14th Dalai Lama, *How to Expand Love: Widening the Circle of Loving Relationships*. (J. Hopkins, Trans.). NY: Atria Books (2005).

The Way You Look at Life *Does* Matter

Jessica Lin

Student

As I write this, it's been two months since the conference, but I still remember many of the resounding lessons that I gathered from the experience. Not a day goes by without the phrase "pain is not avoidable, but suffering is optional" crossing my mind. For me, a mere freshman at Western Connecticut State University, being a part of this conference was the highest of honors. The stories, experiences, and observations from both the panelists and the audience members were mesmerizing, inspirational, and rich with the essence of life. And it didn't matter to me that we, as conference participants, were not able to come up with one conclusive definition for the themes of creativity and compassion. What mattered was that despite the age differences, the disparate backgrounds, and the various areas of expertise, we as a group were able to gather together and go through this "discovery" together. As one of my most respected professors told me, "It's not where you end up that's important, but how you get there that will affect the rest of your life."

Many of the insights that I repeatedly think about from the event fall easily into the category of how an individual views the world and acts as a result of that view. For example, Professor Deborah Calloway said in the first panel—which was focused on the meaning of creativity and compassion—"There is creativity in every moment of your life." I remember hearing her say it for the first time, and as I was writing it down, I realized just how true that statement is. As one of the panelists observed, everyone has a sort of routine, whether that involves getting out of bed at 8:00 a.m., brushing your teeth a certain way, or using the same route to go home or to work every day. A change in any aspect of your life can be creative, although at times it may not be practical. Once again, it all depends on how you look at it. When asked to define creativity, Professor Eric Lewis noted, "Creativity is toward the love of something, not the skill." This was a terrifying but extremely powerful statement. Growing up in a capitalist country, we get the sense that our worth is measured in terms of our marketable skills. As I reflected on his observation, I concluded that Professor Lewis is right. If you don't love what you do, it will be less likely for you to be creative about it, because you see it as a chore that simply needs to be done.

There were so many other important insights that I gathered from this experience. I can review and re-read them when I'm feeling lost, defeated, or in need of motivation. These are not only words of wisdom passed on by those who've actually *lived* these moments of revelation, but they are also creative forms of compassion. At least that's how I saw, and still see, them. When sharing their experiences, each and every single panelist seemed to me to be trying to communicate with each and every single individual at the conference. They were all trying to put into words the feelings that they've had in their experiences, to share those feelings, and tell others that there are different and better ways to look at life. Lastly, the participants were all trying to confirm that they aren't the only ones who have had these feelings.

I lost count of the number of times when I saw both hidden and full-on smiles, nodding heads, and even tears. It was something that I won't try to put into words because the discussions elicited these responses in such great number. All of which reminded me that the way you look at life does matter. It will influence you and those around you in every single moment of your life. As one of the other panel participants, WCSU senior Isabel Lopes, said: "It's what you surround yourself with and what you put out there that's critical."

In thinking through these questions, we use abstract words, starting with compassion, creativity, awareness. One way of thinking about the process is that words and concepts come into being because there is something going on that you want to name or point to. Let's start with the notion that the name or definition that you want to use is totally inadequate; however good it is, it is totally inadequate to what is going on. Add to this the fact that as soon as you apply the definition, the label obscures the fact that that thing that you're naming is holistically interconnected, seamlessly a part of all kinds of other "things" that we have names for. The result is that when you try to pin down your concept too much, you end up getting confused and going wrong. I actually don't think we are confused here. It might look like that sometimes. I think that what has been happening as we discuss these concepts of creativity and compassion, we have been feeling the life going on behind these words, these important words. We're not just discussing them as concepts but rather seeing the vitality of those concepts.

So in the process, I think that I've come closer to understanding creativity and compassion as living things and somewhat closer to understanding the holistic movement going on behind those labels. We can hope to take away the labels, but this is tricky. If you take away those labels, you may just end up with other labels, and I don't know if that helps. I think we're really trying to understand what is meant—has been meant—by those words and the feeling level, the emotional level, the interconnection level of those words. One way to see them is how different people use them, how they talk about them, how they come to understand the differences in perceptions that others have about those words. That's what a number of you were indicating. That's our dialogical process.

—John Briggs,
from the Creativity & Compassion conference

Time to Nurture the Creative Heart

Geshe Tashi Tsering

Buddhist Monk

There is nothing whatsoever
That is not made easier through acquaintance.

—Śāntideva, *Guide to the Bodhisattva's Way of Life*,
chapter 6, verse 14, translation by Stephen Batchelor

It seems clear that here and now, the 21st century should be the time that we start working together on harnessing our creativity and intellectual ability to serve the compassionate side of our nature, our deep human impulse to share others' difficulties.

If we look back over the course of human history, we can see just how much benefit we have gained from using our creativity and intellectual ability to enhance our lives and deal with external problems. Across the world, in various cultures, humans have usually been adept at finding the best ways of meeting the challenges associated with living where they do. At the same time, they have developed methods to help them to contend with the internal problems of loss, fear, dissatisfaction, anger, jealousy, and other negative emotions. Advice about how to deal with these challenges can be found in the religions and philosophies of many cultures across the world. And it seems to me that in these two things, there is not much difference between Eastern and Western approaches.

But in 17th-century Europe, we can clearly see the beginnings of something new, the onset of the scientific revolution that has now swept the world. From isolated beginnings, such as the discoveries of Galileo and Copernicus, even before the 17th century, the working out of this revolution over the centuries has led to extraordinary advances in material development as evidenced in modern technology, communications, and medicine.

At the heart of this revolution was a rigorous training in intellectual and physical observation and in the analysis of these observations, a willingness to question received truths, and a willingness to question one's own findings, analyses, and answers. We think of this as the "scientific method."

Of course, the march of science has not been without problems, and many people still lack the basic necessities of life: food, water, and shelter. And many still live in fear of highly sophisticated weapons and instruments of torture used to oppress basic human rights.

Furthermore, the pristine intellectual tradition of the scientific method has been muddied by the kind of belief system known as "scientism": the idea that only science can provide all the answers to life's questions. It has been further muddied by the belief system known as "materialism," the notion that all life's problems can be solved through material means and that there is nothing other than physical "stuff."

Despite all the material progress of the last few centuries, we still have grotesque inequalities of opportunity; many people still live under the shadow of oppressive political systems and have real problems coping with the stresses and strains that life throws at them. These facts show that there is something missing from our contemporary way of life.

What is that something? The heart of compassion is missing from the mix of creativity and intellectual ability. Our human creativity now needs to focus on our inner world. Somehow in the rush of modern development, we have neglected this—or at least not paid it much attention.

His Holiness the Dalai Lama works extremely hard, traveling all over the world, to share his ideas on how to promote human qualities such as compassion, tolerance and patience. His way of promoting these ideas is, I think, revolutionary.

He is not narrowly seeking to promote the inner values found in Tibetan Buddhism but seeks a genuine promotion of basic human qualities shared across cultures, religions, and philosophies. These qualities and values are truly universal; they are not to be found solely in the East or in the West. They are found regardless of whether someone is a woman or man, rich or poor, educated or uneducated. At the root of all these qualities, he says, is an amazing ability to share a sense of concern for others. And His Holiness suggests that this can be done without associating them with a particular religion. This sense of concern can be universal, and that is what we need now—a universal sense of ethics. We have not just the potential to create universal ethics, but we can also use this amazing creative mind to enhance and cultivate these qualities and values.

His Holiness says that we should place this kind of emotional education at the heart of our current education systems all the way from kindergarten to college. He emphasizes that this is essential for the present day, as well as for the coming centuries. We need to work together to harness our creative ability, intellectual agility, and our compassionate potential and through that build a happy family—starting at the level of individual, family, and local community and gradually expanding more widely to society, country, and all the nations of the world.

To make that happen is not just a question of one or two people who have these tremendous ideas as well as the enthusiasm and charisma to accomplish their goals. Of course even just a handful of people can help, but the broad transformation we seek is very much about people working together, about humanity working together. We must particularly engage with the young—in kindergarten, elementary school, high school, and college—and of course with those who take care of them.

So where do we start? What resources do we have?

I think there are many amazing resources, including all the different Western and Eastern philosophies and religions. From these, we can draw on ethical advice that resonates across cultures, that does not require buying into a particular philosophical or religious worldview. We can promote these and work together to develop and cultivate some form of universal moral ethics, to promote compassionate human beings, compassionate human societies.

This is not just mawkish sentimentality or "motherhood and apple pie." It is perfectly real and perfectly achievable. It is achievable because we have this amazing creative mind. When we look at what human beings have achieved so far with that mind—it is almost unbelievable. Sometimes when I fly in a jumbo jet—600 people and several tons of luggage in the sky at 30,000 feet—I am truly amazed. Two hundred years ago, that would have been impossible to even contemplate. Using our creativity, we have been to the moon. With great effort and hard work, we have overcome or eradicated some of the deadliest and most crippling diseases.

In light of that, there is no reason why we should not be able to promote human qualities such as compassion, love, forgiveness, patience, tolerance, and understanding within ourselves and in other individuals and society.

This is how I see the connection connectivity between creativity and human compassion. And I see there is great hope, great optimism if we work like this together.

What is compassion, where can it be found?
Just stop and take a look around.

—"Compassion," by Makayla, Grade 8

Acknowledgments

I would like to begin our acknowledgments by paying tribute to His Holiness the 14th Dalai Lama for providing inspiration not only for this book, but, more importantly, for inspiring countless lives around the globe.

We want to acknowledge with great emphasis the participants of the Creativity and Compassion Conference who, owing to the Connecticut state budget crisis, came to the conference at their own expense, and then gave even more generously of their valuable time and thoughts to further this inquiry. The WCSU students who joined us were crucial to our discussion. They inspired us older folk in untold ways. In particular, we could not have carried out the conference without Keith Roland and Michael Joel Bosco, our two honors student organizers. They negotiated many a thorny path and plugged many a leaking hole to make the conference happen. We hope that readers will find their own inspiration in the essays the students have written here and in the passages quoted from them while they spoke at the conference.

We would also like to express our gratitude to the scholars, monks, and other writers represented in these pages, who, though they could not attend the conference, spent the hours and meditative sweat necessarily involved in serious writing to provide us with their thoughts on our subject.

Everyone we encountered as we developed the conference and then this book has been remarkably warmhearted, including the Western Connecticut

ACKNOWLEDGMENTS

State University (WCSU) administrative staff, all of whom we wish to acknowledge and thank. These include WCSU President James W. Schmotter, Provost Jane McBride Gates, and former Provost Linda Rinker, who gave us continued encouragement and support.

Thank you to WCSU student Alissa DeGregorio for offering her painting for use on our cover, and to Jason Davis for the cover design. To Peggy Stewart for her photographs of the conference that Karuna Publications designer Clare Cerullo has beautifully fashioned into images to complement our text.

Special thanks to Susan Altabet, who has been the behind-the-scenes guiding spirit and continuous "positive vibe" for both the conference and the book.

Another special thanks to the "Sacred Art Tour of Drepung Gomang Monastery" for its generous donation to fund the conference so that we could have food and drink.

It's hard to know how to properly acknowledge John Cerullo, publisher of Karuna Publications and the chief supporter of this collection. John is an artist as well as editor, publisher, and Buddhist practitioner. His knowledge in all those domains and his gentle, upbeat attention to detail is everywhere infused in this final product.

John Cerullo, myself, and Paul Hackett served as the primary editorial team for corralling the pieces into a collective form. Paul's wonderful contribution to the conference itself was matched by his great contribution as an editor. His incisive intellect is wrapped in a warm and open presence. He made our meetings all go smoothly. As for the copyedit process, so necessary to rounding-off the rough edges and creating consistency to the presentation of all the essays, my thanks to Jeremy Lehrer.

Finally, thank you to the two institutions, Western Connecticut State University and Do Ngak Kunphen Ling Tibetan Buddhist Center for Universal Peace (DNKL) under the spiritual guidance of Gyumed Khensur Rinpoche Lobsang Jampa for their cooperation in putting together the two talks by His Holiness that gave the originating inspiration for this book. It is our hope that these two institutions will be able to work together in the future in the form of a Center for Compassion and Creativity that will extend the reach of the discussion found in these pages.

John Briggs

Contributors

Susan Altabet is currently president of the board of directors at Do Ngak Kunphen Ling Tibetan Buddhist Center for Universal Peace in Redding, Connecticut (DNKL). She works as a professional choral singer in the New York City area and has toured throughout the world with the Gregg Smith Singers since 1984. She teaches voice, flute, and piano at Crestwood Music Education Center in Westchester, New York. She has a music degree from Trinity College of Music, London, in voice and in flute. She is also a longtime dharma student and practitioner.

John Z. Amoroso has maintained a practice as a transpersonal psychotherapist in the Philadelphia area since 1988. He is currently adjunct faculty at Atlantic University, where he directs a degree program in creativity studies and transpersonal psychology. John also continues to pursue his passions for painting and fine art photography.

Daniel W. Barrett, PhD, is an associate professor of psychology at WCSU. He earned his PhD at Arizona State University in social psychology, held a post-doctoral fellowship at the University of Pennsylvania, and received his BA from Wesleyan University. His primary research interests are persuasion and social influence.

Tenzin Bhuchung is a trained Buddhist scholar and a translator (translating between English and Tibetan). He has a Shastri degree (equivalent to a BA with honors) from Tibetan Buddhist University, Varanasi, India. He is also trained in Western academia, receiving a BA with honors from the University of Tasmania, Australia, and a Master's in Asian studies from the University of California, Berkeley. He has more than fifteen years of experience interpreting Tibetan Buddhism to Western students and dharma practitioners in India at the Tibetan Buddhist University and, in the United States and Australia, for some of the most learned Tibetan lamas from all the four traditions.

Michael Joel Bosco is a Western Connecticut State University (WCSU) student and a coordinator of the academic conference on which this book is based. He majors in creative writing and is a member of the honors program, the literary journal *Black & White*, PASS, GSA, and Recreational Council. He is also the cofounder and president of the upcoming WCSU Compassion Club, a staff writer for the student newspaper *The Echo*, and an English tutor at Broadview Middle School. He enjoys composing music and poetry that explore the interconnected nature between love, motivation, and morality.

John Briggs, PhD, is Distinguished CSU Professor Emeritus at Western Connecticut State University, where he was a member of the Department of Writing, Linguistics and Creative Process, and the English Department. He is the author and coauthor of several nonfiction books on aesthetics and physics, including *Fractals: The Patterns of Chaos*; *Fire in the Crucible*; *Seven Life Lessons of Chaos*; and *Turbulent Mirror*, as well as *Metaphor: The Logic of Poetry*. He is also a fine art photographer and a fiction writer, author of the short story collection *Trickster Tales*.

Deborah Calloway teaches at the University of Connecticut School of Law. She practices meditation under the direction of Dzogchen Ponlop Rinpoche. She brings meditation practice and law practice together in her law school course, Contemplative Lawyering. She is currently working on making the transformative power of meditation practice available in prisons.

CONTRIBUTORS

David Capps is a visiting assistant professor of philosophy at Western Connecticut State University. He holds a PhD in philosophy from the University of Connecticut, and his research concerns topics in analytic epistemology and philosophy of language. In his spare time, he enjoys hiking and thinking about poetics. His spirit animal is a tardigrade.

Norman Carey is the director of the DMA program in music performance at the CUNY Graduate Center, where he also serves on the music theory faculty. An active chamber musician, Carey is the pianist of the Prometheus Ensemble. Mr. Carey performed regularly with the renowned violist Emanuel Vardi, and can be heard with Vardi on the recording *The Virtuoso Viola*. Carey's theoretical work concerns mathematical models of musical scales.

Geshe Lobsang Dhargye is a scholar and spiritual teacher. He received his ordination as a novice monk in 1982 from the late Kyabje Ling Rinpoche, the senior tutor of His Holiness the 14th Dalai Lama and the 97th throne holder of the Gelug tradition of Tibetan Buddhism. He then received the vows of a fully ordained monk (a bhikshu) in 1994 directly from His Holiness the Dalai Lama. In 1996, he was awarded the highest monastic degree, that of Geshe Lharampa. Geshe Dhargye then attended Gyumed Tantric College in 1999 to study Buddhist tantra. He received the Ngagrampa degree in Buddhist Tantric Studies. Geshe Dhargye also served in the Education Development Committee of Sera Mey Monastery from 1999 to 2001. He has taught at Sera Mey Monastery and is now the resident teacher at Do Ngak Kunphen Ling in Redding, Connecticut. Venerable Gyumed Khensur Rinpoche Lobsang Jampa is his personal tutor and also the spiritual director of DNKL.

Dr. Stephen Dydo has written music for a wide variety of media. Earning awards such as the Joseph H. Bearns Prize and a BMI Award, he developed computer music at the Instituut voor Sonologie in Utrecht, the Netherlands, under a Fulbright Fellowship and has received fellowships from Meet the Composer and the Johnson Composers' Conference. He received his bachelor's and doctoral degrees from Columbia University and has taught composition and theory at Columbia University, The New School, and William Paterson University. He now teaches at the Greenwich House Music School in Manhattan and the Crestwood Music Center in Westchester, New York. He is a founder and the current president of the New York Qin Society.

Dr. Robert K. C. Forman is a professor of comparative religions at CUNY, who specializes in comparative spiritual experiences. He has been meditating for over 40 years and is the author *of Enlightenment Ain't What It's Cracked Up to Be: A Journey of Discovery, Snow and Jazz in the Soul.* The founder of the Forge Institute for Spirituality and Social Change; Soul Jazz Programs: Fostering Authentic Relationships in Everyday Life; and the *Journal of Consciousness Studies*, he has also received an honorary doctorate from Lund University, Sweden.

Peter Elbow, Professor of English Emeritus at UMass Amherst, has taught at SUNY Stony Brook, M.I.T., Franconia College, and Evergreen State College. He has authored numerous books on writing and teaching. The two major professional organizations in his field gave him awards for "lifetime achievement" and for his "lasting intellectual contribution." He recently published the book *Vernacular Eloquence: What Speech Can Bring to Writing* (Oxford University Press, 2012).

Janet Kathleen Ettele is a musician and author who draws from her background as a student of the Buddhist dharma to bring its teachings into contemporary functional practice through her writing, and the practice of mindfulness through her music. Author of the *How Life Works* series (Diamond Cutter Press), she has published *How Generosity Works* and recently released *How the Root of Kindness Works.* The third book in the series, *How Patience Works*, is scheduled for release in November 2012. Three more books will follow in this series, each a contemporary fable based on the six perfections taught in Buddhism by Master Shantideva. A CD, *Piano Mandalas Compassion,* is a collection of her meditatively improvised music. Ms. Ettele graduated from Berklee College of Music in Boston, Massachusetts, and lives in Connecticut, where she has raised two sons.

Jane M. Gangi, PhD, is an associate professor in the instructional leadership doctoral program, and the author of two books, *Encountering Children's Literature: An Arts Approach*, and, with Mary Ann Reilly and Rob Cohen, *Deepening Literacy Learning: Art and Literature Engagements in K–8 Classrooms.* Her forthcoming book is entitled *Genocide in Contemporary Children's and Young Adult Literature: Cambodia to Darfur.*

Paul G. Hackett is an editor for the American Institute of Buddhist Studies at Columbia University. He earned his PhD in Indo-Tibetan Buddhism from Columbia University and has studied Tibetan language, religion, and culture in both traditional Tibetan and Western academic environments. He is the author of *Theos Bernard, the White Lama: Tibet, Yoga, and American Religious Life*, the book *A Tibetan Verb Lexicon: Verbs, Classes and Syntactic Frames*, and numerous articles on Tibetan language and Buddhist philosophy.

Edward A. Hagan, PhD, has focused his recent scholarship on contemporary Irish and American fiction and essay writing. He is particularly interested in what literary trends tell us about contemporary consciousness. He has just completed a book on contemporary Irish and Irish-American fiction and memoir; it argues that farce is the contemporary writer's tool for puncturing the balloon of triviality in contemporary culture. Hagan authored a 2007 article that argues sports metaphors have become so pervasive in contemporary society that they restrict our ability to think outside the box of winning and losing.

Fredrica R. Halligan, PhD, is a clinical psychologist who has been deeply involved at the interface between psychotherapy and spirituality for over 15 years. As teacher, writer, and therapist, her fascination with comparative mysticism has also motivated her commitment to the interreligious dialogue. Author of the book *Listening Deeply to God*, she has served as director of the Counseling Center at Western Connecticut State University.

Professor Barbara Hesser, CMT, LCAT, FAMI, is the director of music therapy at New York University. She is also the director of the Nordoff-Robbins Center for Music Therapy at New York University. She is the president of the

American Association of Music Therapy and was one of the founders and officers of the World Federation of Music Therapy. She is a board member and vice president of Creative Arts as a Global Resource, Inc. In this capacity, she is one of the directors of the Music as a Global Resource Initiative, an initiative in collaboration with the International Council for Caring Communities (ICCC), UN-Habitat, and other UN partners. She is also coeditor of *Music as a Global Resource Compendium: Solutions for Social and Economic Issues, 3rd Edition.*

Michael Holm graduated Magna Cum Laude from Western Connecticut State University in 2005 with a BA in English/creative writing. In 2008, he returned to earn his teaching certificate in English secondary education and currently works as an English teacher at Broadview Middle School in Danbury, CT. He enjoys writing, drawing, meditating, and appreciating the infinite detail of our natural world.

Dr. Peter Jampel is the director of the Baltic Street Resource & Treatment Center in Brooklyn, New York. He has served as chair of the National Coalition of Arts Therapy Associations (NCATA), president of the American Association for Music Therapy, and coordinator for the 1990 NCATA Conference. He is presently serving as the chair of the Creative Arts Therapy Committee of the Brooklyn Mental Health Council. He is an adjunct associate professor in New York University's music therapy master's program, an adjunct faculty at Touro College, and is associate editor of the publication *Music as a Global Resource.*

David R. Kittay, JD, PhD, is an assistant adjunct professor of religion at Columbia University, where he specializes in teaching courses on Buddhism and on Eastern and Western philosophy. He is also a lawyer, federal bankruptcy trustee, and receiver for the U.S. Securities and Exchange Commission, and is principal of the law firm of Kittay & Gershfeld, P.C. He is the translator of the *Vajra Rosary Tantra* (forthcoming, Columbia University Press) and other books and articles about Buddhism, religion, and law.

Christopher L. Kukk, professor of political science, is the director of Western Connecticut State University's honors program and was the founding coach of the university's Roger Sherman Debate Society. Kukk is a former International Security Fellow at Harvard University's Belfer Center for Science and International Affairs and a 2007–2008 Fulbright Scholar at the University of Tartu in Estonia. His research and publications focus on political and economic relations concerning freshwater resources as well as the creation and sustainability of civil society. Before entering the field of higher education, Kukk was a counterintelligence agent for the United States Army and a research associate for Cambridge Energy Research Associates. He is often asked by the media for his analysis on issues regarding American politics and United States foreign policy.

Eric Lewis is a concert violinist, conductor, music educator, and composer. He received his musical training at the Manhattan School of Music, where in 1965 he formed the Manhattan String Quartet, a group that for 45 years gave internationally acclaimed concert tours, radio concert series, and produced recordings under his direction as first violin. In recent years, Mr. Lewis has performed and recorded with soprano Margaret Astrup (WCSU) in the duo ensemble Delphi; conducts and solos with Elysium Chamber Orchestra; and gives concerts and produces recordings for Centaur Records with the acclaimed Prometheus Ensemble. Professor Lewis has been on the Western Connecticut State University music department faculty for 34 years, during which time he has conducted the WCSU Symphony Orchestra and taught violinists, violists, and chamber music classes. He has given over 1,000 young people's concerts for schoolchildren of all ages; with pianist Howard Tuvelle (WCSU) and Marian Anderson, he formed the Ives Center in 1978.

Jessica Lin is a student at WCSU, majoring in political science and currently looking for a minor. She is part of the WCSU honors program. Some of her interests include foreign languages, communications, and mathematics.

Isabel "Belle" Lopes is currently working as a case manager for Connecticut Junior Republic in Danbury, Connecticut. In that role, she supports and advocates for at-risk youth and their families. She will pursue graduate school in social work and aspires to become a cognitive behavioral and dialectical behavior therapist. She believes compassion and creativity are two of the most important human values: "If we nurture and center these at our core, we will have an un-shakable foundation. If we then use the power of our minds to redirect negativity into love and productivity, we will have a life well spent."

Roland Merullo is a graduate of Exeter Academy and Brown University and is the author of ten novels and four books of nonfiction. His numerous awards include the Massachusetts Book Award in nonfiction and a nomination for the International IMPAC Dublin Literary Award. He lives in Massachusetts with his wife and two daughters. His novel, *Breakfast with Buddha*, was chosen by the Greater Danbury Community for the One Book, One Community read in 2012.

Bill Spontak has taught for the Philosophy and Humanistic Studies Department at Western Connecticut State University since 2006. His interests include political and existential philosophy, the moral consequences of literacy, and the effects of technology on the human condition. Spontak is also a sporadic poet and photographer, intermittently obsessed with thematic clusters of haiku, stills of exhibitionist produce, and Photoshopped renditions of reality. A former member of The Putnam Poets, his poems have appeared in the group's anthologies. His photography is even more reclusive. Spontak's current interests include the aesthetics of craft beer and altered and transcendental states of being.

Keith Roland is a student at Western Connecticut State University (WCSU), majoring in professional writing under the creative writing option, and is a coordinator of the academic conference on which this book is based. He is the current president of *Black & White*, an undergraduate-run literary and art journal at WCSU, tutor for the Writing Department, and an honors student. He is mostly interested in writing strange, poetic short stories and photographing the melding of nature and the man-made.

Dr. Allen Schoen has been a pioneer in the field of integrative animal health care. He received his DVM degree from NYS College of Veterinary Medicine at Cornell University, a master's degree in animal behavior from the University of

Illinois as well as an honorary PhD from Becker College for his contributions to veterinary nedicine. He is the editor and author of three veterinary textbooks and two books for a more general readership. A PBS fundraising TV show was based on his last book, *Kindred Spirits: How the Remarkable Bond Between Humans and Animals Can Change the Way We Live.*

Geshe Tashi Tsering has been the resident Tibetan Buddhist teacher at Jamyang Buddhist Centre, in London, since 1994. He was born in Purang, Tibet, in 1958, and his parents escaped to India in 1959. He entered Sera Mey Monastic University in South India when he was 13 years old, and graduated with a Lharampa Geshe degree 16 years later. Geshe Tashi then entered the Higher Tantric College (Gyuto) for a year of study. Geshe Tsering's teaching career began at Sera, after which he taught the monks at Kopan Monastery, in Nepal, for a year. He went on to the Gandhi Foundation College in Nagpur, India, and then moved to Europe, initially to Nalanda in the South of France. Geshe Tsering teaches in English and is renowned for his warmth, clarity, and humor. Besides Jamyang, he is a regular guest teacher at other Buddhist centers in the UK and around the world; he is creator and teacher of the Foundation of Buddhist Thought, the two-year FPMT correspondence and campus course on the basics of Tibetan Buddhism. Geshe Tsering should not be confused with Geshe Tashi of Chenrezig Institute, Australia.